Proverbs and the Formation of Character

Proverbs and the Formation of Character

DAVE BLAND

Foreword by William P. Brown

CASCADE *Books* • Eugene, Oregon

PROVERBS AND THE FORMATION OF CHARACTER

Copyright © 2015 Dave Bland. All rights reserved. Except for brief quotations in critical publications or reviews, no part of this book may be reproduced in any manner without prior written permission from the publisher. Write: Permissions, Wipf and Stock Publishers, 199 W. 8th Ave., Suite 3, Eugene, OR 97401.

Cascade Books
An Imprint of Wipf and Stock Publishers
199 W. 8th Ave., Suite 3
Eugene, OR 97401

www.wipfandstock.com

ISBN 13: 978-1-4982-2164-1

Cataloguing-in-Publication Data

Bland, Dave.

    Proverbs and the formation of character / Dave Bland.

    xiv + 188 p. ; 23 cm. Includes bibliographical references.

    ISBN 13: 978-1-4982-2164-1

    1. Bible. Proverbs—Criticism, interpretation, etc. 2. Jews—Education—History. 3. Wisdom—Biblical teaching. 4. Character—Biblical teaching. I. Title

BS1465.52 B53 2015

Manufactured in the U.S.A.   10/15/2015

My wife, Nancy, and I would like to dedicate this volume to our grandchildren: Benson, Sloane, Blake Leigh, David, and Joseph.

Our prayer is that each one will, "Trust in the Lord with all your heart, and do not rely on your own understanding. In all your ways acknowledge him, and he will make straight your paths. Do not be wise in your own eyes; fear the Lord, and turn away from evil. It will be healing to your flesh and medicine to your body."
(Proverbs 3:5–8)

"Grandchildren are the crown of the aged." (Proverbs 17:6a)

Contents

Foreword by William P. Brown | ix
Preface | xiii

Chapter One
The Journey of Character Formation | 1

Chapter Two
The Process of Character Formation | 12

Chapter Three
The Content of Character Formation | 41

Chapter Four
The Proverb in Character Formation | 65

Chapter Five
Character Formation through Human Dialogue: (Proverbs 27:14–19) | 91

Chapter Six
Language and Character Formation: (Proverbs 25:11–15; 26:1–9) | 105

Chapter Seven
Wealth and Character Formation:
(Proverbs 15:13–17 and Select Proverb Pairs) | 122

Chapter Eight
Yahweh and Character Formation: (Proverbs 15:33—16:9) | 142

Chapter Nine
Community and Character Formation: (Proverbs 22:6; 31:10–31) | 162

Bibliography | 175

Foreword

Proverbial wisdom continues to be a sorely neglected topic in contemporary moral discourse, at least in North America. The growing field of narrative ethics, for example, has captivated the moral imagination of many an ethicist, theologian, and literary critic. It is widely felt that the proverb, in terms of its moral import, cannot hold a candle to the power of narrative. As scholars, educators, and even political leaders continue their worthy quest to identify those genres that provide the most effective vehicles for shaping moral character, the little proverb is all too often left in the dust. And there it lies to be picked up only by erudite paremiologists, the modern scribes and collators of proverbial lore.

Biblical scholars, too, have been known to exile the proverb to the godforsaken land of the superficial. Relegated to the periphery of biblical theology, the book of Proverbs is often considered a catalogue of simplistic sayings. Whereas the other books of biblical wisdom—Job and Ecclesiastes—are often deemed worthy of theological reflection, ancient Israel's proverbial lore, it is said, largely "tends toward the banal," hardly worthy of "careful study by serious students."[1] A more subtle bias is reflected by those who find proverbs rhetorically significant insofar as they "perform" in narrative contexts. But once captured and placed in a collection, forced out of its narrative habitat, the proverb loses its value. Death by collection, thus, becomes the coroner's report.[2]

Dave Bland thinks that an autopsy is highly premature, and I would heartily agree. Whether featured in a collection or embedded in a narrative, the proverb remains a potent didactic force in contemporary culture.

---

1. Crenshaw, *Education in Ancient Israel*, 232.

2. See, e.g., Mieder, "The Essence of Literary Proverb Study"; Fontaine, *Traditional Sayings*, 54.

Within a collection, the proverb invites lively interaction with the reader in order for its range of meaning to be disclosed. While a particular proverb's significance is prescribed to some degree in a narrative setting, it becomes more fully reader responsive in a collection. As a compact, portable distillation of wisdom, the proverb makes no claim to universal truth or even authoritative guidance, yet it has the uncanny ability to tease the mind and heart, provoking new levels of discernment. As Bland ably demonstrates, both the form and the content of the biblical proverb invite critical engagement and, in turn, foster moral responsibility. Proverbs are as much contextual as they are flexible in application. Perhaps more than any other genre of didactic discourse, the proverb embodies the scandal of particularity within its claim to truth.

That the book of Proverbs features an array of frequently contradictory sayings indicates how the sages dealt with the challenges of day-to-day living. Life, the ancients affirmed, is filled with competing allegiances and bewilderingly diverse situations that demand careful reflection and hard decisions. Small wonder that the book conveys its own *Sachkritik*: it compels the reader to think, discriminate, and act in responsible and realistic ways. Yet the power of the proverb for moral (trans)formation remains untapped in contemporary discourse.

As Bland points out, the first nine chapters of Proverbs have received the lion's share of scholarly attention. Indeed, as I have tried to show in an early programmatic study to which he refers, these chapters (as well as the concluding poem found in Prov 31:10–31) provide a metanarrative for the sayings that constitute the book's center (chapters 10–30).[3] But, in truth, they are only prefatory in relation to the whole of Proverbs; they serve merely to whet the appetite and provide orientation for the myriad of sayings that follow chapter 9. And so it is only appropriate that Bland gives these proverbial snippets of wisdom their literary and theological due, as did the ancient compilers.

The editors behind Proverbs were quite explicit in the way they showcased these sayings. Their introduction to the book concludes with a profile of wisdom's domicile, in which a lavish banquet is prepared for her would-be disciples (9:1–6). What does wisdom require but to leave immaturity at the front door and partake of her feast? "Come, eat of my bread and drink of the wine I have mixed," she beckons (v. 5). Her guests include both the neophyte and the wise. And what does wisdom offer her guests at the table but a banquet of insight and a feast of fellowship? As hostess, wisdom serves a multi-course meal, a curricular cuisine of sayings and instructions. It is

3. Brown, *Character in Crisis*, 22–49.

precisely her rich fare that is featured in the following chapters. To be savored, enjoyed, and digested, these proverbs are the edifying morsels that sustain moral living. More than simply food for thought, they provide the sustenance for righteousness. And what a smorgasbord it is! As food is to be tasted and consumed, so wisdom's discourse is to be heard and appropriated. And it all begins with a diet of discipline taken in small, discrete doses.

Bland's work begins with that diet of discipline. His engagement with ancient wisdom is both wide ranging and urgently relevant. Enlisting the help of many a modern sage, from the philosophical to the down to earth (Hans-Georg Gadamer and Tex Sample, for example!), Bland sheds new light upon these ancient sayings and makes them eminently accessible for any interested reader. Eschewing technical jargon, Bland is able to bring these laconic snippets to bear on some of our most systemic moral challenges, including the lack of community and the narcissistic desire to retreat into uniformity and individualism. He puts to rest all doubts that Israel's proverbial lore is lightweight and pedantic and shows that the tiny proverb is laden with the profound, timely wisdom of the ancients. What is even more remarkable, Bland does all this in a way that is fun and engaging to read, something the sages themselves would have admired.

William P. Brown
Columbia Theological Seminary
Decatur, Georgia

Preface

This book has simmered in the crockpot for a long time. I hope that as a result it is not over cooked but rather the time spent on slow cook has enabled it to absorb the best flavors and ingredients of the research, reflection, and wisdom of others. Hopefully the whole process will yield positive results from following the proverbial advice of "make haste slowly." That, however, remains for the reader to decide.

I have always been fascinated with the pithy proverb, even as a youth. I frequently heard my parents and grandparents utter proverbial sayings as a means of imparting wisdom. I took my fascination more seriously during my graduate work, focusing my dissertation on the sentence literature in Proverbs chapters 10 through 29. That was over twenty years ago. Around 1999 College Press in Joplin Missouri invited me to contribute a volume to their NIV Old Testament Commentary Series on *Proverbs, Ecclesiastes, and Song of Songs*, which I gladly accepted. That commentary was published in 2002 and serves as a foundation for this volume. Even before I published the College Press Commentary, however, I had already been working for several years on this kind of book. It has morphed into different shapes and sizes over the years until settling into its current form.

My goal with this volume is to bring together the best scholarship has to offer from both fields of biblical wisdom and character formation. So this is an interdisciplinary work. The very nature of wisdom calls for an openness to seek insight from all disciplines, experiences, and cultures. That is why the sage in Proverbs seeks wisdom from all corners of the world. The sage, for example, incorporates the best of wisdom material from Egyptian culture (Prov 22:17—24:22) and from foreigners like Agur (30:1) and King Lemuel (31:1). The sage also learns from creation (6:6-8), from observing others (24:32-34), and from listening to others (25:12)—even boring conversations, according to Cornelius Plantinga![4] The wise learn from every experience, culture, creature, community, and resource life offers.

In keeping with the nature of wisdom, this volume brings many different disciplines to bear on the subject of character formation. I of course begin with the book of Proverbs and specifically the sentence literature. This material serves as the source and theological foundation out of which I operate, organize, and develop the volume. Building on that foundation I engage other disciplines that help illuminate, provide fresh perspective, and bring out the contemporary relevance of the sentence literature. These disciplines include the field of homiletics, which I hope will generate ideas along the way for those who preach. The other disciplines I rely on include biblical studies, theology, rhetoric, ethics, philosophy, paremiology, psychology, cultural studies, and education theory. I want to capitalize on the best these disciplines have to offer to the task of shaping individual and corporate character.

In our materialistic culture, success is determined almost exclusively by one's wealth. Not so for the sage. For the wise in Proverbs it is one's character that governs the success or failure of a person. That is why the proverb that makes the observation "a good name is better than great wealth" seems so odd to us (Prov 22:1). It is countercultural. My aspiration is that this book will contribute to this countercultural worldview and enable readers to help put the task of character formation in working clothes.

I want to thank in particular two of my former graduate assistants for their invaluable help in enabling this project to come to completion. Sean Webb, as a critical thinker and a gifted writer, provided fresh insights, identified inconsistencies along the way, and made helpful suggestions for clarifying my thoughts. Steven Gaines, as a careful researcher and thoughtful processor, provided expertise in formatting matters, corrected a number of my inaccurate entries, and made many helpful suggestions to improve the quality of this work. I am indebted to them.

---

4. Plantinga, *Reading for Preaching*, 26.

Chapter One

The Journey of Character Formation

Our culture has a fascination with technology. Several years ago David Wells, author of *No Place for Truth* (1993), spoke about his father, born in 1898, who fought with a sword in the cavalry during the First World War.[1] Though his father is deceased, Wells reasoned it is quite possible that within the living memory of some is contained the shift from fighting with swords to fighting with drones and high-tech weaponry.

We have duplicated that kind of advancement in technology in every corner of life. For example, life expectancy has almost doubled in the last century. Science has eradicated many of the diseases that used to cut life short. In his lecture, Wells observed, "We are no longer cold in winter nor hot in summer. We have food from around the world any time of season."[2]

This wildfire of technological advance is not in itself a cause of concern. The extraordinary conquest of the outward world does, however, cause us to believe that we can duplicate that success in the inward world of the psyche by similar means. Whatever the experience—anxiety, guilt, unhappiness, depression, or lack of motivation—a therapeutic cure exists.

In his address, Wells identified three phases our culture has experienced to arrive at a therapeutic state of mind.[3] First, we have moved from emphasizing virtue to stressing value. The former focuses on normative qualities such as integrity, humility, faithfulness, and self-control. The latter focuses on what is important to me in my life. "Value" emphasizes personal

---

1. Wells, "The Weightlessness of God."
2. Ibid.
3. Wells develops these in more detail in his book *Losing Our Virtue*.

preferences.[4] Second, our culture has moved from identifying individuals as created in the image of God, and thus bound together in community, to identifying individuals by the self, unique from all others and each at the center of her own little world. Third, North American culture has moved from accentuating character to highlighting personality. This transition shifts the focus from internal qualities to external appearances. When specific virtues become habits in a person's life, character results. In contrast personality is defined as "image making," a concern with creating the right impressions.[5]

We have moved from a moral to a therapeutic culture, one that gives primacy to feelings and to finding relief from tension, emotional discomfort, and frustration. The problem with all of this is Christianity's response. Rather than setting out to influence or change culture, Christianity frequently succumbs to imitating the therapeutic mindset. As Robert Wuthnow observes, spirituality now primarily concerns itself with providing therapy. No longer do we look to the church to tell us what choices to make but to confirm for us the choices we already have made.[6] The church in general no longer offers guidance in making daily moral decisions about Christian conduct. Instead religion helps individuals to relieve anxieties or frustrations. We view our relationship with God as a way of enabling us to feel better about the decisions we make and about the lifestyle we choose to live.[7] Wuthnow reaches the following conclusion: "Religious convictions seem to operate at the level of moods and feelings, more so than at the level of morals and behavior."[8]

There is, thankfully, a biblical corrective for this trend. Specifically, the aphoristic sayings which give the book of Proverbs its name are an enduring challenge to a therapeutic mindset that is primarily concerned with making us feel good rather than equipping us to be good. Through these proverbs

---

4. Though making a distinction between "virtue" and "value" can be helpful in understanding our culture's shift in perspective, in later chapters I use the two terms interchangeably. I do, however, make distinctions between "core values" and "personal values."

5. Stephen Covey discovered that for the first 150 years of this country, the key to being successful centered around the development of character. For the past seventy-five years it has shifted to a focus on methods and strategies. Covey, "Seven Habits."

6. Wuthnow, *God and Mammon*, 5.

7. James Davison Hunter makes the observation that when public or private schools want expert advice about moral education, they call on psychologists, psychiatrists, or social workers. The perspective of these professionals is therapeutic; the point of reference out of which they operate is the autonomous self (85–86). Hunter, *The Death of Character*.

8. Ibid., 133.

we enter into the world of the sage and are led on a journey where wisdom[9] is both our guide and our goal. The whole process is one of character formation. Wisdom is not content to leave us as we are but insists that we allow ourselves to be transformed by the power of God.

Character, that cluster of virtues that forms into habits, is a product of one's relationship with God and with other fellow humans. In as much as this character is the natural outgrowth of wisdom, it is important to realize that wisdom, as expressed in Proverbs, is relational. In coming into relationship with God and becoming involved in the lives of others, character takes shape. Character, being shaped by these relationships, in turn rejuvenates them, continually refreshing our love for God and for others. Wisdom engenders character that is both shaped by and shapes community.

THE PROLOGUE

It is necessary that this overarching plan of wisdom should be rooted primarily and overtly in God. The introductory poem of Proverbs 1:2–7 makes this clear:

> For learning about wisdom and instruction,
>   for understanding words of insight,
> for gaining instruction in wise dealing,
>   righteousness, justice, and equity;
> to teach shrewdness to the simple,
>   knowledge and prudence to the young—
> Let the wise also hear and gain in learning,
>   and the discerning acquire skill,
> to understand a proverb and a figure,
>   the words of the wise and their riddles.
> The fear of the LORD is the beginning of knowledge;
>   fools despise wisdom and instruction.[10]

---

9. The idea of wisdom defies any single definition. But speaking in broad terms, wisdom embraces the task of learning how to live successfully. It involves the ability to cope with life's realities, not in the sense of dominating them, but in the sense of navigating the difficulties and assuming responsibility. Wisdom offers direction in connecting individuals to others and ultimately to God. Wisdom knows its limits. God ordered life in a certain way, building moral laws into its scheme. Wisdom seeks to live within those constraints.

10. Unless otherwise indicated, I quote from the New Revised Standard Version (NRSV). Generally speaking, this translation faithfully conveys the thought of the Hebrew text in understandable and contemporary language. However, there are occasions where I offer my own translation because important subtleties in the Hebrew text are not conveyed by the NRSV.

Wisdom grounds moral education in a knowledge of God. The poem discloses this substructure, quoting one of the most repeated lines in the book: "The fear of the LORD is the beginning of knowledge."[11] That the fear of the Lord is the *beginning* of wisdom means that without this relationship one will never acquire true wisdom. This "beginning" is not in the *horizontal* sense of missing the first tire in an obstacle course and just skipping to the next. Rather it is in the *vertical* sense of a ladder. If the student misses the first step of the ladder then progress cannot be made to the next step.[12] What the letters of the alphabet are to reading and notes to music, the fear of the Lord is to wisdom.[13]

In our modern spirituality, "fear" is not typically a stance toward God which is advocated regularly from the pulpits. Nevertheless, Proverbs makes clear that the fear of the Lord is the essence of wisdom. At its most basic level, fearing the Lord means that the center of life is not our world; it is located beyond.[14] To fear God is to realize that there is a moral locus outside of the self—a message which ought to be sounded from the pulpits. The beginning of wisdom is to come to the realization that fulfillment and satisfaction are outside our own power. What we are looking for cannot be bought, sold, accumulated, or invested on Wall Street. Fulfillment is found somewhere else, in Someone else. It is found in pursuing wisdom that comes from God.[15] When we develop the attitude of an inquirer, we are open to receiving God's wisdom, which in turn shapes the character of our life.

This character-forming wisdom, rooted in God, is experienced in community. In studying sapiential instruction, I have discovered the ubiquitous presence of conversation and conflict. Character development flourishes only in a community where healthy confrontation exists. Without the rigors of such an environment, individual character becomes undisciplined. The sages believed strongly in the principle that "iron sharpens iron" when it came to human interaction. Growth comes through struggle, and struggle is manifested as constructive conflict in healthy relationships.

The sages built this concept of conflict and contradiction into the very text of Proverbs. One moment may demand a specific word of advice, but a different moment may demand just the opposite piece of advice. For example, sometimes one must refrain from answering a foolish person (26:4), but

---

11. "Knowledge" and "wisdom" in Proverbs are parallel concepts, and the terms are often used synonymously.

12. Waltke, *The Book of Proverbs: Chapters 1–15*, 181.

13. Ibid.

14. Allen, "Wisdom of the World and God's," 197.

15. Ibid.

sometimes one must respond to a fool (26:5). Sometimes wealth is viewed as unequivocally good (10:15) but sometimes it is a detriment (11:4). In addition, the sages live with the tension that exists between the sovereign Lord on the one hand and the exercise of human freedom on the other (16:1–9). Humans plan their way but the Lord has the final word (16:1). The sages incorporate tension into the very process of instruction itself, often placing contradictory proverbs side-by-side, requiring students to work through the issues for themselves. Character needs a rigorous climate in which to grow.

This hard won wisdom is essentially available to all who are willing to seek it out. The introductory poem does mention two groups specifically, however, that are the intended audience of the instruction in Proverbs. The first group is the "simple" or the "youth" (v. 4).[16] The terms are used interchangeably to describe the inexperienced, the impressionable ones, the ones open to learning. The "simple" include the pliable ones and those easily influenced, but their naiveté leaves them vulnerable to influences from both good and bad sources. That is why in Proverbs the simple are sometimes associated with the fool. They have succumbed to the persuasion of the wrong group.

A second group also receives moral instruction. This group, "the wise" and "the discerning," are those who already possess a level of experience and understanding (v. 5). The "wise" are those who continue to open themselves to constructive reproof and who continue to grow and learn (see 9:8b–9a). In wisdom's world, no one is ever too old to learn. It is true that the older a person gets the less the desire to change due to set patterns established over the years. Still, age is not the most important factor in the ability to grow. According to behavioral scientists, "As long as there is an environment surrounding the person—and always there is that—he or she can change."[17] An increasing number of educators, in fact, are coming to speak of "intelligence" not in terms of IQ, a fixed intelligence quotient set at birth, but rather intelligence defined as the ability to adapt. Life is a long series of adaptations, moves, changes, beginnings and endings, and the wise are those who can make the appropriate adaptations necessary for lifelong learning.

Not only is wisdom open to people of all ages, it is also available to both male and female. True, the social context of Proverbs is a male dominated

---

16. The social context of Proverbs is the world of the young adult (15–25 years of age). This is evidenced in the kind of advice given. Youth are to stay away from gang related activities (1:8–19); they are to avoid the temptress (2:16–19; 5:1–23; 6:20–35; 7:6–27); they are to avoid the overuse of wine (23:29–35); they are to live a disciplined life and not yield to the temptation to slothfulness (6:6–11; 24:30–34). This advice is blunt and graphic, the kind given to young adults, not grade school children!

17. Cited in Clouse, *Teaching for Moral Growth*, 185.

society. The sages in chapters 1–9 address the son. As I have just mentioned, however, an important quality of wisdom is its ability to adapt to different times and contexts. One must read Proverbs with a perspective that sees the sage using the father/son relationship as an example of how wisdom is imparted in a particular transitional setting of life to a particular type of person, the young adult male. Wisdom calls on the reader to implement these educational principles into other settings and transitional moments, for example, between older and younger women or between mothers and sons or fathers and daughters.[18] Wisdom is available to all who possess open hearts and minds and a desire to learn.

The introductory poem also identifies a third group, but, surprisingly, this group lies beyond hope of receiving instruction. Proverbs calls this group "fools." The final line of the poem proclaims, "fools despise wisdom and instruction" (v. 7b). The fool in Wisdom Literature is not inept, clumsy, or slow-witted. Rather in Proverbs the fool is a moral category, one who lacks character.[19] Obstinacy and closed-mindedness characterize the "fool" (1:7). The "fool" is "wise in his own eyes" (26:5). That is, the fool does not rely on the counsel or advice of others. The "fool" creates his own world apart from the faith community. All through Proverbs the fool serves as a foil against which the sage offers instruction directed toward the youth and toward all who cultivate open-mindedness.

In a sense, the category of "the fool" is the most important of all. By showing readers that the only true characteristic that makes one irredeemable is a stance of obstinacy towards God and others, the sage throws wisdom open to the rest of us. The primary qualifications for receiving wisdom are not related to age, gender, IQ, or socio-economic status. What allows us to pursue the character-forming power of wisdom is openness toward God and the wisdom which can be gleaned from the community. So the truly wise ones humbly submit themselves to God. They reflect on and learn from their own mistakes. They make themselves vulnerable to the instructions, observations, and reproofs of others. They see life as a journey in which God's discipline molds them into his image (3:11–12).

In short, the truly wise one is the person who lives life focused not on self but on seeking God (Prov. 3:5–7). This quest naturally generates character, certain wisdom virtues like prudence, self-control, righteousness, and justice (1:3).[20] In turn, these virtues orient and order life in community.

---

18. See chapter 2 under the heading "Educational Process and Context" for further development of this.

19. See Pemberton, "It's A Fool's Life."

20. As Tremper Longman notes, "wisdom in Proverbs is an ethical quality." See Longman, *How to Read Proverbs*, 17.

They enable us to manifest right behavior toward others. While these principles are introduced in the first nine chapters of Proverbs, it is only later in the sentence literature of chapters 10–29 that the sages will attempt to flesh out these virtues into concrete behavior. The sentence literature is the sages' attempt to put righteousness in working clothes.[21] This is what wisdom offers moral education.

This book is designed to help the reader participate in that journey. The intention is to introduce the reader to the world of wisdom, to the process and content of moral instruction, and to the resources available for the formation of character. The interest in the development of moral character in Wisdom Literature,[22] and specifically in Proverbs, has received little attention among scholars. This should not surprise us since many scholars marginalize the book of Proverbs.[23] Contrary to popular opinion, however, Wisdom Literature plays a vital role in the theology of the Old Testament.[24] One of my goals for this book is to highlight the contribution Proverbs makes to the task of character formation in individuals open to a lifelong process of learning. I work at presenting the nuances of the theology of character from the sentence literature in Proverbs chapters 10–29.

Studies on Proverbs frequently gravitate more toward the first nine chapters and the last chapter, known as instruction literature. In reality, however, these chapters primarily serve as the narrative introduction and conclusion to the sentence literature that nestles in-between (10:1–22:16; 25–29).[25] The sentence literature contains the specific instructions upon

---

21. Kidner, *The Proverbs*, 35.

22. Wisdom Literature generally includes the books of Job, Proverbs, and Ecclesiastes.

23 There are a number of reasons why previous scholarship made the book marginal: 1) Canonically, it appears in the third and least authoritative section of the Hebrew Scriptures. 2) Theologically, wisdom does not seem to fit into the frame of the rest of the Old Testament. Gerhard von Rad's emphasis on *heilsgeschichte* and Walter Eichrodt's use of covenant marginalized the Wisdom Literature. Wisdom Literature is deemed anthropocentric. It is centered on human achievement and ability. In the opinion of some, Proverbs is too secular for the rest of the biblical neighborhood. 3) Formally, wisdom is not narrative as is many parts of the Old Testament. How one deals with what appears to be random collections of proverbs is an enigma. The self-contained proverbs have no literary context. They thus give the appearance of moralistic platitudes.

24. Of late the theological tide has shifted and more and more scholars like William Brown, Walter Brueggemann, James Crenshaw, Ellen Davis, Tremper Longman, Leo Perdue, and others have brought Wisdom Literature into the mainstream of study.

25. Camp, *Wisdom and the Feminine in the Book of Proverbs*, 179–208. Michael Fox refers to chapters 1–9 as the "hermeneutical preamble to the rest of the book" (346). Fox, *Proverbs 1–9*. The term "sentence literature" refers to the pithy two-line sentence proverbs located mainly in chapters 10–29.

which Woman Wisdom invites her guests to feast. Yet chapters 10–29 typically have not been taken seriously. The popular consensus labels them as pedantic, secular, and lightweight. William Willimon expresses the sentiments of many when he says, "Generally, I dislike the book of Proverbs with its lack of theological content, its long lists of platitudinous advice, its 'do this' and 'don't do that.' Pick up your socks. Be nice to salesclerks. It doesn't hurt to be nice. Proverbs is something like being trapped on a long road trip with your mother, or at least with William Bennett."[26] The proverbs contain little that deserves serious reflection.

That perspective, however, remains far from true. The reader who earnestly wrestles with these aphorisms, not releasing them until they divulge at least some of their rhetorical power and theological insight will not leave disappointed. They remain an untapped resource for those engaged in the acquisition of wisdom and in the development of character. Consequently this book attempts to usher the sentence literature back into the mainstream of discussion and to show their vitality as a resource in the process of character education. I intend to demonstrate the power of the proverb for character formation both for the individual and for the various faith communities to which we as individuals belong.

PROVERB CLUSTERS

To that end, I approach the sentence literature intending to expand the reader's understanding of how they are edited and collected in the book. It is true that many of the proverbs stand on their own, like words in a dictionary, independent of a surrounding context.[27] Certain pockets of proverbs, however, appear to be intentionally grouped together. I want to highlight some of these proverb clusters. For example, Chapter Five in this book centers on Proverbs 27:14–19. Chapter Six focuses on Proverbs 25:11–15 and 26:1–9. Chapter Seven takes its cue from 15:13–17 as well as other proverb pairs located in the sentence literature sections. Chapter Eight keys in on Proverbs 16:1–9. In these texts it appears that the sages intentionally

---

26. Willimon, *Pastor*, 255–56. Also quoted in his *Proclamation and Theology*, 28.

27. Tremper Longman argues against the current trend to see an intentional organization to the sentence literature. Longman maintains that the sentence literature is more or less random with a few isolated collections here and there. There is, in his opinion, no overarching systematic structure to the book. He observes, ". . . a systematic collection of proverbs may give the wrong impression . . . that life is systematic and that Proverbs was a 'how-to' fix-it book" (p. 40). The lack of structure is intentional and "reflects the messiness of life" (p. 40). He believes the trend to see structure and clusters is imposed rather than discovered. See Longman, *Proverbs*.

grouped together proverbs of like mind. I do not hold to the conviction of Duane Garrett[28] and, to a lesser degree, R. N. Whybray[29] who see almost every proverb in the sentence literature woven into a larger context.[30] But there are occasions in the collections where proverbs are intentionally clustered in larger units. Where a reasonable case can be made for such a context, I want to mine those proverb pockets for what they reveal about the nature and content of sapiential instruction.

CHAPTER SUMMARIES

What follows are eight chapters that introduce the reader to the goal, process, context, content, and resources of wisdom's instruction. In wisdom tradition, all of these components work together synergistically. By their nature each depends on the other. Even though at times in this volume one of these dimensions is highlighted over the other, none exists independently.

Chapter Two briefly identifies the goal and process of wisdom's instruction. The development of character did not ultimately exist for the sake of personal success. Rather it was in order to prepare youth on the brink of adulthood, as well as those with teachable spirits, to serve the larger community and to live in harmony with self and God. In order to accomplish this goal, the sages had at their disposal a number of instructional tools to assist in the process. These tools included, among other things, verbal instruction, negative and positive reinforcement, observation of life experiences, role-playing, and the art of discernment. The process of instruction was initiated within the context of the family.

With Chapter Three, the focus shifts away from the process and more toward the content of sapiential instruction. In contrast to a "values-clarification" approach, which leaves the choice of values to each individual, the sage engages in the practice of teaching specific core values to impressionable minds that in turn help to shape the life of the faith community.

The remaining chapters, Four through Nine, highlight fundamental resources the sages rely on in the educational process. Chapter Four describes the dynamic qualities of the primary oral tool the sages used in their instruction: the proverb. The chapter uses paremiological, rhetorical, and biblical disciplines to probe the inner forces at work in the proverb. The

---

28. Garrett, *Proverbs, Ecclesiastes, Song of Songs*.

29. Whybray, *The Composition of the Book of Proverbs*.

30. Bruce Waltke in his two-volume commentary seeks to demonstrate the interconnectedness of the individual proverbs throughout the sentence literature. See Waltke *The Book of Proverbs: Chapters 1–15* and *The Book of Proverbs: Chapters 15–31*.

proverb possesses qualities that enable it to penetrate heart and mind and do its work in the process of forming character. Such qualities continue to make the proverb a viable tool in the education process.

Chapter Five highlights another key resource in the process: human dialogue. In order to challenge students to grow, the sages engage in the process of verbal exchange between individuals. Wisdom does not believe the formation of character occurs in a vacuum. Wisdom teachers do not give pat answers to perplexing issues of life. Rather students engage in dialogue with the community and out of that exchange make decisions, carry out actions, and create moral order. Students are not shaped in a cookie-cutter fashion. Character is formed in conversation.

Chapter Six explores the role language and speech play in the development of character. In Proverbs, the wise have more to say about the use and abuse of language than any other subject. This should come as no surprise considering the oral culture in which the sages worked. The wise believe that language not only shapes character, it also reveals character.

Chapter Seven accents the theme of material possessions and poverty. The sages were keenly interested in the proper use of wealth. More than any other book in Scripture, Proverbs projects an ambivalent attitude toward wealth and poverty. In and of itself the wise did not view wealth as either good or bad. Rather, it depended on the character of the one using it. Like language, the way one handles wealth not only forms character but also exposes character.

Chapter Eight identifies God as the most fundamental resource for character formation. This chapter highlights what is referred to as the "Yahweh proverbs" in order to better understand the sages' perspective on God's involvement in human life. Yahweh is the ever-present, underlying force at work that initiates and sustains the educational process. The God of the sages does not remain aloof, watching from a distance as events unfold in the life of people. God does not sporadically intervene with a miracle here or there. Nor does the Lord display a cloud by day or a pillar of fire by night so that the people know which direction to go. Instead, the sages' God is involved in the details of daily living, working behind the scenes in the experiences and actions of creation. Yahweh works through human thoughts and decisions, all the while honoring the choices individuals make for themselves. Through such intricate and lovingly patient work, God shapes the character and will of those who remain open to learning.

Finally, I conclude with Chapter Nine and a reminder of the essential role community plays in the whole process, even though I reference its roll throughout the book. Chapter Nine offers a word of exhortation to the faith community to take responsibility for the moral education of its members.

No one party possesses sole responsibility. Rather, parents, families, friends, and the larger community all share a voice in molding individuals into responsible members in God's kingdom.

CONCLUSION

Wisdom as understood throughout Proverbs is not understood as an inherent quality or an object which can be obtained. Wisdom is a trajectory along which the wise grow as they proceed through life. Thus, the wise embark on a fascinating and often unpredictable adventure. Intrigue, disappointment, joy, suffering, conflict, dialogue, and satisfaction accompany every step. It is a journey initiated within the context of the family and perpetuated by the faith community. Wisdom offers no guarantees along the way regarding rewards or financial security or physical well-being, but it does guarantee the kind of character that enables individuals to live responsibly in community and that reflects the very nature of the God they serve. For this reason the wisdom of the aphorisms in Proverbs 10–29 demand a place of critical importance in contemporary discussions of character formation.

Chapter Two

The Process of Character Formation

THE EDUCATIONAL GOAL

C. S. Lewis spoke of a three-pronged approach to morality that in many ways reflects the goals of the sages. First, morality is concerned "with fair play and harmony between individuals." Second, morality involves "tidying up or harmonizing the things inside each individual." And third, moral education clarifies "the general purpose of human life as a whole: what man was made for."[1] Lewis compares these three tasks to a fleet of ships. The voyage of a fleet of ships will succeed only if they do not collide with each other, each ship has its engine in good working order, and they know their destination.[2]

    The goals of the sages can be viewed in a similar vein. Through patient instruction, the sage seeks to fortify youth with wisdom's values in order to enable them to live responsibly to self, others, and God. The values that wisdom teaches, equip a student to live responsibly to self. Wisdom emphasizes not only external actions but also internal attitudes that promote the health of the individual (e.g., 14:30; 15:13; 17:22; 19:1). In addition, wisdom values equip individuals to contribute to the well-being of family and society. The whole of Proverbs is couched in a community context. One's behavior affects the quality of life in that faith community (31:10–31). Finally, the

---

1. Lewis, *Mere Christianity*, 71.
2. Ibid., 70–71.

ultimate goal of the sage is to lead one into relationship with God (1:7). Those who are truly wise learn to trust in the Lord (3:5–7). Wisdom's goals lead one to live morally responsible.

This chapter will explore this process of character formation pursued by the sages. Discussions of the linguistic, historical, and social contexts will serve to augment the analysis. These contexts illuminate the various means by which the sages engage in their program of moral instruction. The sages' methods, to be examined in greater length below, are further illuminated by comparison and contrast to modern theories of moral development.

THE EDUCATIONAL PROCESS AND CONTEXT

Wisdom and Character

In order to understand further this relationship between wisdom and moral education, it is helpful to explore the definition of wisdom.[3] In Proverbs, "wisdom" refers to the ability to negotiate the complexities of life.[4] The wise person is one who develops expertise in living responsibly.[5] Tremper Longman observes that wisdom is closer to emotional intelligence than to I.Q.[6] People with a high I.Q. know facts and excel in the ability to reason and use logic. People with high emotional intelligence possess self-control, persist in the presence of frustration, delay gratification, control moods, think clearly in the face of stress, express compassion, and maintain hope. Such qualities of emotional intelligence are more closely related to the character and goals of wisdom.

Wisdom seeks to discover God's order in life and then proceeds to fit into that order successfully, always acknowledging human limitations.[7] Divine order involves moral behavior. As William Brown properly asserts, the ultimate goal of attaining wisdom is the formation of moral character.[8] This quality of character is the thicker, richer meaning of wisdom, according

---

3. Bland, "Wisdom," in *Baker Illustrated Bible Dictionary*.

4. Bland, *Proverbs, Ecclesiastes, & Song of Songs*, 29.

5. Fox, *Proverbs 1–9*, 32.

6. Longman, *How to Read Proverbs*, 15–16.

7. Stuart Weeks defines wisdom as "the knowledge of how to stay on the path which leads to life, because it is approved by God." See "Wisdom in the Old Testament" in *Where Shall Wisdom Be Found?*, edited by Barton, 26.

8. Brown, *Character in Crisis*, viii. In Brown's most recent volume, he expands the quality of character to include curiosity and wonder (*Wisdom's Wonder*, xi). Crenshaw affirms the following goal: "The goal of all wisdom was the formation of character." *Old Testament Wisdom*, 4.

to Michael Fox.[9] He states, "Proverbs consistently applies the word *hokmah* to wisdom as manifest in the skill and knowledge of right living" in the ethical and pragmatic senses.[10] Near the end of his work, Fox states wisdom's objective succinctly, "And fostering moral character, it is no overstatement to say, is at all times the greatest goal of education."[11]

Folly and Anti-Character

The description of wisdom's counterpart, folly, further affirms its moral dimension. In contemporary American culture we use the terms fool or foolishness to refer to a person's lack of intellectual ability or a person whose actions convey those of a buffoon. We might say of such an imbecile "his elevator doesn't go all the way up." In a series of books that used to be quite popular, Wendy Northcutt gave out "The Darwin Award" to people who do idiotic things, for example: "The terrorist who mails a letter bomb with insufficient postage wins a Darwin Award when he opens the returned package."[12] This kind of behavior our culture labels foolish.

Proverbs, however, uses the term fool differently. Proverbs employs it to describe someone in a morally deprived state. The sage possesses a repertoire of at least a half a dozen different words for "fool."[13] All of them indicate some kind of moral breach and move on a scale from the most morally hardened to the naive.[14] One common phrase the sage uses to describe the fool is one who "lacks sense" (6:32; 9:4; 10:13, 21; 11:12; 12:11; 15:21; 17:18; 24:30). One can also translate this phrase "lacks character."[15] The fool is characterized as the one not open to instruction because he or she is "wise in his own eyes" (3:7; 16:2; 26:5).[16] The fool scoffs at correction and rebuke (9:7, 8, 12; 13:1; 14:6; 15:12; 19:25; 20:1; 21:11, 24; 22: 10; 24:9).

---

9. Fox, *Proverbs 1–9*, 29.

10. Ibid., 33.

11. Ibid., 348.

12. Northcutt, *The Darwin Awards*, 1–2.

13. Crenshaw lists eight words, *Old Testament Wisdom*, 74. Fox lists seven terms in his article, "Words for Folly."

14. Fox, "Words for Folly," 6. See also Fox, *Proverbs 1–9*, 38–39.

15. See Longman, *Proverbs*, 235.

16. It is interesting to note that the etymology of the English word "sophomore" comes from two Greek words: *sophos*, meaning "wise" and *moros*, meaning "fool." A "sophomore" is a fool who thinks he or she is wise, a fitting term for the way a fool is described in Proverbs.

The fool is defensive and refuses to admit mistakes (10:17; 12:1; 15:5). He or she manifests arrogance (cf. 21:24).

Glenn Pemberton provides a helpful synthesis of the fool in the book of Proverbs by gathering references to the character and reconstructing a potential process of how a person deforms into a hardened fool.[17] The first stage involves isolated foolish acts or misssteps that involve lapses into a loss of control on particular occasions. But these isolated flaws do not make one a fool. The second stage, according to Pemberton, is when "folly becomes sport."[18] At this phase, the person starts to repeat the same destructive behavior and begins to enjoy it. The behavior becomes more of a conscious choice. Stage three enters the picture when the individual loses any desire to pursue wisdom. Such a person does not listen to the advice of others because he is convinced he is wise in his own eyes. At this stage the person habitually follows the path of least resistance.[19] The final stage of deformation is reached when the fool loses all respect and honor in the community. The fool is disgraced and there remains no hope for reform.

In contrast to the fool, the wise follow a similar progression of development in the opposite direction except the process is far more demanding. The wise are open to instruction; they cultivate a teachable spirit (1:5; 9:9; 19:25; 21:11). Through discipline and passion to pursue the path of wisdom, they develop qualities of virtue that become habits. When one follows the path of wisdom it offers individuals the ability to negotiate the difficulties of life in a way that enables them to live responsibly before God and others. As a relational quality, wisdom expresses itself through moral conduct that is appropriate for the occasion. Whether choosing the path of wisdom or the path of folly, however, the progression for both is quite similar as expressed in the following rhyme:

> Sow a thought, reap an act
> Sow an act, reap a habit
> Sow a habit, reap a character
> Sow a character, reap a destiny

Proverbs 29:18 and the Gang in 1:8–19

In the absence of instruction that strives toward the goal of wisdom, the moral fiber of a society quickly erodes. An undisciplined person, the fool,

---

17. Pemberton, "It's a Fool's Life."
18. Ibid., 219.
19. Ibid., 221.

wreaks havoc on the larger community. Such havoc is encapsulated in the first line of Proverbs 29:18. Unpacking the meaning of this proverb reveals the consequences of both the absence as well as the acceptance of instruction. The well-known saying reads, "Where there is no prophecy the people cast off restraint; but happy are those who keep the law." The King James Version translates the first line in the most familiar way: "Where there is no vision the people perish." The proverb is frequently understood to mean that where people have no dreams or future goals, they will not survive.[20] This translation, however, renders the proverb impotent. In 29:18 the term "vision"[21] refers either to a word that God spoke to the prophets or to the word the sages spoke to the people. The term does not apply to the imagination or foresight of the people. In fact, the word "vision" or "prophecy" in the first line is parallel with "law"[22] in the second. Consequently verse 18a affirms that where people have no respect or consideration for the instruction of the wise, there is chaos: "the people cast off restraint." That is, there is no discipline.[23] A parallel thought occurs in 11:14a: "Where there is no guidance, a nation falls."

With the second line of the proverb an important shift occurs from the plural to the singular. This shift is lost in the NRSV because it uses inclusive language. A somewhat more precise reading is, ". . . but blessed is he who keeps the law." The verse sets up a contrast between an immoral community (a whole community that has chosen the path of folly) in the first line and a morally responsible individual in the second. The proverb implies that even

---

20. I would say that this proverb is one of the most frequently misquoted proverbs in the book. George Barna uses it to establish a biblical basis for the need for churches to have goals and visions. See Barna, *The Power of Vision*, 11. Curtis Fussell quotes the proverb from the KJV and misinterprets it in a sermon that speaks of the need to have a clear perspective on what Jesus wants in our lives. See Fussell, *Deadly Sins and Living Virtues*, 10. Norman Shawchuck and Roger Heuser refer to Proverbs 29:18 to advocate the necessity of a congregation to develop a vision "of its God-given possibilities" for the future. Shawchuck and Heuser, *Leading the Congregation*, 98, 250. Robert Cueni uses the proverb in the same way. See Cueni, *Dinosaur Heart Transplants*, 62. Gabriel Fackre quotes the proverb from the KJV in the context of encouraging readers to share in the visions that other theologians had as they explored the complex and multifaceted nature of Christ. The point made is legitimate, but the text is misinterpreted. See Fackre, *The Christian Story*, 118. Henry and Richard Blackaby seem to be more on track in interpreting this proverb accurately. See Blackaby and Blackaby, *Spiritual Leadership*, 61

21. The Hebrew term is חָזוֹן. See Amos 1:1; Isaiah 1:1; Nahum 1:1.

22. תּוֹרָה (torah or instruction) here may refer to God's law revealed through Moses. But most likely it refers to the instruction given by the wise, including father and mother.

23. William McKane translates this line as follows: "Where there is no vision people are undisciplined." See McKane, *Proverbs*, 257.

though a society may lose its moral bearings and cast off restraint, an individual who follows sagacious advice can choose otherwise. Such a person maintains strong ethical character even in the midst of a corrupt society.

Proverbs 29:18 offers a personal blessing to the one who adheres to the teaching of the wise. However, the development of moral character is not primarily for the sake of having skills for one's personal success. The book of Proverbs is about those who are willing to venture beyond their comfort zones and embark on a journey that enables them to grow mentally, morally, and spiritually and live responsibly in community (31:10–31). Such a person is one who truly fears the Lord. This is the goal of wisdom's instruction. It is in the context of the family that the journey toward this goal begins.

This is precisely the advice the parents seek to give their son in 1:8–19:

> Hear, my child, your father's instruction,
>   and do not reject your mother's teaching;
> for they are a fair garland for your head,
>   and pendants for your neck.
> My child, if sinners entice you,
>   do not consent.
> If they say, "Come with us, let us lie in wait for blood;
>   let us wantonly ambush the innocent;
> like Sheol let us swallow them alive
>   and whole, like those who go down to the Pit.
> We shall find all kinds of costly things;
>   we shall fill our houses with booty.
> Throw in your lot among us;
>   we will all have one purse"—
> my child, do not walk in their way,
>   keep your foot from their paths;
> for their feet run to evil,
>   and they hurry to shed blood.
> For in vain is the net baited
>   while the bird is looking on;
> yet they lie in wait—to kill themselves!
>   and set an ambush—for their own lives!
> Such is the end of all who are greedy for gain;
>   it takes away the life of its possessors.

Proverbs does not usually talk about such extreme cases that involve felony crimes. The book usually addresses ethical choices related to common everyday decisions such as controlling anger, restraining the tongue, learning patience, and practicing generosity. All the parent is attempting to do in this first lecture is to get the youth's undivided attention.[24] So this lecture intends to generate a shock and awe experience. The admonition is basically, "Do not choose to involve yourself with felons and their criminal activity."

Michael Fox proposes that the unusual scenario causes the youth to ask the question, "Is life really *that* dangerous?"[25] The implied response is, yes it is! The apparently insignificant daily choices one makes lead to a distinct destiny. Decisions made regarding honesty, patience, pride, generosity, anger, greed and other qualities ultimately culminate into life and death matters.

For a couple of years, somewhere between 2012 and 2014, DirectTV ran a series of popular "Get Rid of Cable Ads" on television. The ads always began with some small irritation such as the viewer not able to get cable or record a program on cable or not able to find anything good to watch on cable, etc. This minor irritation then leads to frustration that leads to anger, then to depression, then feelings of dejection, unhappiness, or boredom and ultimately disaster. One of the ads I recall appeared around March of 2014 in which the man's cable is on the fritz. It resulted in causing him tension which led to a lack of sleep, which led him to drive off the road and end up in a ditch, which led him to being stranded, which led him to have to learn how to survive, which led him to eat wild berries, and the wild berries caused him to go berserk and chase butterflies! Small decisions when repeated lead to greater and more serious consequences. The opening poem describing the gang shows the ultimate consequences of earlier decisions its members had made. The rhetorical effect of this poem is not unlike the showing of a video of horrendous car wrecks to Driver's Education students' first learning to drive. It is a way of demonstrating the seriousness of the subject matter.

In this initial lecture, the youth is tempted to become a part of a gang that has no regard for God, others, or for the community. Such a group rejects the instruction given them by their parents (v. 8). They cast off all restraint. They steal, abuse, and mistreat others in order to gain selfishly for themselves (vv. 10–14). They scheme and connive; they act without scruples. They choose the path of least resistance; they choose folly. Their lifestyle, however, is alluring attracting quite a following. They claim to share equally in the spoils of their conquests. They practice the philosophy "all for one and one for all" (v. 14). Yet the father believes that the youth can choose to reject that enticing way of life and follow in the way of sound instruction.

24. Pemberton, "The Rhetoric of the Fathers," 84–87.
25. Fox, *Proverbs 1–9*, 93.

He can maintain strong moral character even in the midst of unscrupulous people. If the son so chooses, according to Proverbs 29:18, he is blessed.

The Familial Context of Education

From the nation's inception, God called Israel to pass on its faith to the next generation. The instruction of youth was a religious responsibility, the very reason for the choosing of Abraham: " . . . for I have chosen him, that he may *charge his children and his household after him to keep the way of the Lord by doing righteousness and justice*; so that the Lord may bring about for Abraham what he has promised him" (Gen. 18:19; italics mine). The book of Deuteronomy indicates that Israelite households followed a general process in carrying out their responsibility to instruct (Deut. 6:4–9, 20–25). Concerning this responsibility, R. A. Culpepper concludes: "Education in ancient Israel . . . was largely informal and related to the family unit."[26]

The book of Proverbs offers a valuable perspective on the efforts of a community to educate those with open hearts and minds in the formation and transformation of character. The setting for the final form of Proverbs is the post-exilic period during the time of the Persian Empire.[27] Before reaching the apex of its contribution to Israelite culture, Israelite wisdom went through several phases of growth and development. The earliest phase was the pre-exilic period of folk wisdom. Israelite clans produced and passed on wisdom sayings within the extended family of the village.[28] The monarchic period initiated the next general phase in which wisdom was developed, nurtured, and incorporated into the court setting.[29] The third phase of development occurred after the exile. It was during this time that the final form of the book of Proverbs took shape. This final phase was the most productive time for Wisdom Literature in Israel.[30]

During the post-exilic period, Israel confronted significant changes that affected its image as God's people. It was a time of transition. Israel no longer had the temple, the monarchy, or the land to depend on for her identity. Israel struggled with how to maintain its sense of community in this environment. The wisdom tradition helped to reshape Israel's former

---

26 Culpepper, "Education," 21.

27 See Gese, "Wisdom Literature in the Persian Period"; Clements, *Wisdom in Theology*; Perdue, *Proverbs*. Patrick Skehan posits a post-exilic editing based on linguistic and structural evidence. See "A Single Editor for the Whole Book of Proverbs."

28. Westermann, *The Roots of Wisdom*.

29. Brueggemann, *In Man We Trust*.

30. See Bland, "Formation of Character in the Book of Proverbs."

nationalistic focus by placing its religious beliefs, so long couched in the form of laws and narrative, in a different literary form (the proverb) and extracting the exclusive language of covenant. As a result, unlike many nations taken into exile, Israel was able not only to survive but also to thrive. Religious and personal identities were not lost but were instead redefined. As Ronald Clements concludes, "In some respects wisdom became a 'transitional philosophy,' maintaining identifiable links with the past, but adapting them to new ways and conditions."[31] So wisdom flourished for a couple of reasons. It succeeded because the original educational function that wisdom fulfilled was heightened during the post-exilic period by the need to instruct Jews, living in a predominantly pagan world, in the religious and cultural ways of Jewish communities. It also thrived because the lack of covenantal language enabled wisdom to ground moral instruction in something higher than Jewish nationalism.[32]

It is within this post-exilic environment, as well, that the family took on new significance. Israel's removal from the land also meant severed ties with the clan structure that had for centuries shaped her lifestyle. From the time they left Egypt, the Israelites' social structure was organized around clans, extended family units known as the "father's house." Such a social system gave them security, identity, and economic stability. But now with Israel dispersed across the Persian Empire, the clan system had less of an influence.[33] Clements' words are most apropos in this regard:

> Taken in a larger context, some useful observations may be made which have a bearing upon the role of wisdom in a biblical theology. The most obvious is that, in the post-exilic period, wisdom appears to have flourished as part of a program of education carried out with the approval of, and probably within the location of, the individual household. Begin early, be persistent and, if necessary, do not shun physical punishment, in order to achieve results. These are seriously repeated maxims for instruction, aimed at parents, instructors and pupils. The very roots of religion and virtue are seen to rest within the relatively small household context of family life. The rewards of adherence to the dictates of wisdom are claimed to include security, prosperity and ultimately happiness. All of this indicates that religion is taken out of its cultic setting and is markedly domesticated. Parents, rather than priests, hold the key to its seriousness and

---

31. Clements, *Wisdom in Theology*, 125.

32. Clements, "Wisdom and Old Testament Theology," 273.

33. The genealogies of Chronicles, Ezra, and Nehemiah, however, do witness to the continued presence of clans during this time.

success! Yet it is never secular in the formal sense, since it recognizes that, deprived of its religious foundations, it cannot succeed and will lack its indispensable starting-point.[34]

The post-exilic period initiated a time of transition for Israel as a people. The household became the focal point in enabling Israel to maintain its identity as God's people. It became the central sphere for the development of moral character.[35]

It is this historical context that lies behind the literary form of the book of Proverbs. The book's formal structure is framed in a familial setting. After the introductory paragraph (1:1-7), the exhortation of the first wisdom poem sets forth the context: "Hear, my child, your father's instruction, and do not reject your mother's teaching; for they are a fair garland for your head, and pendants for your neck" (1:8-9).[36] The book concludes with a picture of the well-ordered house and the wise woman who offers counsel (31:10-31). She is the one who "opens her mouth with wisdom, and the teaching of kindness is on her tongue" (31:26). In addition to this overarching frame for the book, it is noteworthy that the sentence literature of chapters 10:1-22:16 begins with this affirmation: "A wise child makes a glad father, but a foolish child is a mother's grief" (10:1). Such a beginning declaration sets the tone for hearing the sayings in a familial context. Not only that but concern for maintaining the home is woven like a scarlet thread throughout the sentence literature.[37] Clements concludes: "For wisdom the household had become both a school and a spiritual training ground."[38] Even with strong indications that point to the existence of schools in Israel,[39]

---

34. Clements, "Wisdom and Old Testament Theology," 281.

35. See Clements, *Wisdom in Theology*, 123–150; Crenshaw, "Education in Ancient Israel," 614. Michael Fox, comes to the same conclusion: "The family is the primary setting for character education, which is Wisdom's purpose. There is never a hint of a school setting, though scholars have usually regarded this as the locus of wisdom teaching." Fox, "Wisdom and the Self-Presentation of Wisdom Literature," 156.

36. The inclusive language of the NRSV leads the translators to use the word "child." But the literal word is "son," referring to a young adult male.

37. 10:5; 12:4; 13:1, 24; 14:1; 15:20; 17:1, 6, 21, 25; 18:22; 19:13, 14, 26; 20:20; 21:9, 19; 25:24; 27:11, 15–16; 28:7, 24; 29:3.

38. Clements, *Wisdom in Theology*, 143.

39. In brief, there are three major arguments for the existence of schools in ancient Israel: 1. Israel followed the practices of Egypt and Mesopotamia who had schools. 2. The high literary quality of much of the Old Testament is difficult to explain without the existence of schools. 3. Archaeological evidence points to the existence of schools. Fragmentary inscriptions found and dated around the twelfth century BCE seem to be the school exercises of young students.

Bernard Lang is of the opinion there were schools in Israel based on the image the primary responsibility for instruction in the book of Proverbs falls on the family.[40]

Sometimes the reference to the father and son relationship in Proverbs is understood as actually referring to the relationship between a teacher and student. Nevertheless, throughout Proverbs the father, as well as the mother, is assumed to have the responsibility to teach.[41] King Lemuel gives credit to his mother for the instruction he received as a young adult: "The words of Lemuel, king of Massa, which his mother taught him" (31:1). What follows after this heading are examples of the kind of advice the king's mother offered him. In ancient Israel the maternal parent plays an important role in the education of children. This is why the children of the wise woman in Proverbs 31:28 "rise up and call her blessed."

The fact that both parents are frequently cited as fulfilling this teaching role strongly points to the recognition that it was the pupil's natural parents who were involved. The father's reminiscence of his father's teachings in 4:3 further depicts parental, not school, education. So even if Proverbs was composed for use in schools, its literary context is the instruction of the (actual) father to his (actual) son.[42] "Father" means father, just as the parallel

---

described in Proverbs 1:20–33 of Dame Wisdom in the city gate rebuking the young men assembled to learn who were not listening. Lang, *Wisdom and the Book of Proverbs*. However, it is difficult to offer a definitive argument for schools in Israel based on a text that is poetic! Stuart Weeks maintains that no definitive answer can be known from the current evidence, Weeks, *Early Israelite Wisdom*. James Crenshaw concludes that schools existed in Israel. But the evidence does not enable scholars to establish an exact date of emergence or how they functioned. Crenshaw, *Education in Ancient Israel*. G. I. Davies sees the evidence as strongly in favor of schools. Davies, "Were there Schools in Ancient Israel?" Leo Perdue develops his commentary on Proverbs on the belief that the book was a product of the royal and wisdom schools. Perdue, *Proverbs*. See also Clark, "Schools, Scholars, and Students."

40. Carole R. Fontaine draws the following conclusion: "Within the private sphere of the family, the most important sage roles are those that emphasize teaching, and these fall equally to father and mother." Fontaine, "The Sage in Family and Tribe," 164.

Raymond Van Leeuwen remarks, "The social setting of the instructions in Proverbs 1–9 is portrayed as parental address to adolescent 'sons' about to undertake the journey to full adulthood with its responsibilities and rewards. . . . Hence, the primary purpose of these chapters is protreptic: to entice the 'untutored' (פֶּתִי) to a wisely ordered (8:5–21) and godly life (1:7, 29; 2:5; 3:5–12; 8:13; 9:10)," 113. Later he comments, "But our interest lies rather in the explicit, self-conscious function of these texts as instruction to youth in a situation of passage into adulthood." Van Leeuwen, "Liminality and Worldview in Proverbs 1–9," 113, 115.

41. 4:1–4; 6:20–21; 10:1; 15:20; 17:25; 20:20; 23:22–25; 29:15; 30:11; 30:17; 31:26, 28. There are some fourteen references to the mother (אֵם) in Proverbs as it relates to an instructional context: 1:8; 4:1–4; 6:20; 10:1; 15:20; 19:26; 23:22; 23:25; 29:15; 30:17; 31:1.

42. Why are only sons addressed in Proverbs and not daughters? Clearly, Israel's

"mother" (1:8; 4:3; 6:20) must mean the actual mother, not a "schoolmarm."[43] A home, not a school is the *literary* milieu of Proverbs.[44]

Wisdom cultivates a community environment in which moral values are taught. The familial path wisdom takes to achieve its goal involves a journey of rigorous training. Wisdom's process incorporates multiple resources and strategies. But little attention has been given to this untapped reservoir. In order to appreciate its value, one first needs to identify and elaborate on the moral resources of the sages.

THE PROCESS OF "HOME SCHOOLING"

There are a number of specific resources the sage used in the educational process which warrant elaboration: the use of physical discipline, employing wise

---

culture was patriarchal. However, Bruce Waltke suggests that daughters were not as likely to rebel as were sons. The "son is singled out because by nature he is most tempted to stray from the inherited tradition . . . Furthermore, the son will inherit the primary responsibility for his own household's spiritual identity (cf. Num 30; Prov 4:3–4). The daughter was expected to follow her husband's lead." Waltke, "Proverbs: Theology of," 1085. See also Waltke's commentary, *The Book of Proverbs: Chapters 1–15*, 116–17. In addition, the fact that mothers served as teachers indicates that daughters were involved in the process of instruction somewhere along the line.

However one perceives the omission of daughters, the interpretive flexibility and mindset of wisdom calls on later generations that read the material to adjust and to apply the instruction of Proverbs equally to both genders. The reader must also remember that the books of the Bible are occasional. They are addressed to specific audiences and situations. For example, Titus was addressed to Titus. The reader takes responsibility for appropriately interpreting these letters for the church today. One approaches Proverbs in the same way.

Tremper Longman makes an astute observation, "Isolated from the rest of Scripture, Proverbs addresses young men. Once it is included within the broader sweep of Scripture, a fuller application may be sought. After all, though individual biblical books are addressed to specific audiences at the time of their writing, the canon of Scripture is directed to all God's people." Longman, *How To Read Proverbs*, 133.

43. Judith McKinlay studies the proverbs in which both father and mother are mentioned in light of the phenomenon of Hebrew parallelism. She asks some provocative questions. Is parallelism more static in structure in which the second line is equal to the first and thus interchangable? Or is it more dynamic in which the second line expresses new details and perspectives? How these questions are answered determines whether one perceives the parallelism of "mother" with "father" as synonymous and thus interchangable or as antonyms and thus viewed as male and female. In all the proverbs which incorporate the "father/mother" pair, the mother figure is always in the second line. This prompts McKinlay to ask, "Does the woman really live one space below her husband?" See Judith E. McKinlay, *Gendering Wisdom the Host*, 103, 110.

44. Michael V. Fox maintains, "there is no justification for the common assumption that the speaker is a schoolteacher." Fox, "Ideas of Wisdom in Proverbs 1–9," 620.

reproof, implementing oral repetition, the art of discernment, and the skill of observing life.[45] Some of these resources involved a direct and authoritative approach to education. Others were more indirect and interactive. They all worked together in a nurturing family and community environment.

The Rod and Reproof

Proverbs 29:15 refers to the first two resources: "The rod and reproof give wisdom, but a mother is disgraced by a neglected child." The two forms of discipline[46] described include physical and verbal. The first has to do with the use of the "rod" in the process of instruction. Sages promoted the use of physical discipline, as the following proverb graphically depicts:

> Do not withhold discipline from your children; if you beat them with a rod, they will not die. If you beat them with the rod, you will save their lives from Sheol. (23:13–14)[47]

To our western cultural mindset, this proverb seems quite violent, similar to the frustrated parent in the following nursery rhyme:

> There was an old woman,
> Who lived in a shoe;
> She had so many children,
> She didn't know what to do.
> She gave them some broth,
> Without any bread;
> She whipped them all soundly,
> And sent them to bed.

This mother had reached her emotional limit and the way to relieve her own frustration was to give each of her children a sound whipping. Such an arbitrary act of punishment is nothing short of abusive behavior.

As a result of this kind of abuse, the use of physical punishment in the education process poses a major quandary for contemporary American culture where child abuse remains a serious problem. According to statistics compiled in 2014 in the "Child Abuse and Neglect Stats" website 678,810

---

45. See Bland, "Formation of Character in the Book of Proverbs."

46. In Proverbs when the sages speak of "discipline" (מוּסָר) they are speaking of teaching in moral insight and character which includes both physical and verbal instruction. Fox, *Proverbs 1–9*, 34.

47 Eight times שֵׁבֶט (rod) is used to describe physical punishment in Proverbs (10:13; 13:24; 22:8; 22:15; 23:13, 14; 26:3; 29:15). One time the term חֹטֶר (rod) is used (14:3).

children in America suffered some form of maltreatment in 2012.[48] Even among Christian families,[49] it is not uncommon for parents to appeal to the mandate in Proverbs as a reason to inflict bodily harm on their children.[50] Because of the problem, Thomas G. Long concludes that proverbs like 23:13–14 are unwise proverbs.[51] Therefore the whole idea of corporal punishment as an instrument of instruction is not to be tolerated in our North American context.

In spite of its controversial nature, teachers, preachers, and church leaders cannot ignore the subject of physical discipline when addressing the process of moral education. They must educate their congregations regarding how it is used in Proverbs and its ongoing use in Christian homes. At the same time, except for cases of abuse, church leaders do not have the responsibility to decide for parents what they should or should not do regarding the discipline of their own children. Thus, while the church must firmly condemn child abuse and publicly affirm no toleration of abusive behavior in any form, integrity demands that it must also explore the meaning of these proverbs in their theological context before laying the template of child abuse onto all acts of physical discipline and immediately dismissing them.

The most familiar proverb referring to the use of the rod is found in 13:24: "Those who spare the rod hate their children, but those who love them are diligent to discipline them."[52] Often in Proverbs discipline is associated with verbal rebuke or instruction. In this proverb, it is related to physical discipline.[53] The proverb makes a contrast between expressing "hate" on the one hand and conveying "love" on the other. Occasionally, love demands tough action. However, it *never* involves abuse.[54] In Proverbs

---

48. Website: http://www.firststar.org/library/national-statistics.aspx

49. John Goldingay relates an incident where Christian counselors encouraged a mother to spank her children or else "she was disobeying God's command." See Goldingay, *Proverbs, Ecclesiastes & Song of Songs For Everyone*, 57. Goldingay seems to imply that references to the rod or "club" as he translates it in Proverbs "are figurative and hyperbolic" (58). The rod, however, was some kind of actual instrument used to discipline.

50. See Heskett, "Proverbs 23:13–14."

51. Long, *Preaching and the Literary Forms of the Bible*, 62. See also Elliott, *Creative Styles of Preaching*, 94–95.

52. It may be from this proverb that the more contemporary proverb has been coined though it misinterprets the biblical proverb, "spare the rod and spoil the child."

53. Tremper Longman maintains that the rod "is not to be taken metaphorically in the book, but rather as a tool of physical discipline." See Longman, *Proverbs*, 564.

54. The poem in Sirach 30:1–13 is especially egregious with an admonition to parents not to play or laugh with their child and "beat his sides while he is young." Such

physical discipline was administered in the context of a loving family environment. The goal was not the venting of parental anger but the saving of a youth's life from untimely death.[55] Parents follow God's example by observing how God disciplines (Prov. 3:11-12).[56]

The sages had much to say about the self-restraint of anger in the context of discipline. The two proverbs in 19:18-19 demonstrate this close connection:

> Discipline your children while there is hope;
>   do not set your heart on their destruction.
> A violent tempered person will pay the penalty;
>   if you effect a rescue, you will only have to do it again.

The first proverb speaks of the discipline involved in educating one's children. The second observes the severe consequences that come to a person who does not maintain control of anger. While these are both self-contained proverbs, it is instructive that the wise are those who practice self-control, which includes the context of disciplining children.

With the proverbs that speak of physical discipline, one must look at the larger theological context — the virtue of self-restraint (16:32; 25:28) and warnings against excessive anger (14:17) — that underlies much of the teachings of the sage. One should also keep another core virtue of wisdom in mind, namely patience (12:16; 14:29; 15:1, 18), in understanding how the sages implemented the use of the rod. One must conclude that discipline was administered in the context of love, restraint, and patience. Brown concludes that for the sage it is the motive behind the physical discipline

---

admonition must be totally rejected by parents.

55. Kevin Youngblood makes the following observation: "A word is in order about Proverbs' notorious statements regarding physical discipline. To modern ears such statements as "Do not deprive a child of discipline. If you beat him with the rod, he will not die" (Prov. 23:13) sound extremely harsh. Furthermore, such statements, unfortunately, have even been used to justify child abuse. It cannot be said often or emphatically enough that nothing could be further from the sages' intent. While Proverbs does affirm a parent's right, even responsibility, to use corporal punishment when necessary, it also insists that the motive behind this discipline must be love, not anger (cf. Prov 3:12; 13:24). One must further keep in mind that Proverbs is not promoting a type of discipline so much as the principle of discipline in general. The poetic nature of the aphorisms in Proverbs makes liberal use of symbols, such as the rod, in reference to broad concepts. The point of such statements is not the rod is the only divinely approved method of discipline, but that discipline, symbolized by the rod, must be meted out to children in ways appropriate to their personality and situation. For a helpful explanation of this concept see Tremper Longman III, *How To Read Proverbs* (Downers Grove, IL: IVP, 2002), 57." See Youngblood, "Cosmic Boundaries and Self-Control in Proverbs," footnote 2, 140.

56. Longman, *Proverbs*, 565.

that is critical: "edification rather than punishment, love rather than hatred motivates acts of discipline."[57] In addition, he points out that there are no references to children fearing their parents in the disciplining process. That is "fear is evidently not the means" for parents to prompt obedience from their children.[58]

The very quality of wisdom itself demands that parents exercise discretion in how they discipline children. Every child is different. Every family is different. I know of certain families who intentionally chose not to use spanking as a form of discipline. They use other creative means of instruction. These families have raised fine responsible children. I also know of families who intentionally chose to use an occasional spanking as a tool of discipline when their children were young. The spanking was restrained and was administered in the context of love and affection. They too have fine responsible children. Yes, there are extreme cases where Christian parents administer severe spankings to their children claiming to do it in the name of love.[59] Such practice is wrong. Whatever route a parent chooses to go, however, sensitivity to the best interest of the child and a proper loving environment is essential for administering discipline.

The second form of discipline described in Proverbs 29:15 is verbal: reproof.[60] The noun "reproof" appears in Proverbs more often than in any other book in the Hebrew Scriptures.[61] As with "the rod," reproof does not involve mistreatment, be it verbal abuse or persistent nagging. Neither the quarrelsome man (26:17-28) nor the quarrelsome woman (27:15-16) model appropriate verbal behavior. Nor does the use of reproof, like the use of the rod, come in the context of an angry moment. In the context of

---

57. Brown, "To Discipline Without Destruction," 72. Brown also observes that the use of the rod is not about punishment but about discipline. Thus for the sage, the phrase "physical discipline" rather than "corporal punishment" is a better way of describing the act.

58. Ibid., 73.

59. Randall Heskett gives an example of a couple he calls Elmer and Connie who made their children lie on a bed, spread their arms out, and then struck them three to ten times with the "rod of correction." Heskett acknowledges that this is "an extreme example," Heskett, "Proverbs 23:13-14," 181. Extreme examples, however, are exceptions and as exceptions they cannot be used to argue a case against any form of physical discipline as Heskett does.

60. The term "reproof" (תוֹכַחַת) is often paired with the word "discipline" (מוּסָר) in Proverbs (see 3:11; 5:12; 6:23; 10:17; 12:1; 13:18; 15:5; 15:10; 15:32). The Hebrew word for "reproof" is also the word for reasoned argument such as a lawyer would use in a courtroom (cf. Job 13:6; 23:4; Ps. 38:14).

61. It occurs twenty-four times in the Old Testament, sixteen of those are in Proverbs. The verb יָכַח occurs 59 times in the Old Testament. Its most frequent occurrence is found in Job (seventeen times) and Proverbs (ten times).

wisdom and experience, reproof becomes a constructive instrument. The sages describe it as a work of art: "Like gold or an ornament of gold is a wise reprover to a listening ear" (25:12).

Reproof has as its goal instruction in the ways of prudence, righteousness, justice, and equity. In Proverbs offering reproof is a way of holding up experiences of life before young minds in order for them to receive concrete images of how to live responsibly. Through listening to the insights of the experienced, students receive moral training. Though rebuke can devolve into nagging and even verbal abuse (26:17-28), its constructive function is to develop character. In fact, reproof that is forthright but wise is more productive than a superficial demonstration of love.[62] Reproof profits even the advanced student: "The wise when rebuked will love you" (9:8). Reproof finds its theological moorings in the way in which God instructs:

> My child, do not despise the Lord's discipline
>   or be weary of his reproof,
> for the Lord reproves the one he loves,
>   as a father the son in whom he delights. (3:11-12)

In this text a close relationship exists between love and reproof and between the discipline of the Lord and the discipline of a father. The discipline of a loving father reflects the discipline of God.

Fools are held up as the antitype to the receptivity of a rebuke. Because they do not accept reproof, they do not learn from their mistakes or the mistakes of others. To develop a listening ear (25:12) means that one is open to hearing about one's own blunders and missteps.[63] The fool is the one who is defensive and refuses to admit mistakes. The truly wise person desires to know when she has made a mistake and takes steps toward correcting behavior. Thus the sage observes, "Whoever heeds instruction is on the path to life, but one who rejects a rebuke goes astray" (10:17). The wise appreciate insightful criticism because it enables them to live life better and experience more satisfaction.[64] Scoffers do not like rebuke; they will not go to the wise (15:10, 12).

The wise person develops the humility necessary to be open to correction and criticism from others. The wise are in constant dialogue with

---

62. Compare the following proverbs: "Better is open reproof than hidden love" (27:5); and "Whoever reproves a person will afterward find more favor than one who flatters with the tongue" (28:23). See also Ecclesiastes 7:5: "It is better for a man to hear the rebuke of the wise, than to hear the song of fools."

63. As Tremper Longman puts it, "Only the wise are willing to admit mistakes..." See Longman, *Proverbs*, 323.

64. Ibid., 316.

others not only instructing and leading but also learning and following. The wise are good listeners (15:5). Longman expresses the situation succinctly, "If one cannot bear to hear about one's mistakes and take steps to correct them, then one is doomed to be perpetually wrong."[65] Hearing criticism and changing wrong behavior is integral to wisdom.

Oral Repetition and Cultivating Discernment

Woven into the process of reproof is a heavy dose of oral repetition, another resource of instruction. Through continual rehearsal, the sages infuse their instructions into pliable young minds. Thus the young minds memorized the instruction.[66] This is apparently what the sages mean when they exhort students to keep the father's instructions "on your fingers and write them on the tablet of your heart" (7:3; cf. also 3:3; 1:9; 22:17–21).[67] These instructions come packaged in the memory friendly form of the proverb. Parallelism[68] enables the proverb to be tucked away easily in the corners of the mind ready for active duty when the occasion arises. The proverb makes sapiential instruction portable.[69] Even though the sages taught students to develop reasoning skills, to plan for the future, and to think critically, there were times when youth had to make immediate decisions in the heat of temptations and moral dilemmas. A mental storehouse of proverbs provided the resources to meet the demands of such occasions.[70]

---

65. Ibid., 313–314.

66. Charles F. Melchert observes that, "Recent folklore studies reveal that verbal memory in completely oral cultures neither requires nor leads to exact replication. Rather the oral recitation of long works from memory is actually a creative, though tradition-bound, process." *Wise Teaching*, 48.

67. See Lemaire, "Education: Ancient Israel," 309.

68. For a description of parallelism see chapter 4.

69. James Crenshaw refers to this portable quality when he defines the proverb as "a winged word outliving a fleeting moment." Crenshaw, *Old Testament Wisdom*, 62.

70. Walter Harrelson's remarks are apropos (though he oversimplifies the thought process of wisdom): "Wisdom operates without the necessity of synthesis. This is perhaps its most characteristic feature. Humans need both disciplines of philosophy/ logic and phronesis/wisdom thinking. . . . They need the carefully articulated picture of the world and its parts which comes from systematic thought that aims at synthesis. They need equally—and this is my point- the mode of thinking that can stop short of synthesis. That is what the ancient world called wisdom. . . . A society needs to have a large number of observations that can be applied to given situations unthinkingly, immediately, without necessary reference to some coherent scheme of thought within which they fit." Harrelson, "Wisdom and Pastoral Theology," 10–11.

The sages, however, are not only interested in students memorizing oral instruction. They are also quite concerned with youth learning to engage the mind. One is not wise simply because he can quote a lot of proverbs. One is wise because that person knows how and when to appropriately use proverbs. The sages want students to internalize moral values and learn the art of discernment (1:2, 6). The discerning student is the one who develops a "listening ear" (25:12). The sages want to equip students with the ability to think critically.[71] The very quality of wisdom itself invites the reforming and rethinking of ideas. The sages give no pat answers. For example, while the proverbs in chapters 10–15 emphasize the simple, conventional theology of wisdom (wise people prosper, foolish people suffer), those in chapters 16–22 quickly dispel any mechanical or mindless approach to that theology. For example, Proverbs 16:1–9 throws a wrench in the conventional cogs of wisdom, claiming that humans may make their plans but Yahweh has the final say. This cluster of proverbs in 16:1–9 describes the complexity of a world that lives with the tension between human freedom and divine sovereignty.[72] No simple answers exist.

One important manifestation of a lack of discernment is observed in those who developed the habit of speaking before thinking. The consequences result in significant harm inflicted on others (25:20; 27:14). In the same way, the person who does not know how and when to use a proverb displays folly (27:7, 9). The ability to discover what is appropriate for a particular situation is an essential ingredient of wisdom (25:11). In other words, for the sages the development of moral character results from a genuine engagement of the mind in discerning what is appropriate or not appropriate for the occasion at hand.

It appears, however, that some students looked for the path of least resistance to acquire wisdom, as the sage sarcastically observes, "Why should fools have a price in hand to buy wisdom, when they have no mind to learn?" (17:16). Some students believed they could gain understanding apart from using the mind. If they paid the tuition cost, wisdom was theirs for the taking. They viewed wisdom as a commodity, a matter of learning some techniques, accepting certain beliefs, and memorizing a few proverbs. But it was not so in the eyes of the sage. The answers were not cut and dried (cf. 26:4, 5). Students must learn to think. They had to interact with others. Students who accepted the challenge came to realize that understanding is a process by which "iron sharpens iron, and one person sharpens the wits of another" (27:17).

---

71. See Eaton, "Memory and Encounter."
72. See chapter 8 for a more detailed analysis of this text.

Observing the World

The art of discernment is also used to engage students in another process of instruction: the skill of learning to observe life. The strategy of the sage is to provide youth with opportunities to observe experiences at a distance without having to pay the consequences of engaging in irresponsible behavior. The sages do not shelter youth from the harsh realities of life. They want youth to know and experience vicariously the dangers of certain lifestyles. So youth are exposed to the crooked speech of wicked men (2:12–15) and the smooth deceptive words of the wicked woman (2:16–19). Youth witness the violent behavior of gangs (1:8–19) and receive escort into the "red light" district of town (7:6–27). They observe the havoc alcohol wreaks on its victims (23:29–35). They even get a taste of the devastating consequences of a life of indolence (24:30–34). Exposing youth to experiences they can observe in others is a form of inoculation, a powerful means of "receiving instruction" (24:32).

The sage, however, exposes youth not only to negative experiences but to positive ones as well. Youth are given a glimpse of the well-ordered family of Proverbs 31:10–31. All through Proverbs, they observe the ways of the prudent son (10–29). They are exposed to the seven-pillared house of Woman Wisdom and the ordered life she offers (9:1–12; cf., 14:1; 24:3). Youth examine the ways of the ant and see the results of hard work and self-discipline (6:6–8). They learn of the satisfaction that comes from remaining faithful in marriage (5:15–23). They observe creation around them and learn wisdom (30:18–19; 30:24–28). For the sage, then, instruction occurs in observing life. In the process of observing life, one learns to reflect on those experiences with discernment.

PROVERBS AND KOHLBERG'S MORAL STAGES OF DEVELOPMENT

All of the above resources work in synergistic relationship to give students the best possible educational environment. It may be instructional to assess these resources in light of contemporary theories of moral education. Lawrence Kohlberg offers a reputable theory of moral development involving three levels each containing two stages. Kohlberg's levels revolve around what he refers to as the "conventional." By conventional he means the rights and wrongs as they are determined by society. Stress is placed on conforming to cultural rules and expectations. The way in which the moral agent relates to "convention" determines his or her place in the process of moral maturation.[73]

Kohlberg refers to the first level as "preconventional." At this level individuals interpret right and wrong in terms of physical and emotional consequences to themselves rather than in terms of what society says. Morality is that which produces the greatest benefit for the individual. At the midpoint or "conventional" level individuals learn to conform to the social order around them, which includes family and cultural expectations. Individuals at this level have matured to the point where they maintain social expectations regardless of the consequences. The third and most mature level, according to Kohlberg, is the "postconventional" or "principled" level. At this point individuals reason according to the moral principles of justice that possess validity apart from the authority of the individual or the culture. According to Kohlberg, one progresses one stage at a time from the lower to higher levels in the process of moral development.[74]

Do Kohlberg's three levels of moral development provide a framework for understanding the resources wisdom used in the process of moral instruction? Can Kohlberg's scheme of moral stages be constructively integrated into wisdom's educational process and theological perspective? In spite of a number of limitations, the scheme can shed light on ways wisdom approaches moral education.[75] At the preconventional level Kohlberg identifies two stages.[76] Stage one individuals are primarily concerned with avoiding punishment. Wisdom appeals to this stage when the sage resorts to the use of physical discipline, the rod, as well as to certain kinds of reproof that warn or reprimand students. In addition, proverbs that invoke the negative consequences of certain inappropriate behavior operate at this stage. The following represent some of these:

> Folly is bound up in the heart of a boy,
> but the rod of discipline drives it far away. (22:15)

> Evil will not depart from the house
> of one who returns evil for good. (17:13)

> Oppressing the poor in order to enrich oneself,
> and giving to the rich, will lead only to loss. (22:16)

---

73. Kohlberg, *Essays on Moral Development*, 172.
74. Ibid., 170.
75. I will address these limitations at the conclusion of this section.
76. The following description of the six stages is based on Kohlberg's chart. *Essays on Moral Development*, 174–76.

Individuals at stage one do what is right in order to avoid pain inflicted upon them by the one in authority.

The student in stage two responds to what is right or wrong based upon how it satisfies personal needs. Stage two individuals ask the question, "How will this benefit me? How will my life improve as a result of this action?" They think, "God will take care of me and protect me if I live a certain way." They use a morality of exchange approach: "If I do this for them, they might do something nice for me." What is right or wrong is determined by how one will profit or not profit from the decision.

When read in light of Kohlberg's first two stages of moral development, antithetic proverbs pack a double-edged punch offering both negative and positive reinforcement to evoke the desired behavior. Antithetic proverbs contain both an "approach" and an "avoidance" motivation,[77] as the following proverbs illustrate:

> The fear of the LORD prolongs life,
> but the years of the wicked will be short. (10:27)

> Riches do not profit in the day of wrath,
> but righteousness delivers from death. (11:4)

> The righteous are delivered from trouble,
> and the wicked get into it instead. (11:8)

In this system, the antithetic proverbs contain the maximum incentive for doing what is right. They identify both negative (avoidance) and positive (approach) consequences of specific behavior. The sage does not shy away from saying that certain character traits will produce definite consequences (10:24, 28; 11:27, 30; 12:3, 7, 12, 20, 21, 28). The majority of proverbs collected in chapters 10–15 work out of these two stages.

Individuals at the preconventional level focus on meeting personal needs. The conventional level moves beyond this to shift the focus to the community. One resource that enables students to move from the preconventional to the conventional level comes through the avenue of role-playing. According to Bonnidell Clouse, role-playing helps individuals to "decenter" themselves and see experiences from the perspective of others.[78] This is what some of the wisdom poems do in the first nine chapters of the book of Proverbs. They enable students to identify with another person in order to imagine how others might feel. The teachers give both good and

---

77. These are psychological terms that refer to positive or negative motivations to act. See Hildebrandt, "Motivation and Antithetic Parallelism in Proverbs 10–15," for a systematic treatment of approach and avoidance incentives in the antithetic proverbs.

78. Clouse, *Teaching for Moral Growth*, 288.

bad models for students to emulate: the behavior of the gang (1:10–19), the temptress (7:6–27), the sluggard (24:30–34), the woman of noble character (31:10–31), the prudent son (5:15–19; 10:1a), and the hard working ant (6:6–11). These models enable the student to place herself in the position of another situation or person and learn to adapt the values of the community.

Another tool that enables one to decenter self and move to the conventional level is the ability to observe life. The skill of observing experiences, creation, and the actions of others leads one to reflect on those observations and learn the art of discernment. When individuals engage in observation, they must step outside themselves and see life from a different perspective. Both role-playing and observation enable students to move to the conventional level.

Two stages embody the conventional level. Students at stage three are motivated by what pleases others, the respect they receive, in the interpersonal relationships of which they are a part. The question at this stage is, "What will please family and friends?" The sages relied on family and community environment to put pressure on the young to conform. Yet there is reciprocity of joy and satisfaction that exists between the generations of a family: "Grandchildren are the crown of the aged, and the glory of children is their parents" (17:6).

Receiving honor or avoiding shame were some of the most powerful motivational forces to which the sages appealed:

> A gracious woman gets honor,
> but she who hates virtue is covered with shame. (11:16)

> Those who do violence to their father and chase away their mother
> are children who cause shame and bring reproach. (19:26)

> Whoever pursues righteousness and kindness
> will find life and honor. (21:21)

In this shame and honor culture, one's reputation was critical for a productive life: "A good name is to be chosen rather than great riches, and favor is better than silver or gold" (22:1; cf. also 3:35). The sage could very well make statements like, "If you want to live in this family, then this is how you must behave." Or, "If you engage in that kind lifestyle, then you will hurt our family's reputation." The whole of the book of Proverbs is set in a community context that places pressure on the young to conform to its values.

The stage four individual focuses on the rules and laws of the land. At this stage a person moves from the influence of interpersonal relationships to the broader concerns of society. In their instruction, the sages were quite explicit about what behavior was acceptable and what was not in the community.⁷⁹ This may be why memorization played an important role in the instruction process. The memorization of proverbs instilled conventional values of the community into the young minds of students.

At Kohlberg's postconventional level, stage five involves helping individuals see the larger picture and weigh alternatives. Right and wrong no longer appear clear cut. Different circumstances demand different responses. The sages were quite concerned with enabling students to negotiate this dimension of life through developing the art of discernment. Those growing in moral development must grapple with the complexities of life, which many of the proverbs in chapters 16–22 acknowledge. The emphasis at this stage shifts from external restraints to internal control governed no longer by societal rules but by larger principles. One place where these dilemmas find special expression is in the better-than proverbs, where individuals must wrestle with the deeper principles at work in relationships, principles such as commitment, faithfulness and integrity.⁸⁰ The better-than proverbs do not work from a clear-cut right and wrong perspective. Instead they work from a more nuanced scale that moves from good to better:

> A good name is to be chosen rather than great riches,
> and favor is better than silver or gold. (22:1)

> To do righteousness and justice
> is more acceptable to the LORD than sacrifice. (21:3)

Wealth is good. A solid reputation is even better. Offering sacrifices to the Lord may be quite appropriate, but practicing righteousness surpasses it. To seek out what is better among the good requires a level of thinking that at times calls on one to question conventional beliefs.

Another way in which sages required students to struggle with underlying principles was by placing contrasting proverbs side-by-side (e.g., 26:4, 5). Placing proverbs in tension with one another required students to wrestle with what was best in a given situation. Through this phenomenon the sages taught students the art of discernment.

Finally, stage six people emphasize justice and respect for the dignity of others. For Kohlberg, justice epitomizes the ultimate principle.⁸¹ Wisdom also emphasizes the principles of righteousness and justice (1:3; 2:9; 8:20). The sages express concern for what is best for others. At this level, however, from wisdom's perspective and contrary to Kohlberg, the ultimate

---

79. See chapter 3 for more specifics about the content of wisdom's instruction.

80. I deal with the better-than proverbs in more detail in chapter 7.

81. According to Peterson and Seligman, only 20% of the adult population reasons from the postconventional stage. *Character Strengths and Virtues*, 71.

controlling force resides not in a principle but in the One who created it all. In the wisdom scheme of things, stage six people are governed by their relationship to Yahweh. Their trust in God determines everything else they do. The "limit proverbs"[82] express this affirmation. The "limit proverbs" enable students to realize that some things are beyond their control and therefore they must learn to trust: "The human mind plans the way, but the Lord directs the steps" (16:9; see also 16:1; 21:30, 31). Individuals are governed by something larger than personal agendas and societal norms and even principles. Ultimately wisdom is not a set of concepts or principles but a relationship. Proverbs 3:5 epitomizes the perspective of stage six people: "Trust in the Lord with all your heart and do not rely on your own understanding."

The sage desires to integrate students into the life of the community in such a way that they make an ongoing contribution to the community but also that they learn to operate by the larger principles of justice, righteousness, and equity (1:3) which are ultimately based on a relationship with God. Maybe the clearest image of the integration of the community and the Yahwistic dimension is found in the wise woman passage at the conclusion of Proverbs (31:10–31). Here the woman represents those who have wholly integrated wisdom into their lives. Such individuals look after family (v. 15), remain active in the life of the community (vv. 25–27), earn the respect of others (vv. 23, 28–29), practice justice by looking out for the needs of the disenfranchised (v. 20), and ultimately fear the Lord (v. 30).

Kohlberg's six stages can provide a more systematized way of analyzing wisdom's approach to moral instruction.[83] All six stages appear to be present in one form or another in the book of Proverbs. While his model is helpful in illuminating the process of the sages, it is important to highlight some significant differences between Kohlberg's and the sages' approach to moral education. In doing so one sees more clearly wisdom's goals and its holistic approach to education.

First, Kohlberg was interested almost exclusively in moral reasoning and not moral behavior.[84] *Thinking* about moral issues, however, is not a substitute for moral *living*. In contrast, Proverbs is quite concerned with both. On the one hand, a number of the poems in the first nine chapters are devoted to developing the proper attitude toward moral character. In some of the instruction literature, the sage is concerned exclusively with instilling

---

82. See chapter 8 for a definition of "limit proverbs."

83. Hunter, *The Death of Character* (84), summarizes Kohlberg's six stages in the following way: "they tend to evolve from staying out of trouble, to acting out of self-interest, to wanting social approval, to wanting to be responsible in society, to living up to an implied contract, to acting out of principles of social justice."

84. Peterson and Seligman, *Character Strengths and Virtues*, 71.

within youth an appreciation for the value of wisdom (e.g., 1:8–19; 2:1–22; 4:1–9; 4:10–19). On the other hand, much of the material in the sentence literature in chapters 10–29 focuses on concrete actions and behaviors. To emphasize this focus, the book of Proverbs concludes by showcasing what wisdom looks like when it is lived out in everyday life (31:10–31).

Second, Kohlberg gives little attention to the role emotions play in moral development. According to Peterson and Seligman, "Researchers interested in moral development have tended to neglect the emotional and motivational aspects of morality, which doubtlessly influence whether thought is translated into action . . . ."[85] Again in the opening chapters of Proverbs, the sage is quite concerned with generating strong motivations for seeking wisdom (e.g. 2:1–22). Many of the opening poems strive to instill a passion for wisdom within students. Without that intense passion, students will soon weary of the journey and seek the path of least resistance.

Third, Kohlberg's model "overemphasizes abstract rules and principles" (e.g., justice) and "downplays caring and compassion" (e.g., love, kindness, generosity).[86] Proverbs, however, is quite concerned with compassion and kindness and love (e.g., 10:12; 15:17; 11:25; 14:21, etc.).

Fourth, Kohlberg believes that virtues *cannot* be taught didactically. There is no set of core values. The emphasis is on the *process* of making moral decisions. Whereas the sages do employ an informal process in the task of moral education (e.g., physical discipline, wise reproof, oral repetition, the art of discernment, and the skill of observing life), they also taught and passed on specific character virtues. Over and over the sage admonishes youth to listen to instruction from parents and from the wise.

Fifth, Kohlberg's stages of moral development describe a linear process. A person cannot skip over a stage to move to a higher one. An individual goes through these stages in sequence. In this way it seems similar to James Fowler's stages of faith where Fowler argues that individuals move in a linear fashion and systematically through the stages to a more mature levels.[87] But neither faith nor moral development seems to move toward maturity in a straight line. The process is more dynamic and messy. Even though I would argue that the whole of Proverbs moves from the immaturity and folly of the gang (1:8–19), progressing through the messiness of the sentence literature, becoming more complex as the reader works through the book, and finally climaxing with the mature and wise woman (31:10–31), the journey is not a

---

85. Ibid., 72.
86. Ibid.
87. Fowler, *Stages of Faith*.

straight-line trajectory from beginning to end. The journey contains a lot of ups and downs, dead-ends, side-roads, and detours along the way.

Sixth, Kohlberg's scheme is grounded in secular theory and has no concern for the Christian story. It is psychological in its foundation and not theological. The ultimate principle of justice, by which mature people operate, appears to be for the sake of enabling people to reach their full human potential. His point of reference is the autonomous self. There is no interest in imitating the character of God. In contrast, for the sage the very foundation of character formation is rooted in relationship with God (1:7). Apart from that relationship, one's character is something other than what the sages describe.

Even though Kohlberg's scheme possesses several limitations, it still remains helpful in illuminating a number of qualities the sages employ in the process of moral instruction. Imposing the template of Kohlberg's levels onto Proverbs reveals that the sages resorted to a variety of motivations and incentives for developing moral character in others. Even though their ultimate goal was to incorporate individuals into a productive life in the community and to bring them into deeper relationship with Yahweh, they used every stage and available means to do that. The approach taken depended on the level of maturity of the student. In other words, it is not that those who instruct operate only at the postconventional level and ignore all the others. When one operates by the larger principles and out of a relationship with Yahweh, the rules and expectations of the community are not ignored. They are simply viewed from a different perspective. The same is true with the appeal to rewards and punishments. These incentives are not invalidated. They simply are no longer the driving force behind one's behavior.

Depending upon the circumstances, the wise person utilizes all three levels in the instruction process. There are times when it is appropriate to appeal to negative or positive reinforcements in order to stimulate desired behavior. Often it is necessary to challenge individuals to conform to the moral standards (the rules and laws) a particular culture establishes for the welfare of the faith community. It may be quite appropriate on a particular occasion for a parent or a church leader to say to a member, "If you engage in that kind of behavior, you will damage this family's reputation." But there are times when the wise may violate cultural standards for the sake of the higher principle of justice and righteousness. Ultimately, the wise person is the one who "fears the Lord" and conforms to God's will. The truly wise are those whose lives are shaped by the character of Yahweh.

Wisdom devoted much effort to the instruction of young minds. While there is no complete picture of the process, the gravity of the task for parents and youth and faith community is clearly portrayed. Certain contemporary theories of moral development, such as Lawrence Kohlberg's, may provide deeper insight into the motivational forces that lie behind the educational resources used by the sages.

CONCLUSION

The stereotypical view of adolescence in our culture today describes it as a period of rebellion, as a time to "sow your wild oats." Youth, it is believed, have little interest in moral or spiritual matters.[88] Thus conventional wisdom advises, "Leave them alone, be patient, lie low; eventually they will come around." "If they do not have solid instruction given to them prior to the teen years, it's too late anyway." The generation of youth whose parents are baby boomers were referred to as the "abandoned generation" because their parents were so concerned with rebelling against the establishment when they were young that they were careful to impose no ethical standards on their own children.[89] The result? Youth who possess no moral compass by which to navigate the difficult waters of life. In contrast, Proverbs depicts fathers and mothers deeply engaged in the instruction of youth (1:8; 4:1–4; 10:1).

But youth have responsibility as well. They can choose to reject a parent's discipline. Pictures of such rebellious children line the halls of Wisdom's house. Youth can scoff at instruction (13:1). The foolish son (10:1b) offers nothing but grief to his mother. A son's refusal to heed reproof brings shame to his family (29:15). Sometimes the son even abuses his parents (28:24). In contrast, the responsible youth cultivates an attentive ear (2:1–2). Such youth open themselves to receiving instruction (22:17–19). The task is not easy. One must acquire a taste for wisdom. In the initial stages, seeking wisdom and developing moral character may bring nothing but bone-tired weariness (2:3–4). It demands critical engagement of the mind. But those who persevere receive satisfaction. They delight in doing right (2:9–10).

On the other end of the age spectrum, older individuals sometimes use their age as an excuse for not learning and growing. There is a stereotypical belief that older people cannot change. After all "you can't teach an old dog new tricks." Wisdom literature describes individuals who have settled into the later years of life believing they are too old to learn and to change behavior. Job's three friends are classic examples of individuals who settled into a narrow mindset of understanding life and experiences. The writer of Ecclesiastes witnessed certain individuals who refused to learn as they grew

88. Long, "Beavis and Butt-Head Get Saved."
89. Willimon, "Hunger in This Abandoned Generation."

older: "Better is a poor but wise youth than an old but foolish king, who will no longer take advice" (Eccl. 4:13; see also 10:5–7). Yet Proverbs dispels the stereotype and frequently appeals to the older person to continue to seek out wisdom and learning (1:5; 9:8–9; 15:31; 19:25; 21:11). You can teach an old dog new tricks, how to bark lower, walk slower, and scratch harder. One is never too old to learn and never too late to turn.[90]

In Proverbs the primary function of the sage is to prepare those with open minds for living morally responsible lives. Responsibility lies with both the community and the youth in the educational process. Parents and community initiate the process (2:1–2; 4:1–4). They provide the loving, caring environment where instruction can most effectively occur. They offer wise reproof. They engage in role-playing. They give youth a mental repertoire of proverbial lore that enables them to face daily moral decisions responsibly. They actively engage the mind of the youth in the art of critical thinking. They provide opportunities for youth to observe some of the harsh realities of life. They hold up examples of individuals for youth to imitate as well as not imitate. The sages engage youth in a rigorous process of instruction. Theirs is a holistic approach to instruction. As this process unfolds, those who are older also listen, learn, and grow.

---

90. One of my favorite Far Side cartoons pictures a dog on a high wire doing a tightrope walk with the crowd watching below. The dog is riding a unicycle, twirling a hoola hoop around his waist, balancing a jug on his head, juggling three balls with his paws, and gingerly holding a cat in his mouth. The caption below the picture reads, "High above the hushed crowd, Rex tried to remain focused. Still he couldn't shake one nagging thought: He was an old dog and this was a new trick." The person who has cultivated a taste for wisdom is never too old to learn more.

Chapter Three

The Content of Character Formation

Character formation involves a journey; process plays a key role in wisdom's approach to moral instruction a truth which fits well with the image of path or way that the sage is fond of employing (e.g., 4:10–19). Wisdom is not, however, just about going through a process. For the biblical sage, process also involves the communication of a clear set of moral values. Wisdom instruction is not nebulous. It has a specific curriculum to pass on to its students, which in part, is identified in the collections of sayings found in chapters 10–29. In identifying the contents, one gains a better understanding of the type of character the family and faith community seek to build. The "what" in wisdom's agenda is as important as the "how."

WISDOM VERSUS VALUES-CLARIFICATION

Wisdom takes a direct approach to moral instruction in terms of its core values, clearly communicating this core set of values to its students.[1] This flies in the face of certain strands of thought that believe all values are personal

---

1. Significantly William Bennett, the former U.S. Secretary of Education under the Reagan administration, advocates a direct approach to teaching moral values. He argues that being a teacher in public education implies that the one in that position deliberately seeks to influence students for the better through instruction and through example. Bennett, "Moral Literacy and the Formation of Character," 134.

such as a "values-clarification" philosophy.[2] With values-clarification,[3] each individual decides which values are appropriate in order to achieve the person's fullest potential. The highest value in this system is self-actualization. The important question then becomes, which values will bring about self-actualization?

According to values-clarification, the values we hold to are inferred from the choices we make every day. For example, we choose how to use our time, spend our money, and invest our energy. These choices express our personal values. The task is to clarify those values for each individual in order to make life more fulfilling. In the process of identifying one's value system, new values are also discovered and integrated with the old. Therefore values cannot be imposed on an individual from an outside source. They must come from within the person, and thus values cannot be taught. Teachers can only guide students through a process of discovering themselves.

The values-clarification school of thought places emphasis on the process by which individuals become more aware of the values to which they already hold. They focus on the procedure of valuing rather than on the product, "on becoming rather than being, on potential rather than current state."[4] Louis Raths and his colleagues describe one seven-step process of values-clarification:

1. Choosing freely without restriction.
2. Choosing from viable alternatives.
3. Choosing after reflecting on the consequences of each alternative.
4. Being satisfied with one's choice.
5. Publicly affirming the choice.

---

2. Raths, Harmin, and Simon, *Values and Teaching*. This also appears to be the perspective of Lawrence Kohlberg: The "teaching of virtue is the asking of questions and pointing of the way, not the giving of answers. Moral education is the leading of men upward, not the putting into the mind of knowledge that was not there before." Kohlberg, "Education for Justice," 58.

3. Values clarification may not be formally as active a discipline as it was a couple of decades ago. Its principles and philosophy, however, are still vibrant within the field of ethics. Philosopher, Sarah Conrad, makes this statement in an email correspondence on November 12, 2014, "Yes, values clarification is still a central point in ethical discussions. One must be able to identify a value and understand the source of it in order to truly assess the efficacy of it." Conrad is assistant professor of philosophy at St. Cloud State University in St. Cloud, MN. Link to philosophy faculty: http://www.stcloudstate.edu/philosophy/faculty.asp

4. Clouse, *Teaching for Moral Growth*, 303.

6. Acting on one's choice.
7. Incorporating the choice as a habit into one's life.[5]

The first three steps entail the act of choosing a value, the next two include celebrating the value chosen, and the last two call upon the individual to incorporate the value chosen into her life.[6] The whole purpose of the process is to unlock the hidden potential that lies within each individual enabling that person to experience self-actualization.

The values-clarification school has provided a great service in identifying a process for better understanding values, but its weakness is that it leaves to the individual the task of deciding which values to accept or reject. Often what individuals and the church need to hear is not reflections on their own perspective but an authoritative perspective that comes from outside, the authority of Scripture and tradition. Certain moral values are non-negotiable; they are essential for the well-being of the community.

The principles that underlie the values-clarification philosophy strikingly represent a disturbing trend in postmodern ethics and character formation. It is radically individualistic with the locus of ethical truth being placed squarely within each person equally and authoritatively. There is no room for any standards of character imposed from without. While the idea of some external set of principles unnerves postmodern conceptions of uninhibited freedom, one of the most foundation truths of Christian faith is that there is an external authority, God, and as a result there are objective standards to which people are held. The sages, far removed from this particular feature of contemporary culture, had no qualms with assuming a set of finite virtues which the process of character formation sought to inculcate and a set of equally real vices that moral education needed to warn against.

The wisdom community developed a set of values, which it expected its students to adhere. Individuals did not have a choice in picking or choosing from them. Yet even though the sages offer direct instruction about moral values, they do so more often in the form of making observations than issuing commands. To put it another way, in the sentence literature (Proverbs 10–22 and 25–29), there are more "sayings" (observations) than "admonitions" (commands). The sages do not force the values on their students. Wisdom respects the autonomy of the individual, which allows each student the choice of either accepting or rejecting the instruction. In the book of Proverbs evidence abounds of those who chose to reject sapiential instruction. References are made to the rebellious and foolish son and to

---

5. Raths, Harmin, and Simon, *Values and Teaching*, 46.
6. Clouse, *Teaching for Moral Growth*, 306.

the scoffer (10:1b; 13:1; 29:15). Unless individuals are given the option to choose, it remains questionable as to whether they can internalize the values they are taught.

WISDOM'S VIRTUES

Contrary to the claims of William McKane, the religious and ethical dimensions of Proverbs are not later editions.[7] McKane proposes that the earliest proverbs in the collection are secular in nature and it was not until later that those dealing with the religious and ethical issues were added. Proverbs, however, is not a book that only sporadically contains ethical concerns. As Tomás Frydrych argues,

> the whole of Proverbs is essentially about ethics, the distinction between good and evil is truly all pervasive. The book contains no technical advice on conducting any common activity, be it agriculture, skilled work or trade. On the occasions where such daily activities are touched upon, the sages' concerns are confined to their ethical aspects. In no sense, thus, can the book as a whole, or any of its parts, be perceived as a manual for 'mundane realities' (to use McKane's terminology), for such realities are nowhere to be found in Proverbs.[8]

Clearly the focus of the sages is ethical throughout. Still, since Proverbs' intention is not to provide a catalog of virtues it can be a helpful exercise to attempt to systematize, at least in a limited fashion, the core values upheld in the text.

The fundamental content of wisdom, as mentioned in Chapter One, is revealed in the prologue (1:1–7). The recipients of these proverbs receive training in "righteousness, justice, and equity" (v. 3). These are wisdom's archetypal virtues. After Woman Wisdom invites youth to a feast that will serve up these virtues (chaps. 8–9), the youth are treated to the main menu, the dense thicket of individual proverbs that follow in chapters 10–29. These proverbs flesh out the content of Woman Wisdom's teachings.

Significantly, clustered at the beginning of the sentence literature is a series of proverbs describing the paths of the righteous and the wicked (chaps. 10–11). Righteousness and wickedness are relational terms. On the one hand, the wicked are those who advantage self at the expense of disadvantaging others. On the other hand, the righteous are those who

---

7. See chapter 8 for a fuller development of his approach to Proverbs.
8. Frydrych, *Living under the Sun*, 176.

THE CONTENT OF CHARACTER FORMATION 45

disadvantage self for the sake of advantaging others. The sayings that follow specify what the way of righteousness involves.[9] Righteousness has to do with treating others in community with love and loyalty. More concretely, righteousness encompasses such virtues as self-control, patience, diligence, etc. To a degree, "righteousness" overlaps in meaning with the quality of "wisdom." The righteous person knows how to live responsibly before others and before God.

Below is an attempt to itemize qualities of righteousness addressed in the sentence literature. Though by no means comprehensive this ethical inventory is intended to identify some of the most prominent virtues taught by the sages:

- Self-control (13:3; 14:16, 29; 15:18; 16:32; 17:27–28; 18:13; 19:11, 19; 20:3; 21:23; 23:4–5; 25:28; 29:11)
- Humility (11:2; 12:9; 15:33; 16:19; 18:12; 22:4; 27:1; 29:23)
- Patience (12:16; 14:29; 15:1, 18; 19:11; 25:15)
- Diligence (10:4; 12:11, 24; 13:24; 14:4; 21:5; 27:23–27; 28:19)
- Integrity (11:3; 14:25, 32; 19:1; 20:7)
- Prudence (1:4; 3:5–8; 14:8; 15:5, 21; 19:14;
- Faithfulness (16:6; 17:17; 18:24; 19:22; 20:6; 25:19; 27:6, 10; 28:20)
- Generosity (11:24, 25; 14:21, 31; 19:6, 17; 21:26; 22:9; 28:27)
- Cheerfulness (14: 30; 15:13, 15, 23; 16:24; 17:22; 21:15; 29:18)
- Love (10:12; 15:17; 17:9)
- Love Enemies (24:17–18, 29; 25:21–22)
- Contentment (13:11; 14:30; 15:17; 16:19; 17:1; 25:16, 27; 27:1; 30:7–9)
- Considerateness (17:13; 20:22; 24:17–18; 24:29; 25:21–22)
- Compassion (12:10)
- Courage (22:13; 24:10; 26:13; 28:1)
- Curiosity (27:20)
- Appropriateness (15:23; 17:7; 25:11–12; 26:4–5)

9. The largest number of sayings in chs. 10–29 on any single topic deal with the righteous and the wicked. John Goldingay has discovered that the righteous/wicked sayings cluster at the beginning of chapters 10–22. In 10:1–11:13, forms of the root for righteous (צָדַק) appear nineteen times and for wicked (רָשַׁע) appear eighteen times. He concludes that the concentration of righteous/wicked sayings at the beginning of the unit establishes an ethical context for chapters 10–22. Goldingay, "The Arrangement of Sayings in Proverbs 10–15."

- Trust (16:1, 3, 9, 20; 17:3; 18:10; 19:21; 20:24; 21:30–31; 27:1)
- Reputation (22:1; 10:7; 12:8; 21:21; 11:16; 27:21)
- Friendship (3:3-4; 3:27-29; 14:20-21; 16:7; 17:9, 17; 18:24; 19:6-7; 25:17; 27:5, 6, 9, 10, 17)
- Industriousness (10:4,5; 13:4; 14:23; 22:29; 24:27)
- Respect for poor and parents (14:31; 17:5; 19:17; 21:13; 22:2; 22:16; 28:27; 29:13–14; 31:20; 10:1; 15:20; 19:26; 20:20; 23:22; 28:24)
- Virtues of Speech:
- Restraint (10:19; 11:12; 12:16, 23; 13:3; 17:27; 29:20)
- Healing (12:18; 16:24)
- Gentle (15:1, 4; 25:15)
- Gracious (25:11; 15:2; 16:21, 23; 22:11)
- Prudent (10:13; 10:20)

The sages sought to instill these virtues in the lives and thoughts of youthful minds. Each of the above are important virtues worthy of further investigation. There is no systematized way in which Proverbs prioritizes these virtues. So the reader must take care in assigning priority where none has been assigned, even though it is true that some virtues appear with more frequency than others.

Highlighting a selection of these virtues may serve as a way of briefly unpacking the content of what they reveal. For example, the sages valued the virtue of self-control and its close associate, restraint.[10] That the sages express a concern for developing self-control, indicates their understanding of "the enormous power of passion, whether expressing itself as fear, anxiety, anger, or lust."[11] Wisdom views self-control as essential for a person to live a productive life in community. The following proverb is representative:

> Like a city breached, without walls,
>   is one who lacks self-control. (25:28)

---

10. James Crenshaw singles out "the virtues of self-control, restraint, eloquence, and honesty" as those on which the sages focused. Crenshaw, *Education in Ancient Israel*, 2. In a later chapter Crenshaw identifies four other virtues that seem to overlap the four mentioned here: "Both in Egypt and in Israel, four character traits distinguish wise from foolish, good from evil: silence, eloquence, timeliness, and modesty" (71). By silence he means the control of anger, lust, greed, and envy.

11. Ibid., 2.

The first line of this comparative proverb[12] contains an analogy; the second line the subject or referent. The external defense of a walled city is compared to the internal defense of self-control that humans possess. Lack of self-restraint leaves one vulnerable to emotions and desires that wage war within. Self-control enables a person to hold those desires in check and channel them for productive use.

Individuals must exercise restraint in every facet of life. For example, one must restrain sexual passions:

> My child, give me your heart,
>   and let your eyes observe my ways.
> For a prostitute is a deep pit;
>   an adulteress is a narrow well.
> She lies in wait like a robber
>   and increases the number of the faithless. (23:26–28; cf., 21:17; 29:3)

The sage also emphasized the restraint of anger:

> One who is slow to anger is better than the mighty,
>   and one whose temper is controlled than one who captures a city. (16:32)

This better-than proverb[13] makes a contrast between an internal quality and an external possession. The proverb teaches that private conquest of self is more valuable than public conquest of a city. The person who controls the self accomplishes more than the one who controls others (cf., 14:29; 15:18; 19:11; 29:11).

Not only must an individual control feelings of anger but also the use of speech, as the following proverb observes:

> When words are many, transgression is not lacking,
>   but the prudent are restrained in speech. (10:19)

The one who incessantly talks is the one who inevitably gets into trouble. A contemporary proverb expresses the thought succinctly when it announces, "least said, sooner mended." Because such individuals are so busy talking, they are not sensitive to the situation or the individuals around them (cf., 12:16; 13:3; 15:28; 17:27–28; 18:2, 13, 21; 21:23). Restraint is thus critical in every aspect of life, not only sexual passions, anger, and speech, but also

---

12. A comparative or analogic proverb is one in which one line contains a concrete analogy that illuminates a more abstract thought in the second line. A whole series of analogic proverbs are collected in chapters 25–27.

13. See chapter 7 for an explanation of better-than sayings.

decision-making (15:28; 18:13, 17; 20:25), sleep (20:13; 24:30–34), appetite (23:20–21), and thoughts (13:16).

Another important virtue the sages' teach is generosity. The wise show generosity to all people (11:24–26) and in so doing inspire others to generosity (11:25). A wise person expresses generosity especially to those who are poor (14:21). How one treats the poor reflects one's relationship to and respect for God (19:17; 14:31; 17:5). Proverbs 22:9 offers a succinct perspective on this virtue:

> Those who are generous are blessed,
> for they share their bread with the poor.

The phrase "those who are generous" in Hebrew literally reads "a good eye." The ability to see others with compassion leads to expressions of generosity. For the sage, the opposite of the one with "a good eye" is the person with " a bad eye" (23:6; 28:22). This stingy, avaricious person has blurred vision that affects his or her ability to share with others.

Proverbs 21:25–26 contrasts the greedy with the generous person:

> The craving of the lazy person is fatal,
>   for lazy hands refuse to labor.
> All day long the wicked covet,
>   but the righteous give and do not hold back.

Here the wicked and the lazy person are one and the same. They are the ones who continually crave for more. Thus a sharp contrast is set up between the greedy and the generous. The righteous ones demonstrate their righteousness through unselfish behavior.

It may be helpful to highlight one more virtue. The sage holds kindness (or considerateness), especially towards those who would not reciprocate, in high regard. In an uncommon use of the imperative, Proverbs 20:22 directs, "Do not say, 'I will repay evil'; wait for the LORD, and he will help you." The proverb calls on one to suspend the desire to seek revenge. God will deal with the issue in God's own time and own way. The proverb calls on individuals to exercise patience, trust, and spiritual maturity as they face the injustices of life.

The most well known proverb that speaks of kindness in response to an enemy is 25:21–22:

> If your enemies are hungry, give them bread to eat;
>   and if they are thirsty, give them water to drink;
> for you will heap coals of fire on their heads,
>   and the LORD will reward you.

The saying imagines an occasion when the enemy is vulnerable—hungry or thirsty. On the occasion when it is easiest and most tempting to get back at the one who hates you, you are to do the opposite of what your natural instincts call on you to do. Demonstrate acts of kindness, giving the opponent bread and water. The burning or fiery coals may represent the red-faced humiliation of the enemy.[14] Thus the enemy is brought to shame. The admonition is to practice doing good to those who treat you as an enemy.

Self-control, generosity, and kindness represent just of few of wisdom's virtues. Exploring their meaning can help generate deeper understanding and appreciation for them. The most important step, however, is to embody them in life.

WISDOM'S VICES

It is instructive also to look at the counter side of the virtues and identify some of the vices of wisdom. Students can better understand the virtues by identifying the flaws. As with the list of virtues, this list of vices is not exhaustive, but it does give a fairly representative sample:

- Pride (11:2; 13:10; 15:25; 16:5, 18, 19; 21:4; 26:12; 29:23; 30:32–33)
- Haste (13:11; 19:2; 20:21; 21:5; 28:20; 29:20)
- Laziness (18:9; 19:15; 20:4; 24:30–34; 26:13–16)
- Jealousy (14:30; 24:19–20; 27:4)
- Greed (15:27; 21:26; 22:16; 28:3, 22, 25)
- Insensitivity/Inappropriateness (25:20; 26:7, 9; 27:14)
- Anxiety (12:25; 17:22)
- Gluttony (23:20–21; 25:16; 28:7)
- Falsehood (10:2; 11:1; 16:11; 20:10, 23; 20:17; 21:6; 22:28)
- Vices of Speech:
    - bragging (25:14)
    - talkativeness (10:19)
    - gossip (11:13; 16:28; 17:9; 20:19; 18:8; 26:20)
    - quarreling (16:28; 17:1, 14, 19; 18:19; 20:3; 21:9; 22:10; 26:20, 21; 27:15)

14. Some would argue that the image of burning coals is a reference to seeking revenge. Given the number of proverbs that admonish a person not to seek revenge, this interpretation is difficult to accept.

- lying (10:18; 12:17, 19, 22; 14:5; 17:4)
- flattery (26:28; 28:23;29:5)
- slander (10:18; 11:9; 18:8; 19:5, 9, 28)

As with the virtues, let me isolate a selection of these vices. For example, as a flaw pride is one of the most basic sins of humanity. Proverbs 13:10 serves as one example:

> By insolence the heedless make strife,
>   but wisdom is with those who take advice.

The proverb implies that the main product pride produces is strife. So one vice leads to another. In the second line wisdom stands in contrast with insolence or pride. Where the prideful person develops contempt for others' opinions, wisdom gladly receives counsel. Another proverb describes the fault this way:

> When pride comes, then comes disgrace;
>   but wisdom is with the humble. (11:2)

In Proverbs, pride is the fundamental sin of the fool. Humility is the fundamental virtue of the wise. The sages would heartily agree that "pride goes before a fall" (16:18).

Haste is another example of a vice, one that stands counter to the virtue of self-control. The following saying epitomizes the instruction:

> Desire without knowledge is not good,
>   and one who moves too hurriedly misses the way. (19:2)

This proverb declares the inappropriateness of "desire" or passion without knowledge. Enthusiasm must ground itself in reflective thought. Otherwise one engages in activism with no reality base. Such a person is like chaff blown about by the wind (Ps. 1:4). Enthusiasm without understanding easily becomes misguided. Line two intensifies the first line: "one who moves too hurriedly misses the way" literally the Hebrew text reads, "feet that hasten, miss the mark." Haste is highly suspect in wisdom's list of vices. The two lines of this proverb compliment each other. Line one speaks of the inner desires and thoughts. Line two speaks of the outer actions (the "feet"). When internal desires and external actions are not restrained by reflective thought (wisdom), they will not achieve their goals.

One final vice to look at is jealousy. The following proverb describes the physical consequences of jealousy:

> A tranquil mind gives life to the flesh,
>   but passion makes the bones rot. (14:30)

According to this proverb, one's mental state influences one's physical health. A healthy mind brings healing to the whole body. By contrast, uncontrolled passions can destroy the body as quickly as a deadly disease. The wise understood the human being holistically. Thoughts and feelings affect the physical state.

Consider another proverb:

> Wrath is cruel, anger is overwhelming,
>   but who is able to stand before jealousy?" (27:4)

The proverb moves from the harsh emotions of wrath and anger to that which is worse, jealousy! Clearly, anger is harmful, but jealousy serves as its catalyst (cf., 6:34). Jealousy erodes the moral and spiritual fiber of an individual; in the language of 14:30, it rots the bones.

The above are a few representatives of the vices that wisdom opposes. I have at least tried to unpack a partial dimension of their meaning. Looking at both catalogs of virtues and vices can help shed light on the other. It brings a clearer picture of the type of character the sage wishes to develop.

In teaching wisdom's virtues and folly's vices today, part of the education process includes discovering, defining, explaining, and imaging what those qualities look like in the contemporary world. In addition, in keeping with the tradition of wisdom, the education process involves seeing them embodied. Wisdom has as part of its educational philosophy the living out of these virtues. Education, in the world of the sages, is existential and not primarily academic. Wisdom cultivates virtue not merely by engaging the mind but by engaging the whole person in the pursuit of character.

Wisdom calls on families and faith communities to identify the moral values central to the well-being of the community. In the process of naming those values and embodying them in daily life, the faith community develops a clearer understanding of its identity and responsibility. To do this, it is sometimes helpful to look at contemporary resources from other academic disciplines. Such a fresh perspective can provide insight into the virtues found in Proverbs. It can also assist one in incorporating those virtues in contemporary life. With that in mind, the next section will put the virtues described in Proverbs in dialogue with a contemporary model of virtues.

PROVERBS AND THE POSITIVE PSYCHOLOGY MOVEMENT

The sages believe that the one who demonstrates wisdom is the one who gleans from the best culture has to offer. The wise person takes every available opportunity to learn, even from pagan and foreign cultures (e.g., the foreigners from Massa; Prov. 30:1; 31:1). The sages also incorporate wisdom material from Egyptian culture into their thought patterns (Prov. 22:17–24:22). The wise are culturally literate. They do not cower in the face of other cultures. They seek wisdom in any place they can find it. Their search is inclusive. That does not mean, however, that they fully embrace everything they investigate. While the wise are inclusive in their search, they practice discretion in what they accept. Because they hold to a worldview in which the Lord controls the universe and expects certain behavior from them, they filter other belief systems through their Yahwistic lens. They engage in a discerning process in their exploration.

In light of this quality of wisdom, it is profitable to explore a particular model of psychology that is interested in identifying, describing, illuminating, and cultivating character strengths. By examining this model with the background of Proverbs in mind and engaging these two perspectives in dialogue with one another, the positive psychology model might shed light on some of the virtues of Proverbs. In return Proverbs might offer a relevant theological critique of positive psychology.

Two psychologists, Christopher Peterson and Martin E. P. Seligman, have done extensive research in the field of character and virtues publishing it in a volume entitled *Character Strengths and Virtues*.[15] They are part of the positive psychology movement, which is based on the idea of understanding and building on human strengths as a complement to psychology's traditional emphasis on disorder. They state, "What makes life worth living is not ephemeral. It does not result from the momentary tickling of our sensory receptors by chocolate, alcohol, or Caribbean vacations. The good life is lived over time and across situations, and an examination of the good life in terms of positive traits is demanded."[16] The authors feel that psychology has so focused on the pathologies that it does not appreciate the strengths individuals possess to overcome obstacles and make important contributions to family and society.

---

15. Peterson and Seligman, *Character Strengths and Virtues*.
16. Ibid., 12.

The book classifies, describes, and assesses twenty-four character strengths they identify as strengths "valued in most cultures."[17] The twenty-four character strengths contribute to the development of six archetypal virtues mentioned below. The surfacing of these character strengths was the result of an exhaustive research that included brainstorming sessions with a think tank group, review of classic literature, and identification of various inventories of virtues. In regard to the literary sources, Peterson and Seligman focused on the most widely influential traditions of thought in human history (viz., China, South Asia, and the West). They conclude that their review of the literature "reveals a surprising amount of similarity across cultures and strongly indicates a historical and cross-cultural convergence of six core virtues: courage, justice, humanity, temperance, transcendence, and wisdom."[18] They maintain that the primary lesson learned was that, "there is a strong convergence across time, place, and intellectual tradition about certain core virtues."[19]

In light of biblical wisdom's perspective, however, the major limitation of their work is that they believe individuals possess the power within to face and overcome hardships. They leave no place for, nor do they want any place for, the power of God and the faith community to transform character strengths. The spirituality they speak of is a spirituality that emanates solely from within. Theirs is a humanistic perspective. In spite of their secular worldview, their examination can generate insight into the virtues described by the sages and how those virtues might manifest themselves in contemporary lifestyles.

The authors are most interested in developing the twenty-four character strengths. The bulk of the book (500 out of 800 pages) is devoted to exploring and assessing their makeup. What I want to do now is briefly summarize Peterson and Seligman's treatment of the archetypal character strengths and unpack each one with the intention of further illuminating the virtues Proverbs identifies.

With each character strength, the authors go through a battery of items that investigates each one including defining it, offering contemporary examples or paragons of individuals who manifest this strength, and then identifying possibilities for cultivating it. The authors are persuaded that these character strengths can be cultivated. They offer what they call

---

17. Ibid., 6.
18. Ibid., 36.
19. Ibid., 50.

"deliberate interventions" as ways of nurturing a particular strength. Below is a breakdown of their classification.[20]

- Wisdom and Knowledge—
    - Creativity
    - Curiosity
    - Love of Learning
    - Open-mindedness
    - Perspective
- Courage—
    - Bravery
    - Persistence
    - Integrity
    - Vitality
- Humanity—
    - Love
    - Kindness
    - Social intelligence
- Justice—
    - Citizenship
    - Fairness
    - Leadership
- Temperance—
    - Forgiveness and mercy
    - Humility and modesty
    - Prudence
    - Self-regulation
- Transcendence—
    - Appreciation of beauty
    - Gratitude

---

20. With each of the six virtues the authors list anywhere from three to five character strengths. They maintain that an individual possesses a particular virtue if he or she displays one or two strengths within a virtue group (13).

- Hope
- Humor
- Spirituality

With the first virtue, Wisdom and Knowledge, the authors identify five character strengths. For example, the authors identify curiosity and a love of learning as character strengths. They describe these two strengths as openness to new experiences and enjoying the thrill of discovery. Individuals who display them seek out the ordinary in life and are eager to learn from other cultures. The authors believe that one cultivates these qualities through engaging in experiences that the routine of life brings one's way. A person can also nurture them through journaling and reflecting on those experiences. In addition, these qualities are fostered through observing others who have developed a keen awareness and curiosity of the world around them.

Another strength identified under the virtue of wisdom is open-mindedness. This trait is not about being wishy-washy or permissive or the inability to make decisions. This is about the ability to develop discernment, to realize the complexities of life, to use good judgment, and to think critically. The authors cite the psychologist William James as an example of one who manifested this quality. James intentionally recruited other professors to his department at Harvard so that opposite points of view could be represented. Peterson and Seligman suggest that among other things liberal arts education, international travel, and simply learning the habit of listing pros and cons in decision-making are ways of cultivating the attribute of open-mindedness.

The final trait that Peterson and Seligman list is perspective. They define it as the ability to see the big picture and one's role in that picture. Such perspective enables one to hear the views of others, assess what they say, and then offer insightful advice. One of the best means of nurturing this strength is through a mentoring relationship with an older person who manifests the ability to see the larger picture of life and one who is able to understand daily experiences in the bigger context of the world.

The whole worldview of Proverbs fosters all of these strengths. The wise person is the one who develops understanding and discernment (Prov. 1:2, 4–6). Such a person understands that the decisions of life are often complex and require the utmost thought. Seldom does the sage provide "pat answers" (e.g., Prov. 26:4, 5). The sage is not afraid to challenge or question conventional beliefs (16:1–9; 27:1; cf. also Job and Ecclesiastes). In Proverbs, it is the fool who embodies these negative qualities. The fool does not use his mental faculties (Prov. 17:16). The fool is the one who is commonly described as one who "lacks sense."[21] In other words, the fool is the one who displays a total absence of curiosity, open mindedness, love of learning, and perspective (a fitting description of the gang in the opening wisdom poem in 1:8–19).

The next set of character strengths cluster around the virtue of courage. One of them, bravery, includes the ability to face challenges or difficulty or pain with resolve to do one's best under the circumstances. The authors clarify that bravery does not involve just the exceptional acts (they offer examples of people like Joan of Arc and Patrick Henry) but it also comprises the ability to accomplish what needs to be done in spite of fear. For example, doing what is right but unpopular, facing a terminal illness with dignity, and "resisting peer pressure regarding a morally questionable shortcut."[22] One of the basic ways in which bravery is nurtured is by the ability to confront fear. So, for example, if one is fearful of public speaking, the brave thing to do is to give a speech and thus face the fear. The authors suggest that another way in which one cultivates bravery is through offering words of encouragement to the one who faces an apprehensive experience.

This character strength is quite in line with what the sages promote. According to Proverbs, one of the characteristics of a wise person is the ability to take risks, to confront fears. The lazy person in the following proverb is chided for his unwilling to do just that:

> The lazy person says, "There is a lion outside!
> I shall be killed in the streets!" (22:13)

The lazy person is a favorite target of the sages' sarcasm. He imagines the most bizarre disasters occurring in order to keep from stepping out and doing what needs to be done for the day. He envisions the worst-case scenario. Lions are on the prowl in the streets! If he ventures out, he most certainly will be killed. What makes the excuse so ridiculous is that lions did not roam the streets in ancient Israel. In contrast to the fool, the wise were characterized by their boldness: "The wicked flee when no one pursues, but the righteous are as bold as a lion" (28:1). The wicked are paranoid; the righteous are confident. The sages were quite interested in individuals taking risks for the sake of the maturing process.[23]

---

21. See 10:13, 21;11:12; 12:11; 15:21; 17:18; 24:30. *The Message* translates the word "shortsighted" in 10:13. The NIV consistently translates it "lacks judgment."

22. Peterson and Seligman, *Character Strengths and Virtues*, 199.

23. Qoheleth uses the image of investment and farming to advocate taking risks (Eccl. 11:1–7).

Persistence and integrity are other strengths related to courage. Peterson and Seligman describe persistence as the ability to finish what one starts and keep on despite obstacles. "Here it is not fear that threatens action but boredom, tedium, frustration, and difficulty, on the one hand, and the temptation to do something easier and perhaps more pleasurable, on the other."[24] The authors mention Abraham Lincoln as an example of one who persisted to become president in spite of numerous failures. They also relate John D. Rockefeller's story of rise from poverty to wealth as another. Among other things, they say this trait can be cultivated through such apparently little things as children learning to accept responsibility for their failures, cleaning their plate before having desert, and finishing their chores before watching television. Such lessons contribute to forming good habits of persistence in adulthood.

Integrity is another quality of courage. Integrity involves more than just being honest. It means being an authentic person, sincere in one's thoughts and actions. It involves practicing a regular pattern of behavior that is consistent with one's values. Integrity is placed with courage because it highlights the reality that in many situations integrity is not the easy thing to do. It seems that children have a heavier dose of this strength than do adults. Somewhere along the path to adulthood, however, this strength is often lost. Paragons of integrity for Peterson and Seligman include Honest Abe, Eleanor Roosevelt, Albert Schweitzer, and Ralph Waldo Emerson. They also tell the story of a woman named Sojourner Truth (1797–1883) who under life-threatening conditions spoke out in favor of women's suffrage.

The authors claim that there are a variety of ways to cultivate this trait. One is through sports. Sports allow a public forum for discussing behavior involving integrity and honesty (sportsmanship, steroid use, playing by the rules, etc.). Another is through ethics courses taught in med schools and as well as in business and law schools.

Proverbs has much to say about integrity as represented in the following saying:

> The integrity of the upright guides them,
>   but the crookedness of the treacherous destroys them. (11:3)

The internal character of the upright governs their life (cf. 6:20–23). Character is viewed not as a single act, but as a way of life. The following proverb indicates how integrity is cultivated:

> The righteous walk in integrity—
>   happy are the children who follow them! (20:7)

---

24. Peterson and Seligman, *Character Strengths and Virtues*, 202.

Parents who walk in integrity will pass on that lifestyle to their children, who in turn will be blessed by such an example. Children imitate parents. The epigram affirms the interconnectedness of the generations (see 17:6). One generation benefits from another. The process results in the solidarity of values.

Humanity is a third overarching virtue that is identified. Its cluster of character strengths includes three: love, kindness, and social intelligence. Peterson and Seligman mention Brian Piccolo and Gayle Sayers as paragons of the first trait of love (also George Burns and Gracie Allen). As they are described, all three of the character strengths are embodied in the "friend" in Proverbs. Proverbs 18:24 serves as an example:

> Some friends play at friendship
> but a true friend sticks closer than one's nearest kin.

The contrast is between casual friends on the one hand and a close friend on the other; it is a contrast between the appearance of friendship and genuine friendship. The friend who sticks (or clings) closer than a brother reminds one of the story of Ruth, who "clings" to Naomi (Ruth 1:14). The true friend values close relations (Peterson and Seligman define this as "love"), she practices "kindness" (which they define as performing good deeds even in the absence of utilitarian reasons), and she displays "social intelligence" (the ability to be sensitive to another's feelings and motives).

Peterson and Seligman distinguish the fourth virtue, justice, from humanity. Strengths of humanity involve the smaller interpersonal realm (strengths *between*). Strengths of justice comprise the larger community (strengths *among*). The three character strengths they associate with this virtue include, citizenship, fairness, and leadership. Citizenship involves working well as a team player; developing a sense of duty because of solidarity they feel with the group.

The three archetypal wisdom virtues include righteousness, justice, and fairness (1:3; 2:9; 8:20). Within those virtues, to use Peterson and Seligman's terms, is the character strength of community. Wisdom nurtures the building up of community and one's responsibility to that community. The whole task of moral education in Proverbs is placed in the context of family and the faith community (2:1–9 see Chapter Nine). The reason for a youth's moral development is so that she can make a contribution to the larger community. The youth is being trained for good citizenship. Peterson and Seligman offer the practice of volunteerism as one means of cultivating citizenship. Citizenship is also fostered in school through playing team sports, participating in bands, plays, choirs, and other group activities.

Another character strength contributing to the virtue of justice is fairness. Those who practice fairness do not cheat others; they treat everyone with respect. Peterson and Seligman offer Mohandas Gandhi as an example of one who devoted his life to justice and fairness. Gandhi "argued that the same moral standard must apply to colonizer (the British) and colonized (the Indians) alike and to all Indians regardless of their position in the traditional Indian caste system."[25] Fairness, it is suggested, is nurtured through learning to follow the rules in sports, in running meetings, in practicing considerateness whenever we are in a social situation where others are trying to use the same tools or accomplish the same goals as we. It can be encouraged in the home in the responsible training of children. The central factors that promote justice and fairness are open discussions of moral issues and dilemmas, parental style of leadership in the home, peer discourse about moral issues, and schools that display a participatory approach to education.

Proverbs highlights fairness, especially in business practices. Under wisdom's vices above, one item listed is falsehood. The sage condemns dishonesty, fraud, and deceit in all walks of life, especially in business dealings. The following antithetic proverb condemns deception and promotes fairness:

> A false balance is an abomination to the LORD,
> but an accurate weight is his delight. (11:1)

The word "abomination" in Proverbs is imposed as a sanction against unfair business practices and reckless behavior. When the sages could not appeal to specific punishment that would naturally follow irresponsible actions, to speak of something as "an abomination to the LORD" was powerful reproof for engaging in wrong activity.[26] The use of dishonest scales was next to impossible to detect (see 20:10 and 20:23). There were ways of cheating the customer that technically did not violate the law. So the sages might say something like, "Others may not see your deceptive actions, but God does and God abhors your behavior." The wise practice fairness in all of their dealings with others regardless of social status because it builds up the community and reflects the very nature of God. Even though what constitutes acts of justice may vary, the overarching idea of justice remains an important virtue in both Proverbs and positive psychology.

The character traits aligned with the virtue of temperance are designed to equip individuals to refrain from certain destructive thoughts and

---

25. Ibid., 391.
26. See Clements, "The Concept of Abomination in the Book of Proverbs."

actions like arrogance, hatred, pleasures with negative consequences, and damaging emotions. All of these character strengths (forgiveness, humility, prudence, and self-regulation) are deeply rooted in wisdom's paradigm. Here I highlight just one of the traits Peterson and Seligman describe, the quiet character strength of humility and modesty. As the writers explain, humility is not self-deprecation but a persona that "deflects attention from the self and onto other people or circumstances."[27] It is the ability to keep one's accomplishments in perspective. One model of humility they offer is Frank Shorter, the 1972 Olympic gold medalist in the marathon. Peterson met him on one occasion and engaged him in conversation without even knowing who he was. The conversation was spent with Shorter asking Peterson about his graduate studies in psychology.

The authors also suggest Bill Wilson, cofounder of Alcoholics Anonymous, as another paragon of humility. Wilson testifies to his struggles with pride.[28] Yet humility related themes play a central role within Wilson's 12-step AA framework (e.g., admitting personal and moral limitations; making amends; relying on a higher power). Wilson understood the central value of humility. He also, however, understood firsthand the difficulty of attaining this virtue, and he wrestled throughout his lifetime in his attempts to cultivate it. Such a struggle exemplifies the desire to develop humility and the fact that once a person believes he possesses humility, he has lost it.

The authors say that religion can help individuals foster humility by encouraging self-transcendence. Another resource is to provide people with accurate feedback about their strengths and limitations (cf., Proverbs 27:5–6). Religious acts of service, keeping a gratitude journal, realizing indebtedness to others, and developing close relationships with others all help to generate humility.

The sage has much to say about humility and its opposite, pride. The following are a couple of examples:

> Pride goes before destruction,
>   and a haughty spirit before a fall. (16:18)

> The reward for humility and fear of the LORD
>   is riches and honor and life. (22:4)

The second proverb affirms that the one who fears the Lord understands and humbly accepts his place under God's rule. Arrogance gets in the way of instruction. The foolish person is the one who is "wise in his own eyes,"

---

27. Peterson and Seligman, *Character Strengths and Virtues*, 436.
28. Ibid., 461.

a phrase repeated all through Proverbs (e.g., 16:2; 26:5, 12). Humility is essential for youth to acquire in order to learn and grow.

The sixth and final virtue identified by the positive psychologists is transcendence. They classify five character strengths with this virtue: appreciation of beauty, gratitude, hope, humor, and what they call spirituality. Proverbs affirms the value of all five of these. However, I will highlight two of them in the following paragraphs, humor and gratitude.

Proverbs affirms the value of humor and playfulness. The proverbs listed in the category of cheerfulness (in the above list of proverb virtues) relate to this character strength (e.g., 15:13, 15; 16:24; 17:22). Peterson and Seligman list humor with transcendence because, in their opinion, humor enables one to make connections outside of one's self to the larger world. Humor is a sign that we have something in common with others. A humorous person is skilled at laughing, gentle teasing, and bringing a smile to the faces of others. Humor serves a moral good by making the human condition more bearable by sustaining good cheer in the face of despair and by building social bonds.[29] As exemplary of this trait, they mention Bob Hope and the USO shows that were conducted for overseas service men and women. However, for the sages of Proverbs one does not have to be a professional comedian to fully embody this strength. Wisdom is all about that which is ordinary, the ordinary events of daily life and ordinary people. Wisdom believes the ordinary person is fully capable of developing and displaying a healthy dose of humor in interaction with others. Humor is a serious trait that appreciates human imperfections;[30] it also serves as a defense mechanism in adversity. Peterson and Seligman claim that, "a good sense of humor might well be one of the defining features of so-called positive mental health."[31] Just as with the other twenty-four strengths, they believe humor and playfulness can be cultivated to a positive degree and offer two examples of programs designed to do just that.[32]

Gratitude is also singled out as a character strength of transcendence. Gratitude is described as the result of having benefited from the actions of another person, whether it is another human or God. Lou Gehrig is suggested as one who embodied gratitude, especially in delivering his famous retirement speech at Yankee Stadium on July 4, 1939 just 2 years before his death:

---

29. Ibid., 530.
30. Ibid., 595.
31. Ibid., 532.
32. Ibid., 596–97.

Fans, for the past two weeks you have been reading about the bad break I got. Yet today I consider myself the luckiest man on the face of this earth. I have been in ballparks for seventeen years and have never received anything but kindness and encouragement from you fans. Look at these grand men. Which of you wouldn't consider it the highlight of his career just to associate with them for even one day? Sure I'm lucky.... When you have a wonderful mother-in-law who takes sides with you in squabbles with her own daughter—that's something. When you have a father and a mother who work all their lives so you can have an education and build your body—it's a blessing. When you have a wife who has been a tower of strength and shown more courage than you dreamed existed—that's the finest I know. So I close in saying that I may have had a tough break, but I have an awful lot to live for.[33]

Though not many, if any, proverbs speak directly to the character strength of gratitude, this quality is one that underlies much of what the sages teach. Proverbs that speak of contentment assume a sense of gratitude (e.g., 14:30). Often those individuals who possess little are those who are most content and grateful (15:15, 16; 17:1). Those that speak of honoring the Lord and fearing him also assume such a posture (e.g., 3:5; 10:27; 15:16, 30; 19:23). Gratitude serves as the motivation for practicing generosity about which the sage has much to say (19:6). In honoring God one receives a sense of security, which in turn generates a grateful heart. So even though the sages do not use the specific word, gratitude, it under girds much of the motivation for what they do.

One of the values of comparing wisdom's list of character strengths to Peterson's and Seligman's classification is that these psychologists help to flesh out and contextualize wisdom's virtues in contemporary culture. Again education in wisdom's paradigm is not so much an academic exercise as it is a hands-on lived experience involving the whole person. The paragons that they offer with each trait and suggestions for cultivating them can serve to generate ideas for teaching, observing, and experiencing wisdom's virtues. In addition, they include in the final chapter a self-report questionnaire they use to measure the twenty-four strengths of character in an individual. They refer to it as the Values in Action Inventory of Strengths (VIA-IS) and have developed an inventory for adults as well as for youth.[34] They acknowledge limitations to the instrument, but they also identify the degrees of validity.

---

33. Ibid., 525.
34. Ibid., 629–39.

Such an assessment tool may have potential for adaptability in seminaries, synagogues, and churches.

Obviously there are significant differences between the perspectives of Proverbs and positive psychology. For one, Peterson and Seligman are not interested in the theological dimension of life at all. In fact, according to C. Robert Cloninger, "Peterson and Seligman are self-proclaimed agnostics who specifically deny any faith in the divine."[35] This obviously limits their contribution to character formation. For the sage the very foundation of character formation is the fear of the Lord. Again Cloninger observes, "To accommodate the prominent role of faith in the happy life, they recognize it as an alternative to hope on the path to their overarching concept of transcendence. Empirical findings, however, show that the character traits that measure faith, hope, and charity are all interdependent and synergistic in making a person feel good."[36]

Second, and along the same line, their advice and suggestions for cultivating the different twenty-four strengths is limited because there is no faith community that provides support, resources, or modeling. The authors speak often of family as a resource where character is shaped. While valuable to emphasize the importance of the family, it is still quite limited. The family remains isolated and individualized in their scheme. One needs a larger community that can support and nurture family. As someone has observed, a family all wrapped up in itself makes a mighty small package.

In spite of these limitations, Peterson and Seligman's work still holds value in enabling Proverbs' lists of virtues and vices to be translated into a contemporary context by offering insight into the makeup, development, modeling, and cultivation of the strengths. Their work holds heuristic value for generating further insights into how to teach, cultivate, and live out these virtues today.

CONCLUSION

Wisdom is intentional and direct in its instruction. It teaches specific virtues and models how those virtues manifest themselves in life. Through training, observing, modeling, and the use of negative and positive reinforcement people can learn to live morally responsible lives. These values flow out of a particular worldview that shapes an individual's character and the way that individual makes decisions.

---

35. Cloninger, "Book Forum: *Character Strengths and Virtues*."
36. Ibid.

Significantly, wisdom does not spend a lot of time discussing the heavy moral issues in the same way we occupy ourselves today with ethical dilemmas such as cloning, abortion, euthanasia, or environmentalism. Instead its primary interest lies in the ordinary, the routine matters of daily living: patience, trust, contentment, self-control, integrity, generosity, and practicing justice and righteousness.[37]

In order to instill these virtues into our minds and lives, the sages availed themselves of a number of resources that enable us to participate in the formation of character. The following chapters investigate a number of these resources beginning with that little rhetorical form known as the proverb. In order to carry the cargo of wisdom's instructions, the sages depended heavily on the robust quality of the proverb. Because of the process of wisdom's instruction, as well as the nature of its goal, the proverb became the instrument of choice for the sage.

Though small and innocent looking in appearance, the tenacity of the proverb enabled it to carry the primary load of responsibility when the sages offered negative or positive reinforcement or sought to critically engage the student's mind or wanted to convey ideas in a memorable form. The sages harnessed the power of the proverb pressing it into active service in the training of receptive minds and hearts. The next chapter explores the qualities of this resilient and adaptable resident of wisdom's house.

---

37. William Bennett observes that "the formation of character in young people is educationally a different task from, and a prior task to, the discussion of the great, difficult controversies of the day. First things first. We should teach values the same way we teach other things: one step at a time." "Moral Literacy and the Formation of Character," 137.

Chapter Four

The Proverb in Character Formation

THE FORM OF MORAL INSTRUCTION

What rhetorical form does moral instruction assume? Many educators stress the dominant role that narrative plays in the development of character.[1] Katherine Paterson, a well-known award-winning children's author, spoke to a group of us in Atlanta a number of years ago, objecting to the aphorisms and moral advice given her by her parents while growing up:

> I'm sorry to say that moral tales and proverbs and behavior charts did not turn me into a good child. They turned me into a discouraged and occasionally belligerent child. They might have done me in, except for two things. Two very important things. I knew that despite all my failings my father and my mother loved me, and, they gave me stories. Not just moralistic fables, but stories of marvelously real, imperfect people like Abraham and Sarah and David and Samson and Jacob and Peter, both the saint and the rabbit. Stories of bumbling Pooh and fearful Piglet. Stories of reckless, raucous, boastful Toad and Mary Lennox

---

1. William Bennett emphasizes the importance of telling children and youth classic stories from the Bible and from Western Civilization, as well as telling them stories about the great heroes of American history. Bennett, "Moral Literacy and the Formation of Character," 135–38.

whose temper was every bit as bad as mine but who was given the key to a secret garden.²

Paterson believes that narrative serves as the most effective genre for use in the development of character in children. She does not believe that narrative and moral precepts can coexist. In her speech she told of the government of Indonesia inviting her to come and promote the writing of children's books in that country because the children were complaining that there was nothing worth reading. What she discovered was that the majority of books published for children had the "high-minded intention" of teaching children how to behave. Children rebel against reading that kind of material. They know what behavior is expected of them, and they do not like to have their noses rubbed in moral bromides.

Paterson chides those who want to coat the sweet taste of story with the "sour pill of morality." In her own children's books, Paterson writes about human experience as a means of incarnating moral character.³ A genuine story is alive, ever changing and growing as it meets each listener in a unique and spirited encounter. A good story allows children to decide what the story means in their life, a values clarification type of approach. There is no doubt that Paterson's stories are powerful and engaging. For her, narrative and metaphor shape our moral character, not proverbs and rules.⁴ Because proverbs are not viewed as narrative,⁵ they find themselves cast aside like unwanted children. After all, we do not want to engage in moralistic instruction.

But the formation of character is more complex than Paterson revealed, at least in her speech.⁶ The genre of story does not hold a monopoly on developing character. A view that sees narrative as the archetypal genre in moral formation is naive and reductionistic. Developing moral character must involve a healthy use of narrative as well as a variety of other genres, including rules, principles, sermons, liturgical traditions, and proverbs.⁷

---

2. Paterson, "From Story to Stories."

3. She has written such books as *Bridge to Terabithia* and *Jacob Have I Loved*.

4. Stanley Hauerwas is also a proponent of the primacy of narrative from a theological perspective. See his *A Community of Character*.

5. They are not narrative in the conventional sense of the term. But as this chapter will later show there is a narrative-type movement within the two lines of the proverb. From another perspective Alyce McKenzie refers to proverbs as "freeze-dried narratives;" they are condensations of human experiences. *Preaching Biblical Wisdom in a Self-Help Society*, 93.

6. For one perspective on the development of formative education in Israel see Eaton, "Memory and Encounter: An Educational Ideal."

7. Brown, *Character in Crisis*, 18–19.

In the Old Testament, instruction in the formation of character included several literary components and rhetorical genres. First, there was the rehearsal of the mighty acts of God. This was essential to the identity of Israel. However, woven into this narrative rehearsal was a call to a way of life. It was not just the narrative of the mighty acts of God. The narrative included the *interpretation* of the mighty acts. The act and the interpretation of the act belong together. In fact, Jewish tradition understood the Torah to contain these two interrelated components. The narrative dimension, referred to as the *haggadah*, answered the question of identity, "Who are we?" The legal dimension containing commandments and instructions, referred to as the *halakah*, answered the question, "What are we to do?" The Torah does not emphasize one over the other but contains a blend of both. Commands and laws were interrelated in the story.

For example, in Deuteronomy 6:20–24 as the parents recited the exodus story, they concluded with a call to observe the commandments and statutes. The commands and moral principles inform the narrative, and the narrative in turn incarnates the principles. To determine whether narrative or principle is primary is a chicken-or-egg question. That question becomes insignificant when engaging in constructive moral rhetoric. Both forms remain essential. Neither one can stand on its own.[8]

A second rhetorical component in moral education involved bringing these past stories and commands into present reenactment. The liturgical tradition of the Passover Meal, for example, reenacted a past event in the present. In Deuteronomy 26:5–11 when worshippers brought their offerings to God, they engaged in a recitation of the mighty acts of God, identifying with the ancestors of old, bringing the past into the present.

Third, there was a concern to equip the present generation to engage in critical judgment of the past. As I described in Chapter Two, the sages were concerned with cultivating the art of discernment and the ability to think critically. The sages found the form of the proverb especially suited to developing this ability. Frequently sages placed pairs and clusters of proverbs that seem to contradict one another side by side to challenge the student to engage in critical thinking.[9]

---

8 David Greenhaw argues for the interrelatedness of "narrative" and "concept." The hermeneutic process includes a circular movement. A concept is communicated through story and from the story the listener gleans a new concept. However, the implication that Greenhaw makes is that concepts are communicated primarily through narrative. I would argue that concepts are communicated through a variety of genres including proverbs. See Greenhaw, "As One with Authority."

9. E.g., 26:4–5; 18:10–11; 16:1–9; 3:9–12.

All through the Old Testament the education process was reinforced by a variety of genres, including narrative, commands, liturgical practices, and diatribe. Traditional wisdom incorporates narrative and non-narrative material for the sake of character formation. The formation process defies reduction to any single rhetorical genre. The book of Proverbs itself is couched within a narrative frame (chapters 1–9; 31). In addition, there are visual images of good and bad characters sprinkled along the way: the temptress, the sluggard, the fool, the wise son, the wise woman, the drunkard, the proud, the scoffer, the just ruler, the disciplined son, etc. There are also the pithy sayings and aphorisms of chapters 10–29. All serve the goal of moral instruction.

For the sage, however, the rhetorical form of the proverb became most valuable as a tool for instructing others. Proverbs served as instruments of orientation in times of disorientation, particularly during the Persian period. When Israel lost its major institutions, found itself exiled and dispersed abroad, its leaders reframed their beliefs, packaging them not in narratives but in proverbial form to pass on to the next generation. They served as survival tools for Israel in exile.[10] Proverbs have the capacity to clarify the ambiguous, provide stability for changing times, and bring order to disorder.

When handled responsibly, proverbs become valuable resources for instilling within receptive minds principles of proper conduct and character. In the past some of the most popular books on the market have been the H. Jackson Brown series beginning with the first volume entitled *Life's Little Instruction Book*.[11] The series consists of contemporary adages that are, as the subtitle states, "suggestions, observations, and reminders on how to live a happy and rewarding life." The inspiration for these proverbs came on the occasion of Brown's son, Adam, leaving home for college. On that occasion, Brown gathered up his collection and gave it to his son. In the introduction to the booklet Brown makes this observation:

> I read years ago that it was not the responsibility of parents to pave the road for their children, but to provide a road map. That's how I hoped he [Adam] would use these mind and heart reflections. . . . A few days after I had given Adam his copy, he called me from his dorm room. "Dad," he said, "I've been reading the instruction book and I think it's one of the best gifts I've ever received. I'm going to add to it and someday give it to my son."[12]

---

10 This is Clements' thesis in *Wisdom in Theology*.

11. Brown, *Life's Little Instruction Book*, Introduction, np.

12 Brown, "Introduction."

The use of proverbs in moral education, however, has fallen upon hard times. In some circles educators view proverbs as "sour pills of morality," to use Paterson's words. Educators often do not understand how proverbs work or how they influence thought and action. Nor do they understand how to incorporate them into the educational process. What is needed is a better comprehension of how they function in moral discourse and to offer fresh ideas for incorporating them into the process.

HOW PROVERBS FUNCTION IN MORAL DISCOURSE

The Destructive Use of Proverbs

Biblical proverbs are dynamic resources for spiritual growth. Their very nature and the way in which they are incorporated into daily life activate them for spiritual service. They are a part of a rich and honorable tradition, but they do have a darker side. Some users have pressed proverbs into destructive service. The platitudes that Job received from his three friends bear witness to the villainous potential of proverbial sayings (Job 13:12). The friends used proverbs to try and beat Job into submission. In the wrong hands, proverbs possess the power to harm.

During the time of Nazi Germany, Nazi propaganda used folklore to deepen anti-Semitism among the German people. The Nazis used proverbs to "prove" Aryan supremacy over against Jewish "villainism." Wolfgang Mieder provides a sample of anti-Semitic proverbs, which include the following:

> Just as the owl cannot bear the light, so the Jew cannot bear the truth.
> For Jews and ravens all bathing is in vain.
> The Jew corresponds to the human, as the wolf to the flock.
> Jews in the house, are worse than bedbug and louse.[13]

The Third Reich also engaged in promoting the purity of the Aryan race through the use of proverbs:

> Three things make the best couples: same blood, same passion and same age.
>
> Single, sin.
>
> Race sticks to race.

---

13 From Wolfgang Mieder, *Proverbs Are Never Out of Season*, 225–55.

> The apple does not fall far from the tree, as the sheep so the lamb.[14]

Mieder concludes his study of proverbs during the "dark ages" of Nazi Germany with the frightening observation that the publication of such proverbs

> are painful reminders of how proverbs and folklore can be used to influence, manipulate, and poison people's feelings, thoughts, and actions. Proverbs in themselves might be harmless pieces of folk wisdom, but when they become propagandistic tools in the hands of malicious persons, they can take on unexpected powers of authority and persuasion.[15]

The abuse of proverbs during the period of National Socialism is admittedly an extreme case, but even in the routine affairs of daily conversation between people, individuals frequently employ proverbs as objects of misuse.

Most often, individuals carelessly use proverbs to oversimplify complex issues. They use proverbs to express the "definitive statement" on a subject at hand that can stifle any further serious discussion. Sometimes individuals interject a "well-timed" truism in the course of a conversation, such as "God said it, I believe it, that settles it," that brings the conversation to a screeching halt. Such "skillful" handling enables the proverb user to maintain control of the situation. What those listening do not realize is that one proverb never says it all and never was intended to say it all.

Sometimes the abuse of proverbs lies in overuse. Through repeated use, a particular aphorism is made trivial. The user turns into a kind of proverb junkie. In the mouth of this person, any proverb falls prey to the pitfalls of excess. For example, when the user hands out the same advice any time she sees another person caught in a difficult situation (e.g., "It's better to be safe than sorry"), the proverb soon loses its potency. Listeners no longer put any stock in the truism.

Sometimes individuals appropriate proverbs for the sake of demoralizing others, that is, to put them in their place. A number of proverbs or proverb phrases, like the anti-Semitic ones already mentioned, dehumanize people of different races or religions. Because of these common abuses, among others, individuals shy away from intentionally using the pithy sayings. Yet when proverbs are omitted from daily use, a community loses a valuable spiritual resource. When employed wisely, proverbs release compelling truths that capture the essence of the hard experiences of life. Therein lies their rhetorical strength.

---

14. Ibid., 239–40.
15. Ibid., 251.

The Constructive Use of Proverbs

In order to engage proverbs more effectively in the task of moral development, it becomes crucial that individuals understand the functional dynamics that empower proverbs as vital resources for mental, emotional, and spiritual health. By design, proverbs function within a culture to manage social behavior. On the one hand, proverbs are essential for maintaining and controlling order in a community.[16] They enable individuals to say what needs to be said without creating unnecessary social tension.[17] On the other hand, they validate the existing values to which a culture holds.[18] Proverbs can manage potentially harmful behavior as well as affirm constructive behavior.

THE RHETORICAL FUNCTION OF THE PROVERB

So how do proverbs function rhetorically to accomplish their tasks?[19] How do they act upon the hearer? Exploring answers to these questions enables one to further understand the power of the proverb in the educational process. In regard to the biblical proverb, a synergistic relationship among its components enables the proverb to carry out its work. These instructional components include the proverb's memorable form, flexibility, situational quality, familiarity, brevity and wit, and universal appeal.

Memorable

First, proverbs are packaged in a memorable form, that is, they are built on the literary quality of "parallelism" that characterizes the two-line aphorism. Roger Abrahams describes the binary structure succinctly: "The proverb is generally a sentence that is perceptibly broken in the middle."[20] What threatens the vitality of the proverb, however, is the way in which this internal structure has been perceived. The traditional approach to proverbs

---

16. I am also aware that proverbs can function to subvert order. However, that is not their primary purpose in Proverbs. For further treatment of their subversive nature see McKenzie, *Preaching Proverbs*, 41–78.

17. Jacobson, "Proverbs and Social Control: A New Paradigm for Wisdom Studies," 81.

18. See Bascom, "Four Functions of Folklore."

19. Elsewhere I have investigated the rhetorical function of the proverb in Medieval literature. See Bland, "The Use of Proverbs in Two Medieval Genres of Discourse."

20. Abrahams, "Proverbs and Proverbial Expressions," 120.

treats them as inert entities. It views the parallel patterns of proverbs as static, which does not allow for the subtle but dynamic differences that characterize the individual proverbs.[21] Understanding the rich dimensions of parallelism that reside within the proverb yields valuable insight into the way in which the proverb influences thought and action.

The phenomenon of "parallelism" relates to the dynamic quality that exists between the two lines. The second line does not simply repeat the first line but in some way, shape, or form complements it.[22] In relationship to the first line, the second line carries the thought further either by imaging, defining, restating, or contrasting the first line. The second line emphasizes or seconds the first. Or to use a hammer and nail analogy, the first line sets the nail; the second line drives it home. For example, notice the following "antithetic" proverb,

> The righteous one will seek out his friend
> but the way of the wicked ones will wander. (12:26)[23]

The second line intensifies the first by moving from the singular ("righteous one") to plural ("wicked ones"). Furthermore, the first line focuses on seeking out a particular kind of person, a friend. A clear objective exists. However, the second line lacks focus: the wicked ones have no direction. They are those who wander.

Consider another example:

> The sacrifice of the wicked ones are an abomination of Yahweh
> but the prayers of the upright ones–his delight. (15:8)

In this antithetic proverb "sacrifice" and "prayer" are used as synonyms. The proverb moves from a general term for worship to a specific term, namely from "sacrifice" to "prayers." The saying also moves from the singular "sacrifice" to the plural "prayers." Within Hebrew parallelism a dynamic not a static quality exists regardless of whether a saying exhibits characteristics of synonymous, antithetic, or synthetic parallelism.[24]

---

21. The main categories of parallelism include synonymous (the second line echoes the thought of the first), antithetic (the second line says the opposite of the first), and synthetic (the second line expands on the thought of the first).

22. Kugel, *The Idea of Biblical Poetry*. In this work Kugel takes issue with the long-standing way of describing Hebrew poetry. The two lines are not statically parallel. But the second line in some way emphasizes or "seconds" the first line. However, Kugel went to an extreme and identified parallelism even in narrative genres thus collapsing the boundary between Hebrew poetry and narrative.

23. This proverb and the one that follows are my own translation.

24. For a more detailed analysis of the variety of proverbial parallelism see Bland, "A Rhetorical Perspective on the Sentence Sayings of the Book of Proverbs."

The binary construction enables the proverb to possess a memorable quality. Because of that, one can easily retrieve the adage from his or her memory when the appropriate situation arises. Part of the task of moral discourse in any age is to incorporate proverbs into one's memory. For example, individuals, families and churches can develop a simple memorization plan. A person might begin with the list of virtues mentioned earlier in Chapter Three and memorize one or two proverbs from each of the topics (self-control, patience, diligence, integrity, faithfulness, etc.). Consider memorizing them by key words chosen from the proverb rather than trying to remember the verses where they are found. The following proverbs serve as an example. The underlined word or phrase serves as the "key word":

> Like a city breached, without walls,
>   is one who lacks <u>self-control</u>. (25:28)
>
> A <u>cheerful heart</u> is a good medicine,
>   but a downcast spirit dries up the bones. (17:22)
>
> Hatred stirs up strife,
>   but <u>love</u> covers all offenses. (10:12)
>
> One who is <u>slow to anger</u> is better than the mighty,
>   and one whose temper is controlled than one who captures a city. (16:32)

The idea, however, is not just to commit proverbs to memory but to integrate them into the routine of everyday activity and discover ways of making them a part of one's family life. There are different times of the day when a particular proverb might be used. For example, at the evening meal as the family gathers to eat, begin by having someone quote the following proverb: "Better is a dry morsel with quiet, than a house full of feasting with strife" (17:1). A parent could make it a habit at every evening meal to select someone to quote the proverb as the family sits down to the table together. Or in the morning as each member of the family leaves for work or school, a father or mother might ask each one to quote a proverb, perhaps the following: "A good name is to be chosen rather than great riches" (22:1a). A proverb could also be built into the routine activities of preparing for bed. There are many creative ways of making proverbs a part of a family's thought and life. In the process, family members build up a mental reservoir of sayings. Churches can also discover innovative ways of integrating proverbs into the routine of their corporate life together.

It is helpful for individuals store up proverbial advice as a resource for making daily decisions. A proverb says something that is immediately recognized as true. It encourages, can help to clarify the ambiguous, and equips individuals to respond appropriately to other persons, choices, or feelings that unexpectedly arise.

The aphorism is easily tucked away in the corners of the mind ready for active duty when the occasion demands it. The memorable quality of the proverb makes it easy to say and hard to forget. Thus the proverb becomes a valuable teaching aid. Brushing away the deposits from its surface, the proverb reveals a creative as well as complex display of parallelism that has its own way of inscribing itself on the mind.

Flexible

Second, the proverb exhibits flexibility in its meaning. Because of its polysemous quality there is more to the proverb than meets the eye. On the surface the brevity, form, and content of the proverb work together to make its thought something that the hearer can immediately affirm. But its relatively indeterminate nature also fills it with a surplus of meaning.

To understand this quality, compare the proverb for a moment with other literary genres of like kind. Put the proverb on an imaginary continuum with other forms based on the amount of demand that particular form places on the hearer to understand it. The riddle, which places heavy responsibility on the hearer to decode its message, immediately rises to the top of the continuum. Not too many pure riddles exist in Scripture. But the story of Samson in the book of Judges contains a few. Recall Samson challenging his Philistine foes to discover the meaning of his riddle: "Out of the eater came something to eat, out of the strong came something sweet" (Judg. 14:14). The challenge proved to be more than the Philistines could meet. Finally, in order to crack the meaning of the riddle, they resorted to underhanded tactics, namely coercing Samson's wife into telling them what it meant.[25] The riddle, as a literary form, places a heavy burden on the hearer to comprehend its meaning.[26]

A literary form that is not quite as demanding as the riddle is the parable. Think of the parables Jesus taught. Jesus himself says that some things about the parable remain difficult to understand (Mk. 4:11-12). Unlike the

---

25. The riddle refers to Samson killing a lion on one occasion only to return to the carcass at a later time to discover that bees had made a honey comb in it. See Judges 14:14-20.

26. Another example, to what does the following riddle refer? "Throw away the outside, then cook the inside. Eat the outside, then throw away the inside." Without a clue, it is tough to crack the riddle's code of meaning. The answer is corn on the cob.

riddle, however, with the parable there is something for everyone even those who were not disciples of Jesus. At the same time, even to his closest disciples, Jesus sometimes had to explain the meaning.[27]

Much further down the continuum from the riddle and parable resides the slogan. The slogan places no demand on the hearer. It is catchy, easy to remember, and requires no thought to understand as, for example, in the proverbial type phrase "let go and let God." Because of these qualities, political campaigns frequently create and employ slogans.

At the bottom of the literary continuum sits the cliché. Clichés are basically slogans gone to seed. So overused, these unwanted tenants haunt the listener like a worn out song that refuses to leave the mind. If, for example, someone utters the statement "better safe that sorry" before making every decision that arises, it becomes a cliché.

So where does the proverb appear on this continuum? It depends on how the proverb user uses it. On some occasions, a proverb possesses the flexibility to take on the form of a riddle. For example, some contemporary proverbs intentionally remain cryptic. Consider two parents talking to one another about a sensitive subject when in walks their six-year-old daughter. Mom turns to Dad and says, "Little pitchers have big ears." The parents use the proverb as a secret code to remind themselves of the potential harm in discussing this subject in front of their daughter.

On other occasions, some proverbs become more like slogans, easily turning into cheap clichés. A grandmother constantly warns her grandchild about the dangers of taking risks: "look before you leap." The proverb itself is simple and straightforward, but if used over and over again in a particular setting, it quickly deteriorates into nothing more than a worn-out cliché.

Biblical proverbs cover the same kind of continuum. Proverbs 25–27 consists of a series of riddle-like proverbs. In these proverbs, the first line contains an analogy while the second line contains the referent to that analogy. For example, the first line of the proverb in 26:17 says, "One who takes a passing dog by the ears. . . ."[28] The line generates curiosity: Who is the one foolish enough to grab a stray dog minding its own business by the ears? This is the genius of a riddle: Not until the second line do we find out who is the referent and what is its specific meaning: ". . . those who meddle in a

---

27. The following resources develop this perspective on the parables: Crossan, *Cliffs of Fall*. Scott, *Hear Then the Parable*.

28. Unfortunately, again our English versions do not take seriously the form of the Hebrew text. So many of the analogies in chapters 25–27 appear not in the first but the second line. The RSV translates 26:17 thus: "He who meddles in a quarrel not his own is like one who takes a passing dog by the ears." The NRSV follows the Hebrew text and puts it in the correct order.

quarrel not their own." The reader is now clued in. The one who sticks her nose into someone else's quarrel is like someone who grabs a passing dog by the ears. Since the answer to the "riddle" is so easily accessible, however, it is not a true riddle.

Proverbs 1:6 claims that the purpose of the book is to help one "understand . . . the words of the wise and their riddles." In reality, though a few proverbs might possess certain qualities of a riddle, there are no genuine riddles in Proverbs. Yet the prologue claims that this is an important genre in the book. Michael Fox argues that the reference to proverbs as riddles prepares the reader to realize that there is more to these apothegms than meets the eye.[29] They are not just trite or pedantic sayings; these proverbs have depth. Thus the reader should not dismiss them too quickly but carefully study and examine them. On the other hand, there are biblical proverbs that, if not used wisely, could easily become clichés. The proverb, "Pride goes before destruction" (16:18), is not difficult for anyone to understand, but it can become a well-worn phrase if repeated *ad nauseum*.

The flexibility of the proverb also manifests itself in the way that it often possesses more than one meaning. In the United States the familiar contemporary proverb, "A rolling stone gathers no moss," means that one who remains active and on the move will be productive. The presence of moss is a negative image. Such a person lacks initiative and drive. In contrast, in England the image of moss on rocks is quite positive. A stone in a babbling brook with moss draped over it offers a beautiful image of stability and productivity.[30] The flexible nature of the proverb is another rhetorical quality that gives it power to function and to influence thought.

Biblical proverbs also possess this flexibility. This quality makes them well suited for use in moral instruction. On one level, a proverb's meaning appears obvious. That is part of its power. One immediately acknowledges its truth. On another level, the power of the proverb lies in the fact that its metaphorical and poetic nature enables it to have more than one meaning. Proverbs 27:19 serves as one example, "Just as water reflects the face, so one human heart reflects another." The question is does this proverb describe an introspective scenario, a soliloquy, or is it describing interaction between two people? The proverb possesses a quality that requires the reader to dwell on it and probe it more deeply. Thus, one must wrestle for a while with even the most mundane proverb, not turning it loose until it reveals its deeper meaning.

---

29. Fox, *Proverbs 1–9*, 66.
30. See Kirshenblatt-Gimblett, "Toward a Theory of Proverb Meaning," 112–13.

Situational

Third, and overlapping with the quality of flexibility, is the situational character of the proverb. Not only do situations activate the power of the proverb, the proverb also shapes and controls situations. The relationship between the proverb and the situation remains dynamic. Neither one is determinate, but each works together in a dialectic manner to make sense out of the experience at hand. The situation provides a key element in the process of the proverb working to influence and change.

The situational character of the proverb manifests itself in the way in which the same proverb can have an indeterminate number of meanings based on the context in which it is used. The situation and the speaker's intention determine the proverb's meaning and use. Barbara Kirshenblatt-Gimblett expounds on the multi-level meaning of the proverb, "A friend in need is a friend indeed (in deed)." When she asked eighty of her University of Texas students the meaning of this proverb, she received four general types of responses.[31]

To take another example, the proverbial phrase "silence is golden" can be used in different contexts. A parent can employ it to order a child to be quiet. Another person can use it to console a shy partner when awkward pauses enter their conversation. It can be used to express satisfaction or peace of mind when in the stillness of a forest. Or it can be used to express disgust at the constant chatter of a friend or peer. The situations are endless.[32] Taken at face value, the proverb appears to make a simple, once-and-for-all categorical judgment on a particular experience. Its meaning is self-evident. But its meaning is activated when, as Kenneth Burke says, the individual uses it "for promise, admonition, solace, vengeance, foretelling, instruction, charting"[33] or for whatever the situation calls. That is why a proverb is like

---

31. The four meanings include: "(1) Someone who feels close enough to you to be able to ask you for help when he is in need is really your friend; (2) Someone who helps you when you are in need is really your friend; (3) Someone who helps you by means of his actions (deeds) when you need him is a real friend as opposed to someone who just makes promises; (4) Someone who is only your friend when he needs you is not a true friend." Ibid., 113–14.

32. I heard Jeff Arthurs use this example in a paper presented at the Speech Communication Association annual meeting. "Words Fitly Spoken: Rhetorical Characteristics of Proverbs."

33. Burke, *The Philosophy of Literary Form*, 296. Earlier in this work Burke gives an example of the "endless variety of situations, distinct in their particularities," which a proverb may "size up." He says, "To examine one of my favorites: 'Whether the pitcher strikes the stone, or the stone the pitcher, it's bad for the pitcher.' Think of some primitive society in which an incipient philosopher, in disfavor with the priests, attempted to criticize their lore. They are powerful, he is by comparison weak. And they control

a cat with nine lives.³⁴ It continually pops up with another "life" in different contexts.

The situational quality of the proverb often gives it the appearance of contradicting other proverbs. For example, in one context it would be appropriate to counsel, "Out of sight out of mind." In another context it might be more appropriate to advise, "Absence makes the heart grow fonder." But if one simply looked at these two proverbs outside the specific situation in which they are appropriated, they appear contradictory. Proverbs are not absolutes nor are they generalizations. Rather they are "limited" or "partial" generalizations.³⁵ They are statements of truths that are understood situationally. As Alyce McKenzie observes, rather than floodlights that illuminate the whole landscape, proverbs act as spotlights revealing specific experiences of life.³⁶ That is why it is said, "He who knows one proverb knows none." One proverb does not say it all. The user must have a repertoire of proverbs in order to choose the one that fits the occasion. The wise, however, are not wise because they know a lot of proverbs. The wise are wise because they know how and when to properly use the proverbs.

The Israelite sage understood the situational character of the proverb. Its two-line structure ideally equips the proverb for adaptation to different circumstances. For example, it is not infrequent for one of the lines of the proverbial couplet to be altered in another part of the collection. Such overlapping is the case with the following proverbs:

> The crucible is for silver and the furnace is for gold
> but the Lord tests the heart. (17:3)

all the channels of power. Hence, whether they attack him or he attacks them, he is the loser. And he could quite adequately size up this situation by saying, 'Whether the pitcher strikes the stone, or the stone the pitcher, it's bad for the pitcher.' Or Aristophanes could well have used it, in describing his motivation when, under the threats of political dictatorship, he gave up the lampooning of political figures and used the harmless Socrates as his goat instead. Socrates was propounding new values– and Aristophanes, by aligning himself with conservative values, against the materially powerless dialectician, could himself take on the role of the stone in the stone-pitcher ratio. Or the proverb could be employed to name the predicament of a man in Hitler's Germany who might come forward with an argument, however well reasoned, against Hitler. Or a local clerk would find the proverb apt, if he would make public sport of his boss. These situations are all distinct in their particularities; each occurs in a totally different texture of history; yet all are classifiable together under the generalizing head of the same proverb" (2–3).

34. Murphy, *Proverbs*, xxix.

35. Collins, "Proverbial Wisdom and the Yahwist Vision," 5–6; McKenzie, "Different Strokes For Different Folks: America's Quintessential Postmodern Proverb," 207.

36. McKenzie, *Preaching Proverbs*, xvii.

> The crucible is for silver and the furnace is for gold
> so a person is tested by being praised. (27:21)

> All of one's ways are right in one's own eyes
> but the Lord weighs the heart. (21:2)

With the first two proverbs, the second line changes. In the third proverb, the second line is the same as the second line in 17:3. Thus 17:3 has a double overlap. Its first line overlaps with 27:21 while its second line overlaps with 21:2.

Another example is seen in Proverbs 10:15 and 18:11 where the first line in both proverbs is "The wealth of the rich is their fortress" but the second line changes. In 10:15 it is "the poverty of the poor is their ruin," and in 18:11 it is "in their imagination it is like a high wall." Many other examples of overlapping could be cited.[37] The two lines of the proverb equip it to undergo a type of fission. The proverbs constantly divide, reproducing themselves in different shapes.

One explanation for this phenomenon is that in Israelite schools, the teacher would quote the first line of a proverb and, for instructional purposes, expect the student to complete it with a second line.[38] The problem with this explanation is that sometimes it is the first line that is changed with the second being duplicated. A more likely explanation for the overlapping is that it is an indication of the flexibility of the proverbs. One line can be substituted for another depending on what the situation demands. The binary structure of the proverb equips it for adaptation to different situations and enables it to continue to work.[39] The overlapping sayings suggest that the proverbs are to be memorized but not always to be repeated verbatim. They suggest the occasional nature of the proverb and that the user should take responsibility for its creative appropriation. Someone does not become wise simply by memorizing many proverbs. A mark of wisdom is knowing how to adapt a proverb to different contexts.

Together the two qualities of flexibility and situational character contain great potential for the creative use of proverbs today in the educational

---

37. Compare 13:14 with 14:27; 16:2 with 21:2, 14:12, and 16:25. Compare 10:6 with 10:11; 11:14 with 15:22; 15:8 with 21:27; 24:23 with 28:21; 28:12 with 28:28; 19:12 with 20:2; 15:11 with 27:20; 19:5 with 19:9. In the Hebrew text, the second line of 10:8 is the same as the second line in 10:10.

38. Alter, *The Art of Biblical Poetry*, 163; Scott, *Proverbs, Ecclesiastes*, 9.

39. A contemporary example of this is the proverb, "An apple a day keeps the doctor away, a dozen or more he's right at your door." Or "An apple a day keeps the doctor away, an onion a day keeps everyone away." The familiar one line proverb, "Look before you leap," is sometimes given a second line, "and listen to the learned." "Birds of a feather flock together" on occasion is given an additional line, "and fools fair ill with the wise."

process. They highlight the playfulness of the proverb that should be a part of the learning activity. The binary structure of the proverb invites the creative involvement of students as they think about moral qualities. For example, instructors might state the first half of a proverb and call on students to complete the second line in their own way by offering an analogy or comparison or a contrasting thought to the first line. In order to get students to think about the virtue of faithfulness, for instance, an instructor might ask that they complete the following proverbs with an image or comparative thought:

 A friend loves at all times _____(17:17).

 Some friends play at friendship _____(18:24).

One might do something similar with other proverbs in order to surface values:

 A word spoken at the right time is like _____(25:11).

 It is better to live in the cellar of a house, than _____(21:9).

Such exercises encourage imaginative reflection and enable the internalization of moral values.

Wolfgang Mieder and Anna Tóthné Litovkina refer to the phenomenon of the playful alteration of proverbs as "anti-proverbs."[40] Mieder and Litovkina define an anti-proverb as "any intentional proverb variation in the form of puns, alterations, deletions or additions" that turns out to be a didactic statement.[41] Alterations may involve individuals completing a half-stated proverb, as in the following instance: "blood is thicker than water and it boils quicker."[42] Or "A new broom sweeps clean, but an old one gets the corners." Simply changing a single word can alternate the meaning of a saying: "Necessity is the mother of tension."[43] Sometimes all that is needed is to change one or two letters of the alphabet to alter a proverb: "Clarity begins at home,"[44] and "Levity is the soul of wit."[45]

Educators, be they teachers or parents, can capitalize on the rhetorical agility of the proverb in seeking to involve students in the process of

---

 40. Mieder and Litovkina, *Twisted Wisdom*, 3.
 41. Ibid.
 42. Ibid., 54.
 43. Ibid., 2.
 44. Ibid.
 45. Ibid., 55.

examining moral values.⁴⁶ To create anti-proverbs from some of the biblical proverbs can encourage reflective thought on one's own values.

Familiar

The quality of familiarity comprises the fourth attribute that enables a proverb to do its work. Wolfgang Mieder refers to this dimension as "traditionality."⁴⁷ Traditionality includes both "familiarity" and "frequency." The influence a proverb possesses depends on its ability to establish a reputation for itself. The proverb sounds comfortingly familiar to the listener. In addition, a particular culture or community makes "frequent" use of it in the course of instruction and everyday conversation.

E. D. Hirsch in his book, *The Dictionary of Cultural Literacy*, includes a list of facts and information that he believes individuals should know in order to converse intelligently with literate Americans in the United States. These include famous names, significant events, important dates, and proverbs. Not surprisingly, proverbs make up a sizable portion of the catalogue.⁴⁸ Hirsch and his co-authors list about 265 proverbs known to literate North Americans.⁴⁹ The proverbs he includes are those that possess both familiarity and currency (i.e., frequency) among educated Americans. They reflect as well as influence American values. Proverbs also reflect and influence religious values.

The fact that the scribes collected and recorded the proverbs found in 10:1–22:16 and 25–29 witnesses both to their frequency and familiarity among the Israelites and later the Jews.⁵⁰ Quite likely the scribes reshaped the popular folk proverbs used in the oral culture of the day into more artistic literary forms, and also created new proverbs. The reshaping process,

---

46. In a project funded by the John Templeton Foundation, Deborah Holmes developed a program for integrating proverbs into the curriculum of her fourth grade class in order to teach moral values. She writes, "The integration of character development through proverbs to allow ethical reflection, create moral discipline, and teach values through the curriculum will help ten-year-old students develop moral reasoning, self control, and respect for each other" (18). See Mieder and Holmes, *Children and Proverbs Speak the Truth*, 18. I am convinced that such an approach can work for older students as well.

47. Mieder, *Proverbs Are Never out of Season*, 6.

48. Hirsch, *The Dictionary of Cultural Literacy*, 152–215.

49. Ibid., 46–57.

50. Fox says the reason the sayings in the book are called "proverbs" (מְשָׁלִים) is because it is a reference not simply to their rhetorical form but to their currency, "they are well known and in widespread use." Fox, *Proverbs 1–9*, 55.

though, was often based on proverbs already quite familiar in the oral traditions. In addition, the whole process of collecting and editing the proverbs quite likely increased their familiarity as well as the frequency of their use, especially for Jews during the Persian period. Chapters 10:1–22:16 contain approximately 375 proverbs. Chapters 25–29 contain approximately 135 proverbs bringing the total number of aphorisms to around 510.[51] These collections at least give one a sense of their currency in the culture of that day.

Because they strike a chord of familiarity, proverbs possess the capacity to penetrate the ears and minds of those who hear them. This quality makes them well suited as tools of instruction. Emilie Townes offers some specific suggestions on the variety of ways educators might employ proverbs for instructional purposes:

1. Explain human behavior.
2. Serve as a guide for moral conduct.
3. Explain social behavior.
4. Serve to censure or criticize conduct.
5. Give shrewd advice on how to deal with situations.
6. Express egalitarian views.
7. Express finer human qualities or emotions such as generosity.[52]

Though familiarity can lead listeners to tune out a proverb, familiarity can also allow listeners to feel safe with a proverb and therefore open to hearing its instruction.

Brief and Witty

Fifth, the proverb accomplishes its work partially through its brevity and wit. The two work in tandem. A number of "popular" definitions recognize brevity as a part of the quality of the proverb. For example, a proverb is described as "a short sentence based on a long experience;" it contains "a maximum of meaning with a minimum of words." A proverb is "shortness, sense, and salt." The following definition highlights the other dimension, proverbial wit: a proverb is "the wisdom of many and the wit of one." Actually defining a proverb by its "shortness, sense, and salt" includes both qualities of brevity and wit.

---

51. Clifford calculates a total of 512 aphorisms. See his *The Wisdom Literature*, 64.
52. Cited in Sample, *Ministry in an Oral Culture*, 3.

Brevity and wit work synergistically to create proverbs that aesthetically appeal to both heart and mind. Biblical proverbs are characterized by brevity. Unfortunately, few English translations capture this quality. It is not uncommon for a Hebrew proverb, with its binary structure, to contain four words in the first line and three or four in the second.[53]

For example, the first line of the proverb in 21:31 contains four words in the Hebrew text and translates into English in the following way: "The horse is made ready for the day of battle." "Horse" stands as a metonym for preparation for battle. The proverb conjures up images of a soldier preparing for war. The horse must be groomed, fed, and outfitted. The soldier trains and keeps fit, gathers together his provisions, prepares his armor, and sharpens his weapons. He develops a strategy for fighting the battle. Much effort goes into the preparation. But as one reads the second line, a sudden shift occurs. The horse and soldier no longer remain front and center. A third party enters the picture, Yahweh. The second line in the Hebrew text contains only two words. The closest rendition in English might be something like, "Yahweh gives victory." A surprise reversal! After all the hard work spent in training, planning, preparing, and outfitting, it is the Lord who really gives victory. The brevity of the proverb, especially of the second line, is an important part of the way in which it communicates its message.

One other example is Proverbs 27:14: "Whoever blesses a neighbor with a loud voice, rising early in the morning, will be counted as cursing." The first line contains six words, the second three. Using both compactness and humor, this narrative vignette moves from the superficial facade of the person's greeting to how it really affects the neighbor. Again the proverb contains a surprise reversal. Normally a person would think that one friend blessing another results in a welcome reception, but not in this instance. The inappropriateness of the words and the lack of sensitivity on the part of the friend negate the "blessing." In reality the blessing acts as a curse. The sharpness and brevity of the second line drives home the point.

Easily seen from this last proverb, brevity frequently works together with wit.[54] The sage can reach the pinnacle of sarcasm, especially when it comes to proverbs about the fool or the lazy person. The sage in 19:24 observes: "The lazy person buries a hand in the dish, and will not even bring it back to the mouth." This encapsulated narrative embodies a hyperbole that conjures up a humorous image of a person so lazy that he cannot even

---

53. There are exceptions to this. On some occasions the second line may contain more words than the first. This only serves to emphasize the dynamic quality of the proverb.

54. Bascom identifies one of the social functions of the proverb as providing amusement. See "Four Functions of Folklore."

lift his hand to his mouth to feed himself![55] The sage knows all too well that many a truth is said in jest. The *Today's English Version Bible* and Eugene Peterson's *The Message* are especially good in bringing out the levity of some of the proverbs. The following are a few examples:

> Why doesn't the lazy man ever get out of the house?
> What is he afraid of? Lions? (26:13, TEV)

> Getting involved in an argument that is none of your business
> is like going down the street and grabbing a dog by the ears. (26:17, TEV)

> Human desires are like the world of the dead—
> there is always room for more. (27:20, TEV)

> When the wicked die, that's it—
> the story's over, end of hope. (11:7, Message)

> A bonanza at the beginning
> is no guarantee of blessing at the end. (20:21, Message)

> Valuables are safe in a wise person's home;
> fools put it all out for yard sales. (21:20, Message)

The qualities of brevity and wit enable the proverb to penetrate the mind of the hearer allowing it to nestle in for further reflection. In order for cleverness to work, it must be to the point. After all, "brevity is the soul of wit." Without these tandem characteristics, the proverb would be something other than a proverb.[56] The brevity and wit of the proverb once again witnesses to its playfulness, qualities that continue to endear it to contemporary listeners.[57]

---

55. Eugene Peterson paraphrases it in his translation, *The Message*, in the following way: "Some people dig a fork into the pie, but are too lazy to raise it to their mouth."

56. That brevity and wit are an essential part of the proverb is confirmed by the way in which these qualities of proverbs are sometimes exaggerated. Just as political cartoonists exaggerate the outstanding physical features of a politician, so those who make a jibe at proverbs accentuate the quality of brevity and humor. The results are something like the following: "Compounds of hydrogen and oxygen in the proportion of two-to-one that are without visible movement invariably tend to flow with profundity" (i.e., "Still water runs deep"). Or, "it is fruitless to attempt to indoctrinate a superannuated canine with innovative maneuvers" (i.e., "You can't teach an old dog new tricks"). What these highfalutin sayings really demonstrate is that one essential characteristic of the proverb is brevity and wit.

57. Educators would do well to capitalize on these characteristics as they incorporate proverbs into contemporary curriculum on moral development.

Universial

Sixth, proverbs work because they possess a universal appeal. They transcend cultural boundaries. The proverb is "a winged word outliving a fleeting moment."[58] No one culture can claim exclusive rights to a proverb. As far as we know, all cultures have their own proverbial stock.[59] And proverbs familiar to one culture have their counterparts in other cultures.[60] Because proverbs infiltrate all aspects of life and are a part of all cultures, anyone who wishes to understand another culture must know its proverbs. William Penn supposedly claimed that, "The wisdom of nations lies in their proverbs."[61] In arguing the need for scholarship to identify proverbs in current use in American culture, Wolfgang Mieder concludes, ". . . culturally literate persons, both native and foreign, must have a certain paremiological minimum at their disposal to participate in meaningful oral and written communication."[62] What is true of a culture is also true of religion. Anyone who wishes to understand the moral perspective of Judeo-Christian culture must know its proverbs.

Proverbs not only transcend cultures, they also transcend sacred and secular boundaries. Because of the lack of reference to Israel's sacred history, some have said that wisdom is the first cousin to secularism. In reality, the development of Israel's proverbs does not move from individual secular sayings that make no reference to God to Yahwistic reinterpretations of earlier proverbs.[63] Instead the proverbs bridge the gap between the sacred and the secular, not in terms of compromising beliefs but in terms of finding common ground. It is often difficult to distinguish between Israel's proverbs and

---

58. Crenshaw, *Old Testament Wisdom*, 62.

59. B. J. Whiting describes a broad spectrum of cultures and peoples who use proverbial lore and the variety of ways in which they are employed. He acknowledges that certain primitive peoples do not seem to have a store of proverbs. However, he remarks, "It must be borne in mind that it is impossible to be certain of the complete absence of proverbs, because there is always the possibility that proverbial sayings have escaped the attention of foreign observers." See Whiting, "The Origin of the Proverb," 61.

60. The North American proverb, "Too many cooks spoil the broth," has its counterpart in Russian, "With seven nurses, the child goes blind," in Persian, "Two captains sink the ship," in Japanese, "Too many boatmen run the boat up to the top of a mountain," and Italian, "With too many roosters crowing, the sun never comes up." Cited by Pei, "Parallel Proverbs," 16.

61. Marketos, *A Proverb For It*, 15. It has been said, "Tell me the proverbs of a people, and I will tell you their character."

62. Meider, "Paremiological Minimum and Cultural Literacy," 312.

63. Ben Witherington argues that there is no such movement from the secular to the sacred: "If so it seems quite strange in light of Qoheleth who appears more secular and less Yahwistic than Proverbs." See Witherington, *Jesus the Sage*, 21.

the proverbs of other ancient Near Eastern cultures.[64] The Hebrew sage, in traveling abroad, gleaned from the best wisdom other cultures had to offer and adapted the sayings to fit a Yahwistic belief system.

The universal nature of proverbs continues to function so that they connect with contemporary culture. Individuals of religious or non-religious backgrounds find it easy to identify with the practical advice of the common sense sayings. It is not uncommon to find businesses or corporations using them to convey a message or to carry a logo. One can find the following proverb etched in the entrance of the art building at the University of Oregon in Eugene: "By wisdom a house is built, and by understanding it is established, by knowledge the rooms are filled with all precious and pleasant riches." No reference is made to its biblical source (Proverbs 24:3-4), but the saying strikes a common chord.

When public education can no longer openly espouse religious convictions, it still will not take offense in the observation and admonition of a proverb. It is significant that M. Scott Peck proposes that public schools develop programs of mental health education that incorporate the teaching of proverbial lore to the children. He believes that one of the reasons for Alcoholic's Anonymous' success is that they have their own proverbial stock.[65] One place for educators to begin might be with E. D. Hirsch's list of 265 American proverbs.[66] Educators could also paraphrase many of the biblical proverbs into their dynamic equivalents and incorporate them into the learning curriculum. The following list of character qualities offers some suggestions for integrating secular and biblical proverbs into the agenda of moral education:[67]

---

64. Take the following for a few examples:
   a. Be on thy guard against a woman from abroad, who is not known in her (own) town. Do not stare at her when she passes by (the Instruction of Ani, 3:1; cf. Prv. 6:23-30).
   b. As a wise man, let your understanding shine modestly, let your mouth be restrained, guard your speech (Akkadian, Counsels of Wisdom; cf. Prv. 13:3).
   c. He who spoke, but did not [keep his promise(?)], his mouth is a liar (Sumerian Proverb, no. 126; cf. Prv. 25:14).
   d. A good word is a friend to numerous men (Sumerian Proverb, no. 159; cf. Prv. 16:24).
   a. and b. are cited in James B. Pritchard, *Ancient Near Eastern Texts Relating to the Old Testament*, 420, 426. C and d are cited in William W. Hallo, *The Context of Scripture: Canonical Compositions from the Biblical World*, 566-67.

65. Peck, *Further Along the Road Less Traveled*, 141-43. See also Rogers, "The Use of Slogans, Colloquialisms, and Proverbs in the Treatment of Substance Addiction."

66. Hirsh, *The Dictionary of Cultural Literacy*, 46-57.

67. See chapter 3 for a list of wisdom's virtues.

1. Cheerfulness and Contentment:

He is not poor who has little but he who desires much.
Better to light a candle than curse the dark.
He who is rich need not live sparingly, but he who can live sparingly need not be rich.
A cheerful heart is good medicine but a grumpy attitude takes away strength. (17:22)
Contentment makes a body healthy, but jealousy is like a cancer. (14:30)

2. Sensitivity Toward Others:

Apples of gold in a setting of silver are like words fitly spoken. (25:11)
Kind words are like honey, sweet to the taste and good for the body. (16:24)

3. Love:

A friend in need is a friend indeed.
A friend loves at all times, and a neighbor is intended to share trouble. (17:17)
Hatred stirs up strife, but love turns a blind eye to insults. (10:12)
It's better to eat a crust of bread with peace of mind, than to have a banquet with a house full of trouble. (17:1)

4. Self-Control:

Fools rush in where angels fear to tread.
Make haste slowly.
Haste makes waste.
A person without self-control is like a city that can easily be destroyed. (25:28)

5. Gratitude

You don't miss the water till the well runs dry.
A generous person will be enriched, and one who gives water will get water (11:25).

6. Accepting Consequences of Actions

A slack hand causes poverty, but the hand of the diligent makes rich (10:4).
The child is man of the father.
The chickens always come home to roost.
As you make your bed, so you must lie in it.

A word of caution is in order here. Biblical wisdom often upsets the wisdom of this world. As one sifts through a collection of contemporary American proverbs one will find some whose values contradict sapiential morals.[68] Part of the sifting process must involve identifying those proverbs. With some guidance students can discover proverbs that communicate values appropriate to sapiential standards and those that do harm to the moral fabric of a community.

In addition, many contemporary proverbs will also need explanation to younger generations. The words and metaphors may be foreign to them. But that too can be a "playful" educational exercise.[69] It would also be an appropriate and creative activity to ask students to work together in writing their own proverbs that describe or affirm some of the core values.

The six qualities mentioned above function together synergistically. All of them combine forces allowing the proverb to manage social order and to influence thoughts and actions. Far from being harmless clichés, biblical proverbs are potent rhetorical pieces that engage in subtle persuasion. They labor as vital resources in the task of moral education. For example, Vera Jackson suggests that proverbs can serve as intervention tools in helping older adults identify the belief structure on which they make decisions and then assess the value or the harm.[70] Or Harriette McAdoo and Linda McWright describe how grandparents can use proverbs to transfer family values to their grandchildren.[71] Through the use of proverbs in daily interactions with grandchildren at meal times, bedtimes, while brushing teeth and combing hair, family values are passed on.[72] Whether in the home, the church, the classroom, or in therapy sessions, the proverb performs an important function in helping to transfer values and influence the form character takes.

CONCLUSION

The proverb continually exerts its influence on us as our culture experiences a revival in orality. As an oral culture, Israel relied heavily on its stock of proverbial lore as the sages preserved them in various collections. A simple scan through Israel's narrative and prophetic literature reveals their dependence

---

68. One comprehensive resource for identifying and discovering contemporary American proverbs is edited by Mieder, Kingsbury, and Harder: *A Dictionary of American Proverbs*.

69. Mieder and Litovkina, *Twisted Wisdom*, includes definitions of contemporary proverbs. Hirsch, Kett, and Trefil also give a brief definition of each of the proverbs he lists in their *Dictionary of Cultural Literacy*.

70. Jackson, "Proverbs."

71. McAdoo and McWright, "The Roles of Grandparents."

72. Ibid., 35.

on these gnomic sayings.[73] It is quite likely that in the oral culture of Israel, the proverbs were more important for making daily decisions than were the Ten Commandments.[74] The Gospels also reveal that, throughout his ministry, Jesus relied on proverbs to instruct, censure, advise, and encourage.[75]

The electronic media has revived the place of orality in our culture. With the advent of a post-literate culture, the proverb takes on a new significance. Tex Sample maintains that about half of the people in the United States work primarily out of a "traditional orality."[76] By traditional orality Sample means those individuals who still think in terms of an oral mind set, that is those who make reasonable decisions on the basis of three primary resources: stories, the effect of actions on relationships, and proverbs.

Whether we are aware of it or not, people in our culture think and reason proverbially. We make decisions, resolve conflicts, and offer advice based on the proverbial lore we store away.[77] One evidence of this is our love affair with self-help books, which are filled with advice that masquerades as wisdom. Proverbs saturate the literature.[78] The oral dimension of our culture has long been overlooked.

In tandem with other narrative and non-narrative material, proverbs serve as basic teaching tools for an oral culture.[79] They are "the palm oil with which words are eaten" and "the horse on which the conversation rides."[80] In oral cultures, stories and relationships crystallize into proverbs. Proverbs become a means for collecting experiences, making sense of those experiences, and providing reasons for why we do what we do. The Christian community looks for discourse that gives clarity; it seeks out a word that provides direction. Such a community continues to rely on proverbial lore for instruction, guidance, and inspiration.

This means that proverbs take on a whole new dimension in Christian education. Even though many occasions exist when we find ourselves faced

---

73. Carol Fontaine has studied the use of proverbs in the context of Israel's narrative material. Fontaine, *Traditional Sayings in the Old Testament*.

74. Von Rad implies this in his important work *Wisdom in Israel* , 26.

75. See Beardslee, "Uses of the Proverb in the Synoptic Gospel"; Witherington, *Jesus the Sage*.

76. Sample, *Ministry in an Oral Culture*, 6.

77. Tom Long observes, "People live their lives out of proverbs." *The Senses of Preaching*, 36.

78. Arthurs, "Proverbs in Inspirational Literature." See also McKenzie, *Preaching Biblical Wisdom in a Self-Help Society*.

79. In chapter 2 of his popular book, *Amusing Ourselves to Death*, Neil Postman affirms that proverbs are primary instruments in an oral culture.

80. Sample, *Ministry in an Oral Culture*, 3.

with difficult decisions that need long and serious reflection, other occasions require more immediate access to a life principle. We must make a quick decision, give a prompt response, or offer expeditious advice. On such occasions, it is important to have the proper resources necessary to respond responsibly. A storehouse of proverbs serve as one resource an oral culture can draw from in such moments.

Proverbs function not only in times when immediate decisions must be made, they also serve, along with other literary genres, as instruments in the continual process of instruction. In the classroom of life, proverbs urge students to exercise the mental powers of reasoning. When used appropriately, they invite students to challenge conventional wisdom, and to accept, reform, or rethink ideas. When placed side by side proverbs often spar with one another, creating an atmosphere quite suitable for the instruction of youthful minds. To use the language of Lawrence Kohlberg, proverbs can push the learner beyond the conventional level of morality to the "principled" or "postconventional" level.

Not only does wisdom capitalize on the sparring activity between proverbs, it also moves beyond that to rely on the dynamic nature of human interaction to challenge individuals to think and grow. It is essential for dynamic interaction to occur between individuals in order to refine, clarify, challenge, and encourage moral formation. Without such dialogue, the whole process becomes mechanical and stifling, and eventually breaks down. This vitality-infusing dialogue is the subject of the next chapter.

Chapter Five

Character Formation through Human Dialogue

(Proverbs 27:14–19)

The quality of wisdom is acquired through many avenues including the memorization of proverbial lore, prayer, instruction, experience, and observation. One of the most popular views today, however, is that one attains wisdom through a lifetime of quiet meditation. The 1984 movie "The Razor's Edge," based on the 1944 novel by Somerset Maugham, portrays such a perspective. Because of the traumatic experiences he went through in World War I, Larry (played by actor Bill Murray) seriously reconsiders his life and sets out on a lifelong quest for meaning. He explores many different options, many lifestyles. At one point he begins reading the Upanishads and finally travels to India. While there, he climbs a mountain and spends time in solitude, reading, and meditating. The experience transforms him. He leaves the mountain a different, wiser person.

The book of Proverbs would not deny the important place of time spent in personal reflection. But that is not the center of focus for attaining wisdom. Notice where Woman Wisdom resides when first introduced in the book. She dwells in the street, at the marketplace, and in the city gate (Prov. 1:20–33). Wisdom finds herself in a city teeming and bustling with the traffic of human life. According to Proverbs, wisdom is acquired at the hub of human activity. This implies that wisdom is not primarily cerebral. It is first and foremost relational. Through entering into relationship with the Lord (1:7), with parents (1:8; 13:1), with one's spouse (31:10–31), with friends (27:5–6) and with the wise (20:18; 27:17), the student gains wisdom and thus the resources necessary for moral development.

That is why Proverbs places such a heavy emphasis on the value of human interaction. The fool is the one who is "wise in his own eyes" (3:7; 26:5). Fools rely exclusively on self-evaluation and as a result remain morally inept. In contrast, the wise do not depend solely on their own perceptions but rely heavily on the counsel of others. The book of Proverbs makes this clear: "Without counsel, plans go wrong, but with many advisers they succeed" (15:22). Wisdom believes that two heads are better than one (see also Eccl. 4:9–12).

Valuable interaction with others can occur in either adversative or complimentary forms. When entered into with openness, even adversarial dialogue can lead to the refinement of character. Because of a high regard for human ingenuity, even when the other holds an opposing view, the wise seek out the perspectives of others regardless of their cultural background. Yes it is true that sometimes in these encounters interaction goes awry; relationships turn dysfunctional. Nevertheless when individuals and communities seek out the best in others, wisdom is acquired, new insights are gained, and character takes shape. Especially is character formed and cultivated in the heat of conflict.

HUMAN INTERACTION IN 27:14–19

The text of Proverbs 27:14–19 speaks to this phenomenon. The passage contains links that tie its individual proverbs together. For one, all the proverbs in the text describe interaction between two individuals. For another, all through chapter 27 proverbs about the "friend" or "neighbor" dominate. Verses 5, 6, 9,[1] 10, 14, 17, and 19 all portray the value of the friend. Friendship is a key theme in the cluster of proverbs in verses 14–19. Tension and conflict, however, characterize all of these friendships. These links make it appropriate, then, to study the proverbs in this text together as a unit:

---

1. Verse 9b is problematic, as comparing various translations will indicate. The text literally reads "sweetness of his friend from the counsel of soul." The LXX does not believe the line stands in good antithetic relationship to 9a so it emends the text to read, "but the inner being is torn down by trouble," which the NRSV adopts as its reading. But the NIV offers a good interpretation in trying to make sense of the text as it stands: "and the pleasantness of one's friend springs from his earnest counsel." The verse is an analogy. The enjoyment received from the sweet aroma of perfume is compared to the pleasant counsel received from a friend.

> Whoever blesses a neighbor[2] with a loud voice,
>   rising early in the morning,
>   will be counted as cursing.
> A continual dripping on a rainy day
>   and a contentious wife are alike;
> to restrain her is to restrain the wind
>   or to grasp oil in the right hand.
>
> Iron sharpens iron,
>   and one person[3] sharpens the wits of another.
> Anyone who tends a fig tree will eat its fruit,
>   and anyone who takes care of a master will be honored.
> Just as water reflects the face,
>   so one human heart reflects another.[4]

The text brims with vignettes of spirited interaction. The proverbs depict a variety of conflict situations. However, because conflict is painful and because we too often witness the destructive side of it, we find ourselves, to our detriment, taking extreme measures to avoid it.

Such was the case of a disastrous political decision made by President John F. Kennedy in 1961. In that year, the United States embarked upon the now infamous Bay of Pigs invasion of Cuba. The invasion was a plan that called for the secret arming, training, and transportation of an elite fighting force of Cuban exiles. These Cubans, recruited in Miami, received the best training America had to offer. The plan initiated by President Kennedy and a half-dozen advisors representing the best and brightest minds of the time, called for the recruited soldiers to land in Cuba and spearhead a popular uprising against the Castro government.

After two months of deliberation, the group unanimously approved the invasion. After three days of actual implementation, all 1,400 invading troops were either dead or in prison camps. The United States was demoralized, and Castro stood stronger than ever. What happened? This blue-ribbon think tank had made a terrible decision. The advisors were not lazy or evil. Rather they fell victim to what has been called "groupthink."[5] Later, in reflecting on the Bay of Pigs disaster, two of the members confessed that they had had misgivings about it all along, but had remained silent out of

---

2. The word can be translated either "neighbor" or "friend."
3. The same word is used here that is translated "neighbor" in verse 14.
4. Literally this verse translates: "As water, the face unto the face, so the heart of man to man."
5. Janis, *Victims of Groupthink*.

fear of group resentment. Dissident views had been unwelcome. Solidarity took primacy over the decisions and actions of the group.

That is "groupthink." It is a phenomenon to which any group can fall prey when it becomes so concerned with unity that no one can afford to raise honest doubts. Collective thinking replaces independent thinking. Conflict is avoided at all costs, because it is viewed as the enemy of the group. The problem is not an isolated one nor is it limited to politics. "Groupthink" happens among religious groups, synagogues, churches, families, and friends.

Destructive Interaction

The text of Proverbs 27:14–19 addresses this type of dilemma. The proverbs speak of conflict in a variety of relationships: between friends, family, and community. Conflict sometimes is *de*structive. Sometimes it is *con*structive. The first two proverbs (vv. 14–16) describe the former:

> Whoever blesses a neighbor with a loud voice,
>   rising early in the morning,
>   will be counted as cursing.
> A continual dripping on a rainy day
>   and a contentious wife are alike;
> to restrain her is to restrain the wind
>   or to grasp oil in the right hand.

There are times when interaction with others results in harm. Such is the case with the one who blesses a neighbor with a loud voice early in the morning. The blessing ends up being a curse. For one reason, the person blesses in a loud voice. That is, more than likely the person does it for show. For another, the "blessing" is offered early in the morning, a most inappropriate time. What the friend expresses is positive. He extends greetings to his neighbor, offering "encouragement." The problem is, his timing is off! For the sage, timing determines the appropriateness of a word or deed. Timing is everything. Because of the friend's poor timing, his words become abusive; his blessing turns to a curse.

Discord between the parties arises because the one who greets displays no tact. He greets when it is convenient for him, that is, when he is in good humor. The exhilarating songs and words of the early riser translate into nothing more than clanging cymbals to the late sleeper. The friend disguises insults with a lighthearted demeanor.

Still, like many proverbs with their highly metaphoric use of language, this proverb does not limit itself to the behavior of early risers. Beneath the image of the early-morning riser lies a larger issue: the churlish attitude of tactlessness toward others. It is the person who does not know when a joke has gone too far. It is the person who wins, but not graciously, the person who rubs it in. Cheerful words are used to disguise what is really insulting. It is April Fools gone awry. As another proverb crassly expresses it, it is like a person who deceives a neighbor and then says, "I am only joking!" (26:18–19). Such insensitivity creates unnecessary conflict.

Not only are such destructive patterns of interaction developed among friends, they also spring up in the home. Husbands and wives can develop communication patterns that eventually lead to incessant quarreling. Such quarreling simply results from a long-established pattern of insensitivity. Verses 15 and 16 compose one proverb that presents a picture of dysfunctional conflict in the family: the infamous and ubiquitous image of the nagging wife.

In Proverbs women are known by the words they speak. The wise woman offers words of truth and justice to her family and to the poor (31:10–31). The words of "the temptress" lure the simpleton into the snares of death (2:16–19; 5:3–14; 6:20–35; 7:6–27). And finally there is "the contentious woman" who nags; her constant bickering develops her into the in-house critic.[6]

In Proverbs 27:15–16, the contentious woman is notable for the imagery that she evokes. The sages reserve some of their most sarcastic humor for such a person:

> It is better to live in the corner of the housetop,
>   than in a house shared with a contentious wife. (21:9)
> It is better to live in a desert land,
>   than with a contentious and fretful wife. (21:19)

A contrast is set up in these two proverbs: it is better to make yourself vulnerable to the stormy blasts of nature on the outside than to expose yourself to the storms of a quarrelsome spouse on the inside. The imagery in 27:15 is just as colorful and sarcastic: "A continual dripping on a rainy day and a

---

6. In Proverbs not only can women be censorious, men can be just as scathing. Listen to the verbal abuse of a contentious man in Proverbs 26:20–23:
    For lack of wood a fire is quenched
        and where there is no slanderer, quarreling will cease
    As charcoal is to hot embers and wood to fire
        so is a quarrelsome man for kindling strife
    The words of a slanderer are like delicious morsels
        they go down into the inner parts of the body
    Like the glaze covering an earthen vessel
        are smooth lips with an evil heart. (my translation)

contentious wife are alike." The imagery of continual dripping on a rainy day is similar to that used in Ecclesiastes 10:18 to describe a leaky roof: "Through sloth the roof sinks in, and through indolence the house leaks." Eugene Peterson in his modern paraphrase misses the gravity of the figure when he translates the proverb in the following way: "A nagging spouse is like the drip, drip, drip of a leaky faucet; You can't turn it off, and you can't get away from it."[7] The image is not about something that is simply a nuisance with which one must learn to live. It is about a long-established habit that can destroy a whole house. There is an African proverb that describes the dynamics well: "When two bulls fight, it's the grass that suffers." When a spouse nags, everyone around loses.

These two images, the image of the insensitive friend and that of the contentious spouse, depict conflict gone awry. Unfortunately, many people have more negative experiences with conflict than positive. That is the reason why most individuals avoid conflict in the first place. After all, look what it does. It destroys friendships and homes. It destroys churches. Thus an environment is cultivated that nurtures a form of groupthink. Everyone works to soothe the troubled waters, to cover over any differences for the sake of solidarity. We are conditioned to evade any semblance of confrontation or controversy.

Constructive Interaction

Conflict, however, is inevitable, though it does not have to be destructive. Healthy confrontation between spouses, friends, and Christians can lead to growth. Rather than dividing us, conflict can equip us to be a more morally and spiritually responsible community. This is the thrust of the proverbs in verses 17–19:

> Iron sharpens iron,
>   and one person[8] sharpens the wits of another.
> Anyone who tends a fig tree will eat its fruit,
>   and anyone who takes care of a master will be honored.
> Just as water reflects the face,
>   so one human heart reflects another.

In verse 17 the first line contains an old adage: "Iron sharpens iron." The figure depicts someone using metal to sharpen a sword or a farming

---

7. See Peterson, *The Message*. David Atkinson also interprets the image in this verse as a "dripping tap." *The Message of Proverbs*, 26.

8. The Hebrew word is actually "neighbor" or "friend."

implement. The metaphor of steel rubbing against steel in the first line is applied in the second line to the abrasion or friction necessary for personal and moral growth.

As iron sharpens iron, so one friend sharpens another. We experience this in the world of athletics. Athletic abilities are sharpened when athletes engage in competition with others. Wholesome competition strengthens the body. This principle works in the relationship between teacher and student. Teachers challenge students to grow and stretch their mental capacities. The education process requires the student to exercise the mind in the disciplined work of study, dialogue, reflection, and the integration of ideas. When one engages the intellect in interacting with others over issues that matter, mental faculties sharpen.

As pointed out in the previous chapter, proverbs themselves engage in a kind of moral sparring. One proverb offers the admonition to stay out of other people's business: "Like somebody who takes a passing dog by the ears, is one who meddles in the quarrel of another" (26:17). Another is adamant about taking responsibility to get involved: "If you hold back from rescuing those taken away to death, those who go staggering to the slaughter; if you say, 'Look, we did not know this'—does not he who weighs the heart perceive it?" (24:11–12). Or take the tension between two other proverbs. One proverb observes that "The field of the poor may yield much food, but it is swept away through injustice" (13:23), while two verses later another proverb affirms that, "The righteous have enough to satisfy their appetite, but the belly of the wicked is empty" (v. 25). One proverb says poverty stems from unjust treatment. The other claims poverty results from one's own wickedness. The first line of 16:9 suggests that humans make their own plans, but the second line affirms, "the Lord directs the steps." Some proverbs condone bribery (21:14) while others condemn it (17:23).[9] Such is the tension that exists within the ethical language of the sage.

In a similar fashion, one can easily engage in proverb-dueling using popular contemporary aphorisms, firing back and forth sayings that express opposite views on a subject. I can say, "If you lie down with dogs, you'll get up with fleas." But you quickly counter, "If you can't beat 'em, join 'em." Or try this. "You're never too old to learn." Maybe, but "you can't teach an old dog new tricks." Okay. "Variety is the spice of life." Not always because, "You shouldn't change horses in midstream." But you can't deny this: "Birds of a feather flock together." True, but "opposites do attract." What about, "The early bird gets the worm?" You can't argue that, can you? Yes I can

---

9. Sometimes these "contradictory" proverbs are placed side-by-side as in 17:27–28. The first proverb sees silence as a virtue but the next proverb suggests that silence could indicate a person who is a fool just as well as one who is wise.

because it's "the second mouse that gets the cheese!" In the words of Roland Murphy: every proverbial saying needs a balancing corrective.[10] One proverb does not say it all. Diversity of thought, which refuses systemization, is endemic to Wisdom Literature. Wisdom material contains ideas intended to stand in creative conflict.

Proverbial sayings sharpen each other like iron sharpens iron. A lively skirmish energizes them. In fact, the proverb is frequently associated with that which is sharp and aurally penetrating.[11] The Teacher in Ecclesiastes describes "the sayings of the wise" as "goads, and like nails firmly fixed . . ." (12:11).

A word of caution is necessary at this point. It is important to pay close attention to the image used. It is iron sharpening iron not iron sharpening clay or putty. In interacting with others, care must be taken not to impose one's will on a helpless or vulnerable person. In many cases where the other person involved is strong (or strong-willed) and mature, the reciprocal interaction between two parties refines both. Others, however, may come from places where they have been wounded or abused. Those individuals are approached with greater sensitivity.

With that qualification made, the principle of iron sharpening iron is a necessary part of physical, mental, and moral development. But the image of iron sharpening iron is not an isolated image in this text. The proverb in verse 19 compliments it: "Just as water reflects the face, so one human heart reflects another." This proverb, like many, is intentionally ambiguous, though more cryptic than most.[12] We can interpret it in a couple of different ways. Some understand the second line to refer to one person reflecting on her own thoughts.[13] Through introspection, an individual comes to a better understanding of the self. Others understand the second line to refer to two people engaged in reflecting on each other's thoughts.[14] Through interac-

---

10. Crenshaw, "Murphy's Axiom."

11. Compare the following texts where "proverb" is associated with "byword" which literally means "sharp or cutting word": Deut. 28:37; 1 Kings 9:7; Jer. 24:9; 2 Chron. 7:20. See Brown, Driver, Briggs, *A Hebrew and English Lexicon of the Old Testament*, 1042. Also the idea of sharpness is connected with the proverb in Proverbs 26:9: "Like a thorn bush in the hand of a drunkard, is a proverb in the mouth of fools."

12. Because of the figurative and metaphorical language used, proverbs are by nature relatively indeterminate.

13. The second line, McKane says, "has to do only with one man whose self is mirrored in his *lev* [heart], and the meaning . . . is that it is through introspection . . . that a man acquires self-knowledge." *Proverbs*, 616.

14 Robert Alter's analysis of the imagery is especially apropos: "The terseness makes you work to decipher the first verset. Once it dawns on you that what is referred to is the reflected image of a face in water, further complications ensue: Does each man discover

tion, a person comes to a better understanding of the self. So how should the verse be interpreted, as introspection or interaction?[15]

One possibility for determining its meaning examines the context of the proverb. Granted, not all proverbs have a context. Some may be randomly collected or quite loosely connected with their surroundings. This proverb, however, has a thematic connection with the proverbs that precede it. The focus of verses 14–19 is not the individual in isolation but the self in relation to friends, family, and community. In addition, two proverbs located earlier in chapter 27 reinforce the idea of spirited interaction:

> Better is open rebuke
>   than hidden love.
> Well meant are the wounds a friend inflicts,
>   but profuse are the kisses of an enemy.

Within the context of chapter 27, with its heavy emphasis on "the friend" theme, it is more fitting to interpret the reflection of verse 19 not as self-reflection but as inter-reflection.[16] While that may be the case, it is often difficult to separate the process of interaction from introspection. Introspection itself involves an interactive process and vice versa. At any rate, the two work in tandem and individuals come to better understand themselves through the process.

Verse 19 is also thematically connected with another proverb in the cluster. Verse 21 reads: "The crucible is for silver, and the furnace is for gold, so a person is tested by being praised." That is, the kind of reputation that a person develops has much to say about that person. Reputation receives its shape from the furnace of struggle within the community. The community has ways of testing the character of an individual that are just as rigorous as the means used to separate the dross in silver and gold. In exposing our vulnerability to the community, we refine and strengthen character. Thus the image of verse 19 is not isolated. It pervades this chapter and represents the heart of the thought of verses 14–22.

---

the otherwise invisible image of his own heart by seeing what others are like, or, on the contrary, is it by introspection (as we say, "reflection"), in scrutinizing the features of his own heart, that a person comes to understand what the heart of others must be? And is the choice of water in the simile merely an indication of the property of reflection, or does water, as against a mirror, suggest a potentially unstable image, or one with shadowy depths below the reflecting surface?" *The Art of Biblical Poetry*, 178.

15. Longman ponders whether this proverb is about self-revelation or revelation of another. *Proverbs*, 481.

16. Van Leeuwen writes, "The idea is of water as a mirror: man comes to self-knowledge through confrontation with the other." *Context and Meaning in Proverbs 25–27*, 125.

The proverb conveys a potent image: "Just as water reflects the face, so one human heart (or mind) reflects another." When people engage in rigorous interaction with others who reflect with them, offer counter ideas, express alternatives, or just listen, they discover new insights. Thoughts are clarified. A former teacher of mine was fond of saying, "The thought process is not complete until the idea is verbalized," meaning that, until individuals can explain or express their thoughts to others, they do not understand them as well as they think. When thoughts and ideas are clarified to others, we better understand them ourselves.[17]

The proverb in verse 19 revolves around the image of water, incorporating two dynamic qualities of human nature. Unlike the predictable reflection in a mirror, reflection on the surface of water is ever changing, a quality also characteristic of people. And unlike the mirror, the reflection in water implies depth.[18] More is there than meets the eye. A parallel proverb makes a similar observation: "The purposes in the human mind are like deep water, but the intelligent will draw them out" (20:5). The image is of a deep well. It takes a person with a bucket and long rope to draw out the water. In the same way, it takes time, patience, and one who is indeed a friend to plumb the depths of another's thoughts.

The images of iron sharpening iron and one person reflecting the mind of another are complementary images. They describe the constructive conflict necessary for growth to occur. Character is sharpened when individuals put defensiveness aside and engage in open discussion about life issues that will lead to stronger faithfulness. Sometimes when iron sharpens iron, sparks fly. But when two friends in conflict have the best interest of the other in mind, such conflict results in good. Character does not develop in a vacuum but only in community with others.

The principle of two people "sharpening" or challenging one another is a key principle in the process of moral education. In Lawrence Kohlberg's scheme, at the postconventional level, a student interacts with the complexities of life.[19] Right and wrong do not always fall into nice neat categories. Students learn to think critically, to listen to and interact with the views of others that may be in opposition to their own, in order to sort out the most appropriate course of action for the occasion. In interacting with others' views, individuals operate on Kohlberg's "principled" level.

17. I agree with the old German maxim, "The best mirror is an old friend."
18. See Alter's remarks on this verse in n. 252.
19. Lawrence Kohlberg said that one needed the environment of a supportive or "just community" in order to nurture moral development. See Howard, "Lawrence Kohlberg's Influence on Moral Education in Elementary Schools," 54–55.

That sages encouraged students to interact with one another demonstrates the concern they had for teaching individuals the art of discernment. They did not devote themselves exclusively to the use of negative and positive reinforcements. Nor were they content with students regurgitating ideas simply learned through rote memory. Rather the sages demonstrate an interest in equipping students to process ideas through spirited interaction with others.

One other relationship is described in this text: the relationship between master and servant. Verse 18 observes: "Anyone who tends a fig tree will eat its fruit, and anyone who takes care of a master will be honored." Like verse 17, the first line of this saying contains a folk proverb, and the second line applies it to the master/slave relationship. The image is that of a farmer caring for his crop. The responsible farmer will eat the fruit of his labor. In the same way, the worker who looks after and protects his master's interests will also receive honor.

What is the meaning of this proverb in the context of 27:14–19? A couple of characteristics should be noted. The proverb, like the others, speaks of a particular relationship, a master/servant, employee/employer relationship. In this case, it is a difficult relationship between unequal parties. The potential for conflict is great. Whenever a relationship is unequal, the likelihood for abuse increases. The one who possesses power can easily misuse it, but the inferior party can also create problems.[20] A servant, for example, could be lazy, irresponsible, obnoxious, or disrespectful, all of which could lead to serious confrontation. This proverb focuses on the servant's potential for being irresponsible, for not tending to his master's property and well-being. In contrast, the servant who literally "watches his master," that is, who has the best interest of the owner in mind, is one who brings about order and harmony in the relationship. A lot of sacrifice, hard work, and effort lie behind the success of this unequal relationship. A lifetime of respect and concern for the owner's welfare results in honor.

Obviously in this type of unequal relationship conflict and problems are approached differently than in a relationship of equals. The subordinate must approach conflict indirectly. A direct approach more than likely will not only fail but also result in censure or estrangement.

Some maintain that the proverb is an effective tool of discourse for addressing difficult issues between unequals, namely because proverbs are indirect. The qualities of anonymity, impersonality, obliqueness, metaphor,

---

20. Note the contentious wife in verses 15–16. Israelite culture was a patriarchal world in which women had less status than men. However, the contentious wife could still create a lot of problems for the husband and the family because of her obnoxious behavior.

and sometimes humor contribute to their indirectness. Arland Jacobson argues that, "proverbs allow people to say what needs to be said without creating additional social tensions."[21] The need to depersonalize speech is especially important when a party brings a sensitive subject before a superior. The proverb allows us to let off steam indirectly without upsetting the social order. Thus to know proverbs and to have a mental stock of them can make us more competent in unequal relationships.

"Anyone who tends a fig tree will eat its fruit, and anyone who takes care of a master will be honored." By itself, this proverb could have any number of meanings and references. Thus we see the highly metaphoric nature of proverbs, especially the proverbs in this text. In taking seriously the surrounding context, however, it could refer to the normal tension of relationships.[22]

CONCLUSION

Proverbs 27:14–19 presents a powerful cluster of images revolving around conflict and interaction in a variety of relationships among friends, family, and community. A couple of the proverbs describe a dysfunctional picture of people in conversation. Others depict strong relationships that have implicitly resulted from healthy conversation. The former images depict relationships divided by conflict, the latter ones are bound together by it. Only when "iron sharpens iron" can an individual or community mature. Moreover, when humans understand what takes place in the give and take of conversation, they can no longer approach it lightly. As a faith community, we are not simply talking about sharing information and ideas, we are dealing with the production of a moral universe.

Christian character does not develop in a vacuum but only in interaction with others. Healthy tension and struggle must also be a part of church life in order for that community to mature. Here is a scenario of the way in which two different churches might face difficult issues. There is a conflict brewing in Northside Church. Should the church add a new wing to the auditorium? Group A is for it and so is Group B. But Groups C and D are not. There is another conflict: Should they bring screens and PowerPoint into the public worship? Here, however, Groups A and C want the technology but

---

21. Jacobson, "Proverbs and Social Control: A New Paradigm for Wisdom Studies," 81.

22. Eaton sees 27:17–18 as a proverbial pair. He claims the referent of both is a tutorial debate that takes place between a teacher and student. *The Contemplative Face of Old Testament Wisdom in the Context of World Religions*, 26.

Groups B and D do not. Still a third conflict: Should Christians participate in the political arena? Groups A and D say yes but Groups B and C say no. There are also other issues at stake besides these! Confusing? This church is a maze of intertwining relationships. If you had just arrived in town and were looking for a church, would you choose Northside?

Before you decide, look at Southside Church. It's about the same size and demographic makeup as Northside. This congregation also disagrees over similar issues. But at Southside there are just two distinct groups. The people in A group are in general agreement on all the issues and the people in B group oppose them on those issues.

Now if you were seeking a church in which to partner with in ministry, would you be more interested in Northside or Southside? Despite the complexity of the interaction, the Northside Church is healthier in terms of conflict management. There is more "cross-stitching" interaction going on among many different people and groups. The Southside Church is less complicated in its interaction. But the lines are clearly drawn: there is Group A and there is Group B. The church is polarized. Little interaction takes place between the two sides. At Northside some members find themselves in disagreement about some issues but in agreement on others.[23] There is healthy dialogue. The dynamic of iron sharpening iron is actively at work at Northside.

Dynamic and continual interaction is a part of any community wanting to grow morally and spiritually, and dissonance remains endemic to that process. A principle in conflict management states the following paradox: If you want to have less conflict in your relationships, try to have more. This does not mean that we try intentionally to get people angry. More precisely, it could be stated: If you want less conflict, invite disagreement.[24] Being open to different opinions on various issues and experiences is a sign of a healthy family, a healthy friendship, and a healthy community. Engaging constructively in conflict indicates that we take each other seriously. When iron sharpens iron, individuals grow, and the faith community is able to create an environment governed by righteousness, justice and equity.

Wisdom is fundamentally relational. We come to understand who we are through interaction with others. We engage others in sparring, conflict, and discussion and out of that interaction grows new understanding and insight. We are able to see things from a different perspective. Hans-Georg Gadamer refers to this phenomenon of interaction as "play." Engaging in

---

23. This scenario is taken and paraphrased from a video entitled, "Conflict in the Church," produced by the Mennonite Central Committee.

24. Ibid.

"play" is a participation in a kind of dialectical movement. As one participates in the dialectic, the player becomes absorbed and lost in the activity. In the context of being totally absorbed in the "play," new meaning arises from the experience. In the play of conversation humans do not simply reproduce information or regurgitate ideas, but collaboratively produce new understanding.[25] John Stewart puts it this way, "By engaging both proactively and responsively in the play of language events, humans participate" in creating their world.[26] They cannot create any world they want because they are constrained by the limits of wisdom as well as by the sovereignty of God. But within these constraints, humans can create an order that manifests the virtues of wisdom and reflects God's glory.

---

25. Gadamer, *Truth and Method*, 102–3.
26. Stewart, *Language as Articulate Contact*, 119.

Chapter Six

Language and Character Formation
(Proverbs 25:11–15; 26:1–9)

L anguage reflects character. Jesus affirms this when he announces that:

> The good person brings good things out of a good treasure, and the evil person brings evil things out of an evil treasure. I tell you, on the day of judgment you will have to give an account for every careless word you utter; for by your words you will be justified, and by your words you will be condemned. (Matt. 12:35–37)

But not only do words reveal character, they also shape character, both our own as well as others. In the epistle of James, the writer acknowledges the negative influence of the tongue when he makes the following observation:

> With it we bless the Lord and Father, and with it we curse those who are made in the likeness of God. From the same mouth come blessing and cursing. My brothers and sisters, this ought not to be so. (James 3:9–10)

At the same time words both reflect and shape character. In the process of interacting with others, we reveal who we are, and the words we speak influence the lives of others for better or for worse.

The sages understood this dynamic. Consequently, they had much to say about the virtues and vices of the tongue.[1] Wisdom acknowledged the centrality of language in the process of moral instruction. More is said about

---

1. See the list of virtues and vices in chapter 3.

speech and the organs of speech (lips, mouth, tongue) than any other subject in the sentence literature. The sages studied words and proverbs and engaged in dialogue with others in order to shape the lives of their students.[2] They understood the proper stewardship of speech as a vital resource for moral well-being. The sages knew well the power of language to influence others.

THE PERSUASIVE POWER OF WORDS

Proverbs 25:11-15

The sages knew that one who learns how to use words has the power to influence and persuade others for better or for worse. Oratorical skills played and continue to play a crucial role in the position and respect leaders receive in elder-led communities in the Middle East. Timothy Willis concludes that the most important characteristic local elders in these communities possess is their skill of persuasion.[3] The Old Testament frequently documents the value of verbal skills for the wise that sat in judgment in the city gates of ancient Israel (cf., Job 29:7-11, 21-22). In line with this tradition, one of the primary functions of the sage was to train the young in the proper use of words, mainly by entering into dialogue with them and by modeling the power of language through their own instruction.

The cluster of proverbs in 25:11-15 presents a series of images describing the persuasive power of words. The wise person simply does not throw out ideas but discovers ways of making those ideas rhetorically appealing:

> A word fitly spoken,
>   is like apples of gold in a setting of silver.
> Like a gold ring or an ornament of gold,
>   is a wise rebuke to a listening ear.
> Like the cold of snow in the time of harvest,
>   are faithful messengers to those who send them,
>   they refresh the spirit of their masters.
> Like clouds and wind without rain,
>   is one who boasts of a gift never given.
> With patience a ruler may be persuaded,
>   and a soft tongue can break bones.

---

2. In Ecclesiastes the Teacher is described as one who "taught the people knowledge, weighing and studying and arranging many proverbs. The Teacher sought to find pleasing words, and he wrote words of truth plainly" (12:9-10).

3. Willis, "'Obey Your Leaders,'" 323. Willis argues that the NRSV translation of Hebrews 13:17, "Obey your leaders" should be translated "Be persuaded by your leaders."

Though the proverbs in this cluster do not form a tight unit, it is nonetheless valid to examine them together for at least two reasons. To begin with, as a unit, they are disconnected from the preceding verses. Chapter 25:1–10 is structured more along the lines of a series of narrative vignettes. With verse 11 the structure reverts to the single sentence proverb and the use of comparative or analogic parallelism. By default verse 11 begins a new section. Additionally, a common theme loosely holds the group together. The proverbs in verses 11–15 generally revolve around the subject of the persuasive influence of words.[4] Verses 11 and 12 and verses 13 and 14 each form a proverb pair. Verse 15 is not a part of a pair but is thematically related to the previous two pairs.

Chapters 25–27 are made up mainly of analogic proverbs that use rich images and metaphors. Typically these proverbs contain a comparison in the first line with the second line identifying the object of comparison. The proverb simply lays the comparison alongside the object, often without the use of the conjunction "like" or "as." The NRSV, however, typically adds the particle and also sometimes reverses the order of the two lines, stating the referent first and then making the comparison. This detracts from the anticipation that the proverb intends to create with the comparison in the first line. In contrast, a translation of 25:11–12 that follows more closely the sequence and brevity of the Hebrew text might read:

> Apples of gold in settings of silver,
>   a word well turned.
> A ring of gold and a trinket of fine gold,
>   one who gives wise reproof to a listening ear.

Compare the way in which the NRSV translates these same two proverbs:

> A word fitly spoken
>   is like apples of gold in a setting of silver.
> Like a gold ring or an ornament of gold
>   is a wise rebuke to a listening ear.

With verse 11 the NRSV reverses the order of the lines putting the analogy last. And while it keeps the order of lines in verse 12, the NRSV adds the connecting word "like." Throwing a common image or experience alongside a moral statement without explanation requires the student to work

---

4. Huwiler has argued that "speech and silence" is a common theme that holds the text of 25:11–20 together as a unit. *Control of Reality in Israelite Wisdom*, 214–30.

to connect the two.[5] It is part of the education process. English translations often muffle the artistic challenge the analogic proverbs present.

The comparisons used all through chapter 25 come from the everyday experiences of life. When such images are placed alongside the virtue or vice described in the second line, the meaning clarifies and the thought penetrates the open-minded person. The interaction between the two lines of the proverb models the kind of verbal interaction the wisdom teacher expects to occur among students.

A closer look at the contents of 25:11–15 discloses the persuasive power of words. Verses 11 and 12 use the image of precious metal as an analogy for proper speaking and listening. Both proverbs describe the crafting of gold into an aesthetically pleasing piece of artwork. In one case (v. 11), the beautiful golden artwork is inlaid on a silver frame. Such a masterpiece of human art is compared to the artistic use of words. When used aptly, words can generate a response similar to that of experiencing a beautiful work of art. When read in tandem verse 11 describes a word fitly spoken and verse 12 a word fitly received.

Verse 11 does not detail the kind of word spoken. Is it an encouraging word? Or is it a word of confrontation or instruction or reproof? It really does not matter because the word spoken was right and necessary for the occasion. Verse 12 may indicate that it was a word of rebuke. In Proverbs a rebuke covers a variety of speech forms including warning, correcting, instructing, and exhorting (cf., Prov. 1:9–19). But a rebuke does not involve nagging or scolding or demeaning speech. The rebuke given here is wise, meaning it was the word necessary for the occasion. But notice the team effort in the education process. Successful instruction requires a teacher who delivers a "wise rebuke" and a student who develops a "listening ear." When the two come together, they are compared to a precious piece of jewelry. The process of molding and shaping the character of another individual open to change is truly a work of art.

It may be helpful to pause for a moment and place a foil against this verbal piece of artwork and view the negative counterpart to it, that is, the destructive power of words. Verse 20 forms a stark contrast to the beautiful *objet d'art* portrayed in verses 11–12. Proverbs 25:20 juxtaposes two analogies before identifying the referent in the third line:

---

5. In his translation, Alter keeps the order of the two lines as they are found in the Hebrew. He also works to keep to the terseness and compactness of Hebrew parallelism. *The Wisdom Books*, 191.

> Removing a garment on a cold day
>   vinegar on a wound[6]
>   and singing songs to a sad heart. (my translation)[7]

The first two lines describe the shock received from an outside element. Taking your coat off on a cold blustery day and exposing yourself to the forces of nature shocks your system. Like climbing out of a sleeping bag on a frigid winter morning, your whole body shivers in response. The second image creates the same kind of shock: applying vinegar to an open wound. The immediate response is a cry of pain.

These two images create a curiosity in the reader and set the stage for the third line, which finally discloses the proverb's focus. Just as shocking as the physical forces on the body, or perhaps even more so, is the emotional shock that occurs when someone sings a lighthearted song to another who anguishes over a grieving heart (cf., Ps. 137:1-4). The heavy-hearted person receives a shock to the system—mental and emotional—when platitudes are employed in an untimely effort to cheer. The one who offers the words of consolation demonstrates no sensitivity to the grieving person. Whether intentional or not, the "comforter" ends up doing more harm than good. The consoler's words demoralize the other person and trivialize the grief process.

What a contrast this proverb paints to the earlier word picture. With the earlier picture, persuasive words artistically employed mold the character of another for good. In the last portrait, words carelessly spoken destroy the morale of another. In the process of words doing their work on others either to destroy or build up, much is revealed about the character of the one employing them.

The second proverb pair, 25:13-14, offers another angle on the power of speech:

> Like the cold of snow in the time of harvest
>   are faithful messengers to those who send them;
>   they refresh the spirit of their masters.
> Like clouds and wind without rain
>   is one who boasts of a gift never given.

---

6. The Hebrew text reads "vinegar on soda." The idea is that the two are incompatible, adding one bitter thing to another. The word can, nevertheless, also be translated "wound." McKane, *Proverbs*, 588.

7. The LXX adds another line after the last one, which the NRSV follows: "Like vinegar on a wound is one who sings songs to a heavy heart. Like a moth in clothing or a worm in wood, sorrow gnaws at the human heart" (NRSV).

While verses 11–12 speak of the elements of nature (i.e. gold and silver) that have been artistically molded and shaped by humans, verses 13–14 speak of the forces of nature beyond human control: the weather. Some translators question the reality of the image in 13a and the improbability of snow during harvest season, but the image does not have to be a reality or an actual event. It may simply be a figure depicting unexpected and pleasurable refreshment. Beverage commercials sometimes depict their drink bringing the refreshing relief of a snowstorm during the scorching summer heat. This proverb imagines the relief harvesters receive from the heat of the day by something cold and refreshing. That image is used as an analogy to describe a master who receives refreshment simply from knowing he can depend on his messenger to relay the message faithfully. The master knows the message will be communicated with integrity.[8]

Whereas verse 13 describes the character of a reliable messenger, verse 14 describes the unreliable braggart. The proverb focuses on the one who makes empty promises. Such promises are like clouds that appear on the horizon over a parched country but bring no rain.[9] The person who speaks words with integrity contributes to the well-being of a community. The person who makes empty promises contributes to its demise. As the old World War II proverb put it, "Loose lips sink ships." By the words they speak, both the reliable messenger and the unreliable boaster reveal their inner character. Only in an environment of integrity can growth truly occur. In the same way that a greenhouse nurtures the growth of flowers, so integrity nourishes the emotional and spiritual growth of the individual.

Verse 15 stands by itself in the structure of this text. It is not paired with any proverb before or after it, but its thought ties it to the theme of the two previous pairs:

> With patience a ruler may be persuaded,
> and a soft tongue can break bones.

With proper use of discourse, someone of lesser status can exercise influence over someone of greater status. Through proper restraint of words,

---

8. Davis identifies a dominant messenger contemporary Christians face today and that is the public media. As a messenger the media is more concerned with creating sensationalism than with telling the truth. She rightly maintains how it is the church's responsibility to teach its members to become "critical consumers." She also urges the church to encourage young people with potential media gifts to use their gifts not to become celebrities but to be "faithful messengers" for God. *Proverbs, Ecclesiastes, and the Song of Songs*, 132–33.

9. Some contemporary counterparts to this image might be when we say of someone he's, "all talk and no action." Or in Texas, "All hat and no cattle." Or in the California racing world, "All show and no go."

an individual can influence a leader who holds a position of power. Such a one can challenge the person with political clout to consider other ideas. The second line uses figurative language to express the power of such language: "a soft tongue can break bones." The softest member in the human body fractures the hardest! Wisdom believes that, ultimately, brains are better than brawn. The proper control of words can effect change in those who occupy the most powerful positions.

The meaning of this proverb is seen in action in a parable the Teacher in Ecclesiastes tells in 9:13–16. The parable is about a powerful king who laid siege against a small town in which only a few inhabitants lived.[10] The king could have conquered the city easily except for the presence of a poor wise man. But the Teacher says the poor man "by his wisdom delivered the city" (v. 15). The Teacher does not detail how the wise man saved the city, but given the nature of wisdom and the ability of the sages to use words, it seems likely that he used some kind of diplomacy to persuade the great king not to destroy this little town. A proverb following the little example story seems to confirm this: "The quiet words of the wise are more to be heeded than the shouting of a ruler among fools" (v. 17). The king encountered a wise man who, through restraint and tact, persuaded the king to spare the city, thus demonstrating that "with patience a ruler may be persuaded."

The text of 25:11–15 describes how words not only reflect but also shape character. The text depicts the persuasive power of words through proper control and restraint. Such restraint is like a work of art (v. 11), a beautiful piece of jewelry (v. 12), and a satisfying refreshment (v. 13). When such words are under control, they can influence even the most politically powerful individual (v. 15). With proper control, the reproving words of a sage can change decisions and lives (v. 12). However, when such words are not under control, they become destructive. They can drive a person even to deeper despair (v. 20). They undermine the solidarity of the community (v. 14).

In the early days of naval warfare, the military lost more sailors to the kickback from their own cannons after they were fired than from enemy cannon fire. After a cannon was fired, it would frequently come roaring back and break loose from its seat on deck. Sailors standing behind the cannon were crushed or burned or knocked overboard. The military tried all kinds of ways of securing the cannons but they would still break loose. From that experience was coined the phrase "loose cannon." Words have a similar

---

10. Scholars debate over whether the text actually says the wise man rescued the city or whether he did not deliver it because the city ignored the advice of the wise man. I favor the former position. See my commentary, *Proverbs, Ecclesiastes, Song of Solomon*, 375–77.

destructive capacity when people fail to keep adequate control over them. When employed at the wrong time or for the wrong person, words become loose cannons, free from their moorings and wreaking havoc in people's lives. Words are tools to bless or curse others. They possess the power to build or to tear down character.

SPEAKING THE APPROPRIATE WORD

Proverbs 26:1–9

The persuasive power of words becomes most evident when those words are spoken at the right time. The ability to understand what the occasion calls for reveals much about the speaker's character. It indicates that an individual has moved beyond a focus on self to the ability to perceive the bigger picture of life. That person operates from the "principled" level, and sees more clearly how various components in the environment fit together in a particular situation. Individuals who know the significance of contextualization value the uniqueness of others.[11] They take seriously the interaction with others in a way that respects others' God-given talents.

The sages have much to say about the quality of appropriateness, especially as it relates to words. Consider the following proverb: "To make an apt answer is a joy to anyone, and a word in season, how good it is!" (15:23). The person who speaks an appropriate word for the occasion is the one who has de-centered self and penetrated the world of others. She practices righteousness and justice in a way that contributes to the health of the community.

The cluster of proverbs in 26:1–9 speaks to this quality of appropriateness. The text describes appropriate and inappropriate uses of words and actions:

> Like snow in summer or rain in harvest,
>   so honor is not fitting for a fool.
> Like a sparrow in its flitting, like a swallow in its flying,
>   an undeserved curse goes nowhere.
> A whip for the horse, a bridle for the donkey,
>   and a rod for the back of fools.
> Do not answer fools according to their folly,
>   or you will be a fool yourself.
> Answer fools according to their folly,
>   or they will be wise in their own eyes.

---

11. See chapter 2 for a description of Lawrence Kohlberg's principled or postconventional level of moral development.

It is like cutting off one's foot and drinking down violence,
    to send a message by a fool.
The legs of a disabled person hang limp;
    so does a proverb in the mouth of a fool.
It is like binding a stone in a sling
    to give honor to a fool.
Like a thorn bush brandished by the hand of a drunkard
    is a proverb in the mouth of a fool.

The cluster of proverbs in this unit extends through verse 12.[12] For the sake of a more manageable text, however, I focus on the first nine verses. Except for the second, each of the proverbs in verses 1–12 contains the catchword "fool." Following this group, another cluster of proverbs (vv. 13–16) gravitate around the catchword "sluggard" or "lazy person" (NRSV), thus setting it off from the first twelve verses. In the Hebrew text, both groups of proverbs conclude with the phrase, "wise in their own eyes" (vv. 12 and 16).

A thematic component also links verses 1–12 together, expressing a common concern for properly timing certain actions and words: bestowing honor on a person of dishonor (vv. 1, 8), expressing malicious words to an innocent person (v. 2), punishing one who deserves it (v. 3), knowing how to give an appropriate "answer" (vv. 4–5), the proper care in sending "messages" (v. 6), and the proper use of "proverbs" (vv. 7, 9). The text describes the sapient who understands the importance of fitting the words to the occasion.

In contrast, the fool does not understand what is germane for the occasion at hand. The fool speaks folly (v. 3), does not faithfully convey a message (v. 6), and does not know how to use a proverb (vv. 7 and 9). Understanding what is appropriate is one distinction between the wise and the fool. The sage takes special interest in the ability to discover that which is suitable.

The little collection in 26:1–9 represents this preoccupation. The first three verses serve as an introduction. Certain things just do not fit. In fact, in and of themselves they are good, but the timing is off. The first proverb sets up an analogy: "Like snow in summer or rain in harvest, so honor is not fitting for a fool." Snow on a hot summer day and rain in harvest are out of place. Good in and of themselves, these elements cause harm because they come at the wrong time of the year. Similarly, praising someone for engaging in foolish behavior is not "fitting."[13] Verse 1 compares the disorder

    12. All the proverbs in this cluster, like most in chapters 25–27, are comparative in form with the first line giving an analogy and the second line specifying to what the analogy refers.

    13. The same Hebrew word is used in Proverbs 17:7: "Fine speech is not <u>fitting</u> to a

that sometimes occurs in nature with disorder that occurs in society when people bestow honor on the wrong person. Such an experience happens when, for example, an individual is promoted to a position for which he is incompetent, sometimes referred to as the Peter Principle. It also occurs when society lavishes certain athletes, politicians, or religious leaders with honor when their lives do not exemplify strong character. Like the rain at harvest time, praise heaped upon the wrong person destroys the moral foundations of a community.

The next proverb describes just the opposite phenomenon, dishonoring an innocent person: "Like a sparrow in its flitting, like a swallow in its flying, an undeserved curse goes nowhere" (v. 2). A fool can use malicious words to attack a person who does not deserve it, but because others know the words come from a fool, the dishonor does not take root. Finally, the third proverb describes something that *is* fitting: punishment for fools: "A whip for the horse, a bridle for the donkey, and a rod for the back of fools." Fools, like dumb beasts of burden, do not learn from verbal instruction. To use a rod on the back of fools raises an ethical issue, especially when it is essential to take a strong stand against any form of abuse whether physical or verbal. The rod, however, was always implemented in the context of love, patience, and self-control. For the sages not to use physical discipline with prudence and when needed was an act of abuse.[14] In disciplining a fool, subtlety does not work. One must take a more direct approach.

Living by wisdom involves interpreting events, people, and actions in light of what specific occasions demand. Wisdom does not follow fixed rules. It operates within specific contexts responding to particular quandaries. In speaking of that which is fitting for the occasion, the first three verses set the tone for understanding the proverbs that follow.

The thrust of verses 4–9 describes the foolishness of certain words or sayings because they are out of place. For example, sometimes proverbs themselves are misused. The sage remarks in verse 7, "The legs of a disabled person hang limp; so does a proverb in the mouth of a fool." The saying compares the legs of a handicapped person with the proverbs of a fool. Like the useless legs of a paraplegic, a proverb spoken by a fool rolls impotently off the lips. The adage dissipates silently in the air because of the ineptitude of the user. Søren Kierkegaard tells a parable of a man who escaped from an insane asylum. The escapee knew he must disguise himself, otherwise he would be caught and sent back to the asylum. He thought that if he could come up with a maxim everyone would acknowledge as true, no one would

---

fool, how much less is false speech to a prince" (emphasis added).

14. See chapter 2 n. 55.

recognize his insanity. Finally he settled on a phrase: "The world is round." So to everyone he met he stated, "The world is round, the world is round." Needless to say, he was immediately discovered and returned to his former confinement.[15] A proverb or proverb-like saying in the mouth of fools sounds ridiculous.

A proverb not only sounds ridiculous in the wrong hands, it can also turn destructive. The saying in verse 9 overlaps with verse 7: "Like a thorn bush brandished by the hand of a drunkard is a proverb in the mouth of a fool."[16] Here the analogy moves beyond impotence to a proverb used to do damage. Wielding a thorn bush in hand, with no control over his faculties, the drunkard[17] endangers not only himself but also everyone around him. He thrashes about inflicting injury to everything within reach. As a drunk driver behind the wheel of a car can turn the vehicle into a deadly projectile, so proverbs become lethal weapons in the wrong hands. When used as propaganda to discredit another race, religion, lifestyle, or person, proverbs maim and destroy. Even without that kind of malignant intent, a proverb untimely spoken is dangerous.

In the hands of individuals not taught to interpret people or experiences in context, proverbs inflict harm. Thus a parent grieving over the waywardness of a youth receives a scolding from a well-intentioned advisor who unequivocally states, "If you had only trained her in the way she should go she would never have departed from it" (cf. Prov. 22:6)! The advisor brandishes the proverb like a thorn bush in the hand of a drunkard.

Some wield the weapon of a proverb to suppress others. So one says to another reeling from a mistake, "Well, after all, you reap what you sow," or, "You made your bed, now you must lie in it." Proverbs are sometimes intentionally used to put another person in his or her place. In the 1992 movie "Sister Act II," Whoopie Goldberg plays the role of a lounge singer who comes to a parochial school to teach music to a rowdy group of teenagers. The Catholic mother in charge takes one look at the singer, and exclaims, "You are a living example that you can't make a sow's ear into a silk purse." The nun used the proverb to put the new arrival in her place.

In an ethnographic study on the way in which certain African communities use proverbs, Ojo Arewa and Alan Dundes quote a Nigerian student:

15. Kierkegaard, *Concluding Unscientific Postscript*, 174.
16. The *English Standard Version* translates the first line this way, "Like a thorn that goes up into the hand of a drunkard . . ." This translation interprets the saying to refer to the damage that is being done is primarily to the drunkard and not to others. For further explanation, see my commentary, *Proverbs, Ecclesiastes, Song of Solomon*.
17. The drunkard was not usually a down-and-out person but often one in power and one who possessed wealth. See Waltke, *The Book of Proverbs: Chapters 15–31*, 353.

"I know the proverbs, but I don't know how to apply them."[18] If one does not know how to use proverbs, then they degenerate into something less than tools for instruction. When used wisely, however, proverbs serve as valuable resources for mental and spiritual development. When used wisely, they exhort, comfort, confront, clarify, and censure, all in the best interest of the individual and the community. To use proverbs appropriately is a mark of sagacity, social intelligence, and responsibility.

Irony, nonetheless, resides in the proverbial form. On the one hand, the proverb speaks wisdom. On the other hand, it requires wisdom to use it and hear it appropriately (25:12). The wise person is not wise simply by knowing a lot of proverbs but by knowing the appropriate time and context in which to use them.

At center stage in 26:1–9 stands a pair of proverbs providing a clue to discerning the nature of appropriateness.

> Do not answer fools according to their folly,
>   or you will be a fool yourself.
> Answer fools according to their folly,
>   or they will be wise in their own eyes. (vv. 4–5)

Initially these proverbs appear confusing, seeming to give contradictory advice.[19] The first one counsels the student not to answer a fool. The very next one advises just the opposite! Perplexing! Which is it?[20] Do we just average it out and take the middle of the road? Like a man with one foot on a block of ice and the other on a hot stove who responds to the question about how he's feeling, "On the average, I'm fine." Is this the admonition of "moderation in all things"?

The problem here is not one of contradiction or moderation but of appropriateness. Both admonitions demand that we comprehend the importance of timing. These two "contradictory" proverbs intentionally placed

---

18. Arewa and Dundes, "Proverbs and the Ethnography of Speaking Folklore," 70. They comment: "In European courtrooms, of course, lawyers cite previous cases to support the validity of their arguments. In African legal ritual, an advocate of a cause uses proverbs for the same purpose. Here clearly it is not enough to know the proverbs; it is also necessary to be expert in applying them to new situations. The case usually will be won, not by the man who knows the most proverbs, but by the man who knows best how to apply the proverbs he knows to the problem at hand."

19. Such contradiction is not uncommon in the Proverbs collection. Compare the following proverbs: 18:10 and 18:11; 15:22 and 19:21; 13:23 and 13:25; 22:6 and 13:1; 26:17 and 27:5–6; 10:4 and 12:9; 10:12 and 25:5, etc.

20. Aitken says that the Rabbis solved the problem of 26: 4 and 5 by making verse 4 refer to worldly matters and verse 5 to spiritual matters. *Proverbs*, 104. It is also these two proverbs that made some Jewish scholars question the inclusion of book of Proverbs in the canon.

side-by-side state powerfully that timing is everything. The sages do not instruct students to respond to situations mechanically, grasping for some stock response or pat answer. Rather they instruct students to do reflective thinking and to learn the art of discernment.

Once again, dueling proverbs demonstrate the process at work. A few years ago I heard a man talk about his family gathering together for Thanksgiving dinner. Everyone crowded in the kitchen and busily prepared the meal bumping elbows and bodies. Suddenly his grandmother hollered out, "Too many cooks spoil the broth." Everyone scattered, leaving her to prepare the meal in a more orderly manner. Then after the Thanksgiving dinner, as she walked into the kitchen with a load of dirty dishes, she announced, "Many hands make light work." All came running to help clean up.[21] Dueling proverbs!

To a couple anxious to wed, a marriage counselor might advise, "Marry in haste, repent at leisure." To another couple dragging their heels that same counselor might say, "Happy the wooing that is not long in doing." The advice given is based on consultation with the parties involved, an understanding of the situation, and on prayerful consideration for what is best.

Even though some may be more adept at proverbial use than others, everyone can develop elementary skills in employing proverbs in conversation. Tex Sample relates a story told to him by Sister Ann Nielsen, a missionary in Africa who had collected several thousand African proverbs. A man from Malawi left his tribal home to make money. He was away for three years and had no contact with his wife. Upon his return, his wife had a child that was clearly not his. Wanting to divorce his wife and take all her belongings, the husband took her to court. An uncle defended her and won the case with what seems to have been a proverbial coup. He said: "If you leave your hoe in the rain for three years, it will rust."[22] He stated his case powerfully: it was not the wife's unfaithfulness but the husband's abandonment that was the wrong.[23]

Wisdom does not reside in the pithy sayings as much as it resides in the one who uses them. The most succinct definition of a wise person is one who knows what to say at the right time. The definition extends beyond just the use of proverbs to address an individual's responsibility in speaking words appropriate to the occasion.

---

21. I cite this story in *Preaching Character: Reclaiming Wisdom's Paradigmatic Imagination for Transformation*, 181.

22. While in our American culture this proverb is clearly demeaning of women, in the African context, it is not. Also, it fit the occasion and in the end kept the wife from further abuse.

23. Sample, *Ministry in an Oral Culture*, 38.

Initially the responsibility to say the appropriate thing seems beyond the average person's ability. Most of us would find ourselves saying something like, "I can never seem to find the right words." Or "Why didn't I think of that?" Or "I wish I would have said that." Diderot referred to this experience as *l'esprit de l'escalier* ("the wit of the staircase").[24] It is the experience of thinking of the right words to say too late, usually as you climb the staircase to bed at night. But this common human anxiety misses the mark.

The art of finding the right word for the occasion does take thought and experience. Nevertheless, even novices can discover a good beginning point, usually by offering a word of encouragement. Seldom is encouragement out of place. Several years ago, I heard Lamar Alexander, the senator from Tennessee, speak at a banquet in Memphis. He told of his long time friend Alex Haley, author of *Roots*, who was a frequent visitor to the Alexander's home as Lamar was growing up. Haley was such an encourager. The family always looked forward to his coming because he lifted everyone's spirits. On one occasion Haley was asked, "What's your secret for being so encouraging?" He replied, "There's no secret to it. I simply find the good in others and praise it." Haley used that phrase frequently in his advice to family and friends. The advice can at least serve as a starting point for learning to speak the right word, simply seeking out the good qualities in others, and praising them.

The proverbs in verses 4 and 5 not only acknowledge the significance of right timing, they also acknowledge that humans possess a limited capacity for understanding the best response in a given situation. The text gives no definitive answer about when or when not to respond to a fool. Why, because wisdom knows its own limits.[25] Wisdom cannot dictate how to respond in every situation. The wise were well aware of humanity's limited ability to know what is fitting. There are no rules, no pat answers, given in this text for knowing the right time because life, relationships, and experiences are dynamic, ever changing. The sage is sensitive to such ebb and flow.

Be aware, however, that the ability to cultivate appropriate timing is not a method but an art. The ability comes not through following a set of rules or guidelines but through engaging in conversation itself. It comes in the act of "play."[26] For example, John Angus Campbell asks how does a speaker acquire the concepts of timing and the sense of what is appropri-

---

24. Referenced by Tom Long in "Preaching the Pronouncement Stories in Luke," 39.

25. The worldview of Proverbs allows a place for learning to live with and appreciate the ambiguities of life: "Do not boast about tomorrow, for you do not know what a day may bring" (Prov. 27:1). This is developed further in chapter 8.

26. Gadamer, *Truth and Method*, 102–103. For the idea of "play," see the conclusion in chapter 5.

ate in any given context? This practical knowledge is not easily conveyed through applying some general principles. Rather the speaker becomes absorbed in the "culture of the game" and understands what the other players are saying, not just from their perspective but also from the speaker's particular stand. Out of this, the speaker develops a keen sense of timing.[27] Individuals acquire competence in timing through the continual give and take experience of conversation.

Conversation, however, is not something we *use*, like a tool we put down whenever we no longer need it. Rather conversation and language itself is an experience that shapes our identity.[28] It is central to who we are. John Stewart concludes, "human worlds are collaboratively constructed (modified, developed, razed, reconstructed) in speech communicating."[29] We make sense of our world and help others make sense of theirs through language. This act of interpreting the world is in part an act of appropriation. No one individual can do it alone. It can only be accomplished in relationship. We learn what is appropriate in concert with others. In the process of collaborating with others, we learn to manage and speak to the incongruities of life.

The sage entered into life's "messes" and relationships ready to make the best judgments possible based on the available resources. None of the interpersonal conflicts described in Proverbs 26:1–9 are resolved by appeal to a universal rule. The text implies that resolutions come through engaging in discourse. The sage struggles to understand her world through talking with others to whom she relates in community. Sages interpret events and experiences in the context of the believing community, giving them a new and vibrant perspective. This engagement not only equips students to respond to the world around but also, in part, helps them to create a new world.

Students grow in wisdom based on their ability to interpret life experiences, to respond appropriately to them, and, in the process, they create a moral community that manifests justice, righteousness, and equity. In spite of all available resources, however, the one who truly demonstrates wisdom acknowledges that only God knows what is appropriate in every situation. "No wisdom, no understanding, no counsel, can avail against the Lord" (21:30).

---

27. Campbell, *Quarterly Journal of Speech*.

28. For a more nuanced development of this thought, see Stewart, *Language as Articulate Contact*.

29. Ibid., 111.

Once again, the proverbs in this text affirm that the wise are not wise because they have accumulated a lot of knowledge and experience. They are wise because they know how and when to use their experience, at least within the limits of human understanding. One of Emily Dickinson's poems expresses well the mind-set of the sapient:

> Tell all the truth but tell it slant
> Success in circuit[30] lies
> Too bright for our infirm delight
> The truth's superb surprise
> As lightening to the children eased
> with explanation kind
> The truth must dazzle gradually
> Or every man be blind[31]

The wise share their knowledge, experiences, and insights with others; they are, however, sensitive to how much the other person can understand and accept. That is, they do it with a "slant."[32] An effective teacher instructs students at *their* intellectual level. A wise parent explains sensitive subjects at the child's mental and spiritual level of maturity. Full disclosure can morally cripple the recipient.

True wisdom is the ability to discern what is fitting. As one wise man said, "For everything there is a season and a time for every matter under heaven: a time to be born, and a time to die, a time to plant, and a time to harvest.... A time to keep silence and a time to speak..." (Eccl. 3:1–9).

CONCLUSION

The sages believed in the persuasive power of words. Through words one can either destroy or build up another. In times of crisis words can demoralize or function as a source of healing. Through words students developed the character of integrity. The sages called on students not to make empty promises but to keep their word. Through words they also learned self-control. One who demonstrates restraint in speech can influence the lives of others. The proper use of language equips students to learn and develop

---

30. I agree with Daniel R. Barns, who maintains that "circuit" means circumlocution. Successful truth-telling lies in indirect revelation. "Telling it Slant: Emily Dickinson and the Proverb," 459.

31. Johnson, *The Complete Poems of Emily Dickinson*, 506–7.

32. "Slant" is not a reference to deception in the use of the truth. Rather using the geometrical term figuratively, the word refers to sharing the truth at an angle, that is, in a gradual manner.

sensitivity toward others (cf., 25:11 and 20). They also learn when to speak and when to keep silent (26:4–5).

The authority the sages possessed was not based on arbitrary commands or a "thus says the Lord" statement but on the ability to use words persuasively (25:15). They tailored their instruction to the maturity level of the student and tapped the potential for growth. Students did not independently acquire skills in the artful use of language. Instead, through collaborating with others in dialogue, they learned to identify and to express what was appropriate for the occasion. Learning the language of wisdom involved a team effort. On the one hand, it took wisdom to know how to exhort or offer rebuke (25:12). On the other hand, it took a "listening ear," that is, an open mind, to receive the instruction properly (25:12).

Even though no direct mention is made of God in the texts we have looked at in this chapter, the sages maintain a strong commitment to the presence of the Lord. They naturally assume God plays an intimate role in the collaborative process, of opening the minds of the young, and of granting wisdom to the teachers. It requires wisdom both to speak and receive formative instruction. The process forever changes those willing to take the risk of entering into the dialogue.

Chapter Seven

Wealth and Character Formation
(Proverbs 15:13–17 and Select Proverb Pairs)

All through the biblical wisdom tradition, the sages teach that things are not always as they appear. What at first glance looks like an exciting lifestyle can actually be little more than an impoverished existence. Through the eyes of faith, one task of the sages is to distinguish between what is authentic and what is facade.

The sages, for example, warn against the enticement of the beautiful temptress with her seductive ways: "Do not desire her beauty in your heart, and do not let her capture you with her eyelashes" (6:25). In the end, the sages reveal that "charm is deceitful, and beauty is vain, but a woman who fears the Lord is to be praised" (31:30). The sages warn against the appealing look of alcohol: "Do not look at wine when it is red, when it sparkles in the cup and goes down smoothly" (23:31). Furthermore, some people are quite skilled in fooling others with their eloquent speech, as the sage can testify to from experience: "Like the glaze covering an earthen vessel are smooth lips with an evil heart" (26:23). Humans can even fool themselves into believing their actions are good when they may actually be a cover for selfish motives: "All deeds are right in the sight of the doer, but the Lord weighs the heart" (21:2).

For the wise, however, one of the most common deceptions relates to the possession of wealth. The rich think wealth gives them security (18:11) and the poor fall into the temptation of believing that it is the answer to all their problems (30:8–9). Trust in wealth can subtly erode the moral fiber of an individual and a community. It is unsurprising, therefore, that the sages take special interest in employing their strategy for character formation—particularly the cultivation of moral discernment—on the topics of wealth and the acquisition of material possessions.

WEALTH AS REWARD FOR THE RIGHTEOUS

In Proverbs, wealth and poverty are mentioned more frequently than in any other section of the Old Testament.[1] What receives special attention is the delusive nature of wealth. Not all that glitters is gold in the sages' dictionary. What makes the issue of wealth especially complex is that, in and of itself, wealth is not evil; it is morally neutral. Sometimes wealth is ill gotten and thus corruptive, but other times wealth is a sign of blessing from God. This latter view represents the conventional wisdom of the sages, at least in its most basic formulation.

Traditional wisdom teaches that the Lord will provide material well-being to those who honor God. Certain instruction poems reach this conclusion. The paradigmatic observation is Proverbs 3:9–10:

> Honor the Lord with your substance
>   And with the first fruits of all your produce;
> Then your barns will be filled with plenty,
>   And your vats will be bursting with wine.

In fact, through the first six chapters of the sentence literature (chaps. 10–15) the idea that godly character produces positive consequences dominates:

> In the house of the righteous there is much treasure,
>   but trouble befalls the income of the wicked. (15:6)
> The blessing of the Lord makes rich,
>   and he adds no sorrow with it. (10:22)
> The crown of the wise is their wisdom [riches],[2]
>   but folly is the garland of fools. (14:24)

In addition, poverty sometimes results from corrupt character, which evokes divine punishment:

> Misfortune pursues sinners,
> but prosperity rewards the righteous. (13:21)

> Poverty and disgrace are for the one who ignores instruction,
> but one who heeds reproof is honored. (13:18)

---

1. Washington, *Wealth and Poverty in the Instruction of Amenemope and the Hebrew Proverbs*, 1.
2. The Hebrew text has "riches" and not wisdom.

But most often, the sages attribute poverty to laziness:

> A slack hand causes poverty,
> but the hand of the diligent makes rich. (10:4)

> Go to the ant, you lazybones; consider its ways, and be wise. Without having any chief or officer or ruler, it prepares its food in summer, and gathers its sustenance in harvest. How long will you lie there, O lazybones? When will you rise from your sleep? A little sleep, a little slumber, a little folding of the hands to rest, and poverty will come upon you like a robber, and want, like an armed warrior. (6:6–11)

In laying out the fundamentals of wisdom in the poem of 6:6–11 and the sentence literature of chapters 10–15, the sages appear to conclude that wealth comes as a reward for the diligent. Poverty is a product of the foolish and the lazy. One's economic status simply reflects one's character. But that does not mean that to know whether someone is truly righteous, all one needs to do is to look at her level of income. Once again, appearances are deceptive.

WEALTH AND THE PROCESS OF CHARACTER FORMATION

Proverbs addresses the hard economic decisions individuals must make in terms of the use of wealth and how those decisions affect their relationship with God and others. The sages walk readers through a process of thinking critically about wealth as a means of maturing character.

The book begins with the image of a gang (1:8–19). By far the easiest path to follow is the lifestyle of the gang. This band promises instant gratification of one's desires without any sweat. They promise exciting adventure (v. 11–12), instant wealth (v. 13), and camaraderie (v. 14). This gang embodies the vices of greed and violence. They steal, abuse, and mistreat others in order to selfishly gain wealth for themselves (vv. 10–14). Ultimately, their greedy lifestyle results in their own downfall; they "kill themselves" (v. 18, NRSV). The sages conclude with this observation, "Such is the end of all who are greedy for gain; it takes away the life of its possessors" (v. 19). Proverbs thus begins with a full-blown image of the destructive power of greed. It destroys community; it destroys the self.

From this destructive beginning, the book works its way through a plethora of instructions, sayings, and admonitions building to the final image in chapter 31:10–31, the woman of wisdom. The family of this woman has acquired financial security. Her acquisition and use of wealth stands in stark contrast to that of the gang. The whole obsession of the gang was to obtain more and more: "we shall fill our houses with booty" (1:13). For this woman, wealth does not appear to be her ambition in life. In many ways it was merely incidental. She and her family took a different perspective on wealth. She developed a lifestyle of generosity opening her hands to the poor (31:20). She has developed what the sages earlier refer to as "good eyes" (22:9).[3] Her primary focus was on the fear of the Lord which moved her to serve others. In the process of demonstrating diligence in her work, the by-product was prosperity. In the process of caring for family, reaching out to the poor, offering counsel, and instructing others, God blesses her family materially. But again, prosperity was not the *goal*. The goal was developing a lifestyle that identified the family as one that truly feared the Lord (31:30).

Cradled between the two images of the gang and the woman of wisdom is the sages' pedagogy for moving individuals from a lifestyle of greed to a lifestyle of generosity. The journey from the gang to the wise woman is arduous, complex, and not orchestrated in a nice step-by-step process. In chapters 1–9 the parents prepare the youth to face the challenge. In these initial instruction poems, the parents' voices dominates. The son is silent; the son listens. The parents persuade and instruct and guide. They prepare the son for the hard choices and the complexities in life he will face.

Beginning with chapter 10 the proverbial landscape suddenly shifts. At that point the book moves from instruction poems to the sentence literature, the pithy one-line proverbs. The son and readers move from listening to the persuasive appeals from the father to the responsibility of making his own decisions. As Yoder points out, the single proverb in chapters 10–29 places more interpretive demands on the reader than do the instruction poems.[4] The reader must now discern the appropriate context in which the proverb fits. In addition these chapters move away from the parental home to the larger community. They move from imposed parental discipline to voluntary discipline. Both the son and the readers must now take responsibility for their own actions and the tough decision they face. They are not alone, however. If they listen to the faith community, they will continue to receive the support they need to make wise decisions and form good habits of character. They move toward embodying the lifestyle of the wise woman.

As youth move out into the world on their own, they confronted with a plethora of resource material through which they must sort. Chapters

---

3. Proverbs 22:9 reads, "Those who are generous are blessed, for they share their bread with the poor" (NRSV). The term "generous" is literally the Hebrew phrase "good eyes." The wise woman of chapter 31 has developed good eyes.

4. Yoder, *Proverbs*, 110–11.

10–29 contain a storehouse of virtues and character strengths. This is the core of Proverbs. Contrary to popular belief, the collection of sentence literature is not completely haphazard.[5] There is a progression of movement in terms of the rhetorical form of the sentence literature, from simple antithetic proverbs that dominate chapters 10–15, to a more challenging mixture of proverbs in chapters 16:1–22:16, to the most complex assortment of instruction, analogical, antithetic, synthetic, and synonymous proverbs in chapters 25–29.[6]

Not only is this true of the rhetorical movement, it holds true for the content as well. The various themes dealt with by the sages seem to intentionally move from a simple to a more complex treatment. William Brown observes that, "Generally, the greater the variety of forms in a given collection, the more encompassing and complex the overall moral setting in which the various sentences and instructions are set."[7] The first Solomonic collection (10–15) exhibits the least variety with a predilection for clearly defined categories of righteous and wicked behavior. Then Brown remarks, "Splashes of gray are in greater evidence in the moral nuances conveyed in the latter collections than in the black-and-white world of the initial antithetical section. Stereotyped polarities are tweaked and, in some cases, transformed."[8]

This is true with the sages' teaching on wealth. The instruction regarding wealth begins with an elementary understanding of its theological nature in chapters 10–15. At this initial phase, wealth is a reward for righteous living and poverty the consequences of indolence. Near the end of the first Solomonic collection (ch. 15), however, the focus begins to shift. More ambiguity is introduced into the instruction. With the entry of the better-than proverbs near the end of the first collection (15:13–17; see below) and with their concentration in 16:1–22:16, material goods are viewed more indeterminately. Life gets a little more complicated; the value of wealth is qualified.

The better-than proverbs take the desirable physical quality of wealth and place it in the context of strife or chaos. Suddenly a reversal occurs. The desirable element is no longer as attractive. The less desirable physical component (e.g., a little income, a dinner of vegetables, poverty) becomes the better way because an atmosphere of peace and tranquility accompanies it. A comparison is made between combinations of negative and positive elements. In the better-than proverbs, the sages make value statements about

---

5. Crenshaw argues that it is. *Education in Ancient Israel*, 230.
6. Van Leeuwen, "Proverbs," 105.
7. Brown, "The Pedagogy of Proverbs 10:1—31:9," 180.
8. Ibid.

the more important dimensions in life. For example, "A good name is to be chosen rather than great riches, and favor is better-than silver or gold" (22:1). That is, one's reputation is more important than simply amassing stocks and bonds.

The most complex proverb collection is the Hezekian collection of chapters 25–29. Its perspective on wealth is multifaceted. The rich are chastised for their arrogance (28:11). Even kings are critiqued for their treatment of the poor (28:3; 28:15). In this collection, certain kinds of wealthy people are actually a menace to the community (28:8) and share a common bond with the wicked. The poor are commended for their integrity (28:6). Those who use their wealth to serve the poor are rewarded (28:27). Knowing the rights of the poor is what separates the righteous from the wicked (29:7). In Brown's words, "Of all the collections featured thus far in Proverbs, the Hezekian series looks most critically on wealth and most sympathetically upon the poor."[9] This collection describes the rich as greedy and the poor as righteous.

The sages' perspective on wealth and poverty is complex. They call on readers to wrestle with these perplexities, come to understand what is appropriate for the occasion, take ownership of their conclusions, and act on them. The sages equip readers with the ability to think critically. The very quality of wisdom itself invites the reforming and rethinking of ideas.

At the same time, the sages did not practice a values clarification approach leaving everything up to the individual to decide. Certain behavior, like greed, destroyed community life; it was not a gray area. Avarice is the way of the wicked while the righteous practice generosity. The sages were clear about their goal of moving individuals from those controlled by greed to those shaped by generosity. That task, for Proverbs, is a moral enterprise. They achieved this tension between strong, concrete values and critical, situational thinking with two techniques: the better-than proverbs and the disputational proverb pairs.

WEALTH AND THE "BETTER-THAN" PROVERBS (PROVERBS 15:13–17)

Proverbs' understanding of wealth and poverty is more complex than what traditional wisdom taught. Wealth may not always be a blessing from God. Poverty may not always be a curse. This ambiguity is highlighted in the sayings known as the better-than proverbs. In the sentence literature, one of the first better-than sayings appears in a small cluster of proverbs in 15:13–17,

9. Ibid., 174.

which comes near the end of the antithetic proverbs in chapters 10–15. Up to this point, the antithetic proverbs taught the fundamental ABC's of wisdom: one who fears the Lord will, generally speaking, prosper. Those who choose to follow a different path will find themselves laden with poverty and problems. With the entry of this cluster of proverbs, however, material goods are viewed more indeterminately. Life gets a little more complicated. Readers are introduced to the ambiguities of life's experiences. Things are not always what they appear to be. Two better-than proverbs, with their more obscure tone about the value of wealth, come at the conclusion of a group of proverbs describing an ambience of cheerfulness in the face of difficult experiences:

> A glad heart makes a cheerful countenance,[10]
>   but by sorrow of heart the spirit is broken.
> The mind of one who has understanding seeks knowledge,
>   but the mouths of fools feed on folly.
> All the days of the poor are hard,
>   but a cheerful heart has a continual feast.
> Better is a little with the fear of the LORD
>   than great treasure and trouble with it.
> Better is a dinner of vegetables where love is
>   than a fatted ox and hatred with it. (15:13–17)

This proverb text contains features that loosely connect the material together. The proverbs throughout chapter 15 as a whole display an overarching theological tone.[11] Beyond this general observation, a couple of other characteristics hold the proverbs together. For one, the specific text of 15:13–17 is stitched together by a series of verbal links[12] and by the image of eating (vv. 14, 15, 17). For another, two motifs are prominent. First, four of the five verses (vv. 13, 15–17) are concerned with creating an environment of cheerfulness regardless of external circumstances. Verse 17, which gives its own definition of the nature of a feast, may be an application of verse 15. A feast is a meal eaten in the context of love. Second, the proverbs of verses 15–17 address the ambivalent dimension of wealth.

The text introduces a common proverb form, the better-than proverb (sometimes referred to as "comparative sayings"). In the book of Proverbs,

---

10. More literally "a cheerful face." An inner happiness or peace of mind shows itself externally in the face.

11. Verses 3, 8, 9, 11, 16, 25, 29, 33 are all Yahweh proverbs. See chapter 8 for explanation of Yahweh proverbs.

12. Note the following links and common vocabulary terms: "heart" (לֵב also translated "mind," vv. 13, 14, 15); vv. 15–17 all contain the word *tob* (טוֹב; "cheerful" or "better"); vv. 16–17 are linked by their syntactical form (better-than proverbs).

there are basically two types of better-than sayings. On the one hand, some "better" proverbs make a simple comparison in which X is said to be better than Y as in the second line of 19:22b: "... it is better to be poor than a liar." On the other hand, more elaborate ones are based on the following formula: X is better with A than Y is with B. The comparative proverbs of 15:16–17 belong to the more elaborate type:

Contrary to traditional wisdom, in the better-than proverbs the sages give no pat answers. Wealth and poverty remain mixed blessings. The comparative proverbs take some desirable physical situation or circumstance and place it in the context of strife or chaos. Suddenly a reversal occurs. The desirable element is no longer as attractive. The less desirable physical surrounding becomes the better way because an atmosphere of peace and tranquility accompanies it.[13] A comparison is made between combinations of negative and positive elements. In the better proverbs, the sages make value statements about the more important dimensions in life. For example, "A good name is to be chosen rather than great riches, and favor is better than silver or gold" (22:1). That is, one's reputation is more important than simply amassing stocks and bonds. Accumulating wealth is good, but developing character is better.

A "solid majority" of the better-than sayings are concerned with wealth.[14] The first comparative proverb to appear in the book (not in the sentence literature) contrasts wealth with wisdom: "Happy are those who find wisdom, and those who get understanding, for her income is better than silver, and her revenue better than gold" (3:13–14). These comparative proverbs set conventional wisdom on its head. It is by no means always true that those who practice righteousness, justice, and equity will become prosperous. Wealth's value is thus relative. In 15:16 it is not that "little" is better and "much" is worse. The point is that the scale of material prosperity (from little to great) is subordinated to the character scale (from turmoil to fear of the Lord). This is the general contrast set up in the majority of the comparative sayings. The proverb in 16:8, a parallel of 15:16, reflects from experience: "Better is a little with righteousness, than large income with injustice." The comparison is between "little" and "large income." Again in

---

13. Bland, "Rhetorical Perspective on the Sentence Sayings of the Book of Proverbs," 75.

14. Huwiler, "Control of Reality in Israelite Wisdom," 90, 129. In looking at Egyptian influence on the better-than sayings in Israelite wisdom literature, Glendon Bryce compares the twelfth-century writing of Amenemope with the Proverbs collection. He maintains that in Amenemope there are nine better-than sayings. Five of the nine deal with the subject of wealth and poverty. Of the twelve comparative proverbs in Proverbs 15–22 six deal with riches and poverty (pp. 347, 349). Bryce, "'Better'–Proverbs."

itself, "little" is not better than "large." "Little," however, is juxtaposed with righteousness and "large" with injustice. Now a value judgment must be made in order to choose the better of the two. One is forced to rank these attributes on a scale from good to better. The choice is not always obvious. For the teacher of wisdom, the issue of poverty served an important heuristic function, enabling the student to contemplate more clearly the conditional quality of wealth and the value of wisdom.

Israelite wisdom developed a values scale. The sages were not shackled to a fixed way of evaluating experiences. Value choices are not always between good and evil. Often, as in the "better" proverbs, the choices are between good and better. Youth needed education in making these choices. As Glendon Bryce maintains, wisdom is based on insight and experience, not on law.[15] Of all the provisional values in life about which the wise had to make choices, riches were the most provisional of all.

The comparative sayings reveal that relationships are more important than material goods.[16] They subordinate external qualities to internal character. Community and character transcend creature comforts. This is the locus of thought in the cluster of proverbs in 15:15-17. So a cheerful heart has a continual feast even though, physically speaking, there may be little to eat. As a result it is better to have only the bare essentials of life and a healthy relationship with God, than to have great wealth and turmoil with it. The proverbs in 15:16-17 are the first of many comparative sayings (found mostly in chapters 16–22) that maintain the priority of community and character over possessions acquired without spiritual value. They act as an archetype for the following comparative sayings:

> Better is a little with righteousness,
>   than large income with injustice. (16:8)

> How much better to get wisdom than gold!
>   To get understanding is to be chosen rather than silver. (16:16)

> It is better to be of a lowly spirit among the poor,
>   than to divide the spoil with the proud. (16:19)

> Better is a dry morsel with quiet,
>   than a house full of feasting with strife. (17:1)

---

15. Bryce, "'Better'-Proverbs," 343-44.

16. There is an intentional word play in Hebrew on "good" or "better" (טוֹב). The same word can be used to describe material wealth as in 28:10. But the irony in the better-than proverbs is that it is used to describe internal well-being.

> One who is slow to anger is better than the mighty,
> and one whose temper is controlled than one who captures a city. (16:32)[17]

> What is desirable in a person is loyalty,
> and it is better to be poor than a liar. (19:22)

> It is better to live in a corner of the housetop,
> than in a house shared with a contentious wife. (21:9)

> A good name is to be chosen rather than great riches,
> and favor is better than silver or gold. (22:1)[18]

The better-than sayings disclose some fundamental principles regarding one's perspective on wealth. Wealth is by no means bad in and of itself. Wealth properly acquired has worth, but there are better things in life than riches. These include the importance of relationships and related virtues like a good reputation, wisdom, righteousness, humility, self-control, contentment, harmony, generosity, and love. Wealth can easily distort one's sense of values, causing individuals to lose sight of that which is more important. Additionally, wealth often carries with it unwanted baggage such as strife, a false sense of security, pride, lying, hatred, trouble, and indifference to others. Robert Wuthnow gives an important piece of advice to religious leaders in this regard. If leaders want to call for church members to restrain their appetite for more money, "the most effective way of doing this is by pointing out the sacrifices one would have to make to become rich, rather than directly challenging the desire for wealth."[19]

The better-than sayings in 15:16–17 claim that personal relationships are more important than material possessions. Poverty is not a desired state but it is more desirable than confusion or hatred. The sage does not tell the reader to avoid rich food or great wealth, but to place them in the proper perspective. If one must choose, spiritual health is always preferred over physical health. In a nutshell, the message of the better-than sayings is that a little with righteousness is better than a lot with strife.

---

17. Notice that within each line of this proverb there is a move from the internal to the external, from one who has control over her emotions to one who is able to control others. *Today's English Version* translates the proverb this way: "It is better to be patient than powerful. It is better to win control over yourself than over whole cities." Note Bryce's paraphrase: "Better is a man who controls his temper than a famous soldier, and a man of self-control than a war hero" Bryce, " 'Better'–Proverbs," 349.

18. In addition, see 21:3.

19. Wuthnow, *God and Mammon in America*, 129.

A Closer Look at 15:15–17

The proverbs in 15:15–17 contrast two value systems which reveal themselves in two different lifestyles. Take a closer look at these proverbs:

> All the days of the poor are hard,
>   but a cheerful heart has a continual feast.
> Better is a little with the fear of the Lord
>   than great treasure and trouble with it.
> Better is a dinner of vegetables where love is
>   than a fatted ox and hatred with it.

They depict a life lived on only the bare necessities: "All the days of the poor are hard." The poor live on the edge of survival. How can there be anything good about such an existence? There is nothing good about it, at least not in and of itself, but an inner resilience of character enables the individual to excel regardless of the external circumstances. Those who cultivate the mental and spiritual resources within create a feast that can never be depleted. Taken in context with verses 16 and 17, the continual feast of verse 15 includes an environment where one is nurtured by a close relationship with God (v. 16a) and by the community of family and friends (v. 17a). These resources continually nourish the one who possesses only the bare essentials of life.

The contrast in verse 15 (cf. also v. 13) is not between the joy and sorrow that humans occasionally feel. The contrast is between the choices of two sets of dispositions. On the one hand, is an anxiety-laden spirit that dampens the surroundings. On the other hand, is an inner spirit of resilience that maintains strong morale regardless of the circumstances. Such persons display mental toughness. The mentally disciplined person manifests a spirit of contentment that reveals itself through an atmosphere of encouragement and deep-seated joy. Within an environment of cheerfulness, love, and security one sees more clearly the priorities of life.

The proverb in verse 16 states the sapiential principle in general terms: material prosperity is subordinate to religious faith. Verse 17 applies that principle to the specific context of family: personal relationships are more important than experiencing the finest cuisine at every meal. These sayings use the metaphor of food to contrast two styles of life that are polar opposites.[20] A whole worldview is symbolized by what we do at the meal table. The fatted ox, the banquet of roast beef, represents the first worldview. Such a meal epitomizes a consumer mentality where the focus is on pursuing the good life: the accumulation of more real estate, more wealth, more

---

20. Brueggemann, "What You Eat is What You Get: Proverbs 15:17."

comforts, more luxuries, the pursuit of a bigger house, a better car, a nicer neighborhood. Such pursuit represents a particular frame of mind driven to succeed, to work long hours, to be aggressive, ambitious, career focused. Yet the commitment to increasing one's standard of living automatically carries with it anxiety, tension, quarreling, and exhaustion. Such a lifestyle assumes the qualities of a black hole, engulfing its prey in a world of materialism. Perspective on life is lost. Priorities are jumbled. Relationships become strained. On the one hand, one gets more than one bargained for: strife, anxiety, and discontentment. On the other hand, what one gets with roast beef is often much less than expected: discord and the insatiable desire for more. As a more contemporary proverb observes, "He is not poor who has little, but he who desires much."

"Beef with hatred" personifies the environment of a busy family.[21] They arrive home for dinner too tired to care much, too exhausted to communicate, too preoccupied to invest in each other. Beef stands as a metonymy for the fast, affluent way of life. It takes more energy, more work, more production, more competence, and more time, to generate lots of beef for the table. Little remains to expend on friends and family. Such an environment breeds tension, insecurity, disorientation, and strife.

Eating practices reflect the character of a family and of a standard of living. Among teenagers our culture has faced an epidemic of eating disorders such as anorexia and bulimia. We now know that individuals do not *have* anorexia or bulimia; they often are disorders that stem from dysfunctional relationships.[22] They are an indication of dysfunctional families and of a dysfunctional society. In our culture, beef with strife signifies an excessively ambitious lifestyle, which results in great cost to the physical body and extracts a heavy toll on the family.

A "dinner of vegetables" represents the second value system and stands in stark contrast to the dinner of beef. The sage does not advocate here a cholesterol-free diet. The concern is not primarily with preventing heart disease. The proverb suggests an alternative way to live, one that brings wholeness. "Vegetables with love" sounds like a lifestyle, a standard of living that is plain and simple, where people have time for each other.

Nevertheless, we do not need to live in poverty conditions to embrace the values of this proverb. The proverb calls on us to pull back from our unrelenting pursuit to increase our standard of living. It calls one to prioritize

---

21. Ibid. Cf., Brueggemann, *Texts Under Negotiation*, 87–89.

22 Cynthia Rowland McClure, herself a victim of an eating disorder, maintains that eating disorders often point to family and past hurts, such as abandonment or neglect, abuse of all kinds including sexual, physical, emotional, verbal or spiritual, unrealistic expectations from parents, or lack of nurturing. McClure, *The Courage To Go On*.

relationships over riches. The proverb reminds individuals that wealth is measured not by the quantity of physical possessions but by the quality of one's character.

Whether rich or poor, if increasing our standard of living remains the priority in life, then we cannot have roast beef without quarreling and strife. There are some things in this life that we just cannot have without other things trailing along. "Vegetables with love" symbolizes a well ordered home that nurtures health and well-being for the whole family. It is an environment of contentment, security, peace, and cheerfulness; an atmosphere where love rather than strife reigns supreme. It is a family that has incorporated the priority Jesus talked about to his disciples: "Do not be anxious for your life, saying 'What shall we eat?' or 'What shall we drink?' or 'What shall we wear?' For the Gentiles seek all these things; and your heavenly Father knows that you need them all. But seek first his kingdom and his righteousness, and all these things shall be yours as well" (Matt. 6:31–32).

Proverbs 15:15–17 sets before the reader powerful images of two feasts. On the one hand, a succulent meal of prime beef lures us to its table. But it comes at a price that even the wealthiest cannot afford. On the other hand, there stands the image of a simple meal of vegetables. From all appearances it does not look like much. When you set your feet under this table, however, it overflows with love and expressions of genuine care for one another. The trio of proverbs depicts an environment of contentment that no longer depends on external circumstances or material wealth.

WEALTH AND THE DISPUTATIONAL PROVERB PAIRS

The comparative proverbs place the extrinsic value of wealth in tension with the intrinsic values of relationships and moral character. They teach that wealth possesses only relative worth. This instruction is not, however, confined to the comparative proverbs. Not infrequently the sapiential teachers place two contrasting or "disputational"[23] proverbs side by side to address the subject of wealth. These proverbial pairs also demonstrate that Proverbs does not subscribe to a simplistic dogmatism about material goods. Raymond Van Leeuwen remarks that, when individual proverbs are interpreted by themselves, one often concludes that "the tidy dogmatism of Proverbs does not correspond to reality."[24] The reason is that one proverb never says it all.

---

23. Washington, *Wealth and Poverty in the Instruction of Amenemope and the Hebrew Proverbs*, 193.

24. Ramond Van Leeuwen, "Wealth and Poverty," 28.

The sages frequently resort to an "intentional disputational technique" in which they place contrasting proverbs close to one another so that one can correct or interpret the other.[25] Such a technique was quite useful in the education of youth. It served as an exercise for training youthful minds in the ability to discern, to think critically. Sages do not give pat answers. Youth need exercise in the process of deciding right and wrong, good and better, for themselves.

Several proverbs on wealth and poverty have a disputational relation to one another. Take for example the following proverb pair in 14:20-21:

> The poor are disliked even by their neighbors,
>   but the rich have many friends.
> Those who despise their neighbors are sinners,
>   but happy are those who are kind to the poor.

These two verses are held together by the catchword "neighbor." Verse 20 appears to be a neutral observation about things as they are. Because of their poverty, the poor have no friends, but people flock to the rich. Verse 21 serves as a critique or a corrective to this social phenomenon.[26] In other words, it stands as an ethical response to the social inequity of verse 20. The proverb pair highlights two different ways of behaving toward the neighbor who can either be despised or treated with kindness.

Chapter 22:7-9 contains another dueling cluster of proverbs:

> The rich rules over the poor,
>   and the borrower is the slave of the lender.
> Whoever sows injustice will reap calamity,
>   and the rod of anger will fail.
> Those who are generous are blessed,
>   for they share their bread with the poor.

Verse 7 observes the fact of life that the rich have power over the poor, but then verses 8 and 9 bring in the ethical dimension to this relationship. The responsibility lies with the rich to practice generosity toward those who live a life of poverty. The "generous" are, literally, those who have developed a "good eye." Wealth, when used by those with a "good eye," becomes a constructive resource.

The value of wealth is critiqued in the interactive proverb pair in 18:10-11:

---

25. Washington, *Wealth and Poverty in the Instruction of Amenemope and the Hebrew Proverbs*, 193.

26. See further 14:31, "Those who oppress the poor insult their Maker, but those who are kind to the needy honor him."

> The name of the LORD is a strong tower;
> the righteous run into it and are safe.
> The wealth of the rich is their strong city;
> in their imagination it is like a high wall.

Here the NRSV appropriately interprets verse 11 by stating that it is only in the "imagination" of the rich that wealth gives security. The Hebrew text contains a play on words that highlights the contrast. The righteous in verse 10 place their security in the Lord and they are "safe" (literally "exalted"). The wealthy in verse 11 place their trust in riches and they imagine that it acts "like a high wall" (literally, wealth "exalts" them). The rich think their wealth protects them, but appearances are deceiving. True security lies in those who rely on the strength of the Lord.

Certain proverbs, by themselves, appear to promote an ethic that is primarily concerned with protecting one's own financial interests. Proverbs condemning the practice of surety[27] seem to promote such a self-interest mentality, but another proverb juxtaposed to the surety proverb often tempers its thought. Such is the case with the following disputational pair in 17:17–18:

> A friend loves at all times,
> and kinsfolk are born to share adversity.
> It is senseless to give a pledge,
> to become surety for a neighbor.

The catchword "friend" or "neighbor" (the same word in Hebrew) connects these two proverbs. Not offering surety to a neighbor does not necessarily indicate selfishness.[28] Rather to engage in such a venture was a precarious business practice that jeopardized the security of one's own family. Going surety indicates a lack of forethought. It spreads the disaster rather than containing it. That does not, however, relieve one of one's responsibilities to the friend or neighbor (v. 17). Especially in times of crisis, a friend was to come to the aid of a neighbor. Verse 17 serves as a check on the person in verse 18 who might use the admonition against going surety as an excuse for not helping the neighbor, but the sage mandates that a person use money wisely, even when offering help to another.

As the dispositional pairs demonstrate, the sages did not believe in the mindless submission of students. Dissonance and dialogue were a necessary

---

27. Surety is the practice of taking responsibility for someone else's debt if she is unable to pay the debtor. For a more extended treatment of surety see Proverbs 6:1–5.
28. Scherer, "Is the Selfish Man Wise?"

environment for character formation to occur. The teachers actively engaged students in the process of assessing the proper use of wealth.

Dialogue continues to play a vital role in enabling individuals to assess the value of wealth. Through interaction with others in the faith community, new understanding is produced regarding one's responsibility to wealth. Robert Wuthnow, for example, urges individuals to engage in critical self-reflection and discussion about economic issues with others in order to loosen the grip materialism holds on our culture. He advocates entering into small group formats in order to reflect on priorities and to bring spiritual values to bear on economic issues.[29] Banding together with other seekers challenges us in the politics of economic values. Through serious dialogue we hold one another accountable for how we use and distribute material wealth.

THE PRAYER OF THE WISE

Individuals engaged in the process of moral development must learn to hold to wealth tenuously. One's economic situation serves only as a means to a greater end: the development of integrity that images the nature of God. The use of wealth, like language, reflects character. The disciple nurtures an attitude toward wealth that strengthens her or his dependence on God. This is the prayer of the sage in 30:7-9:

> Two things I ask of you;
>   do not deny them to me before I die:
> Remove far from me falsehood and lying;
>   give me neither poverty nor riches;
>   feed me with the food that I need,
> or I shall be full, and deny you,
>   and say, "Who is the LORD?"
> or I shall be poor, and steal,
>   and profane the name of my God.

In this prayer, the worshipper requests two things: the removal of falsehood and lying and to be kept from extreme economic conditions.[30] The reason the worshipper requests no "riches" is the desire to accumulate too much and forsake the Lord (v. 9). Living a life of luxury was one of the

---

29. Wuthnow, *God and Mammon in America*, 266.

30. Duane Garrett says the two requests are to possess neither poverty nor wealth. The falsehood and lies refers to the deceptiveness of poverty and wealth. *Proverbs, Ecclesiastes, Song of Songs*, 238.

temptations of youth highlighted in chapters 1–9 (e.g. 1:8–19). Such a life leads one to forget God.

On the other hand the worshipper prays that neither will the Lord give him poverty, lest he "steal, and profane the name of my God" (v. 9). The "poverty" referred to here is abject poverty, a desperate hunger. This is not the poverty described in the sentence literature that speaks of a modest existence: "Better is a dinner of vegetables where love is than a fatted ox and hatred with it" (15:17). The worshipper simply asks the Lord to "feed me with the food that I need" (which Jesus may be alluding to in his prayer in Matt 6). The incentive for the request is to honor the Lord. The goal that the sage seeks is moral discipline for the sake of Yahweh.

That discipline is reflected in concrete behavior as one reaches out to the poor and oppressed. It is reflected in one's refusal to engage in unethical business practices. Such people do not use "false weights" or deceptive means of making more money. They practice integrity in their economic dealings with others. They practice restraint and self-control in financial matters.

Moral discipline as a way of serving the Lord is the very goal the sages started with in the instruction of their students. Proverbs 3 begins with the father admonishing his son to heed his instructions, "for length of days and years of life and abundant welfare they will give you." Then the father continues with a series of instructions that puts wealth and poverty in proper tension with each other. The sage states the general view in 3:9–10.

> Honor the Lord with your substance
>   and with the first fruits of all your produce;
> Then your barns will be filled with plenty,
>   and your vats will be bursting with wine.

The sage believes that godly character made for a richer, fuller life, which included material security, as evidenced in the life of the woman of noble character (chapt. 31).

Still, virtuous character did *not* guarantee material prosperity. Immediately thrust alongside this instruction, another disputational proverb gives a counter image. That is to say, following the image of righteousness with prosperity portrayed in 3:9–10 comes the image of righteousness with poverty in 3:11–12:[31]

> My child, do not despise the Lord's discipline
>   or be weary of his reproof,
> For the Lord reproves the one he loves,
>   as a father the son in whom he delights.

---

31. Van Leeuwen, "Wealth and Poverty."

This saying is also found in Deuteronomy 8 and Hebrews 12. Both texts provide breadth and depth to the meaning of the saying. In Deuteronomy 8, Moses reflects on the way in which God led the people of Israel through the wilderness for forty years. God humbled them, let them go hungry, and then fed them with manna. What was God's purpose? So that Israel would know that "as a parent disciplines a child so the Lord your God disciplines you" (8:5). God's discipline sometimes resulted in a subsistence living. God wanted Israel to trust in the Lord.

The other text in Hebrews 12 comes immediately after the litany of the great heroes of faith in chapter 11 who suffered for their faith. The writer then quotes Proverbs 3:11–12, followed a little later by this commentary:

> Now, discipline always seems painful rather than pleasant at the time, but later it yields the peaceful fruit of righteousness to those who have been trained by it. (12:11)

Righteousness, justice, equity, and godly virtues often can only develop on the anvil of suffering and deprivation. There is no guarantee that, materially speaking, one will recover and prosper. Recall the Jerusalem church in Acts. That church demonstrated righteousness, equity, and generosity for all. They sold their possessions and distributed the proceeds to those who had need (Acts 2:43–47). Yet this most generous church did not become wealthy as a result. Actually they remained in poverty. Paul spends three years of his life raising funds from Gentile churches to help the church in Jerusalem. Virtuous character does not guarantee material prosperity.

So the wisdom and prosperity of 3:9–10 is juxtaposed with the wisdom and poverty of 3:11–12.[32] But both texts flow out of the preceding admonition of 3:5–8, which calls for rich and poor alike to put their trust in the Lord, not in wealth:

> Trust in the LORD with all your heart,
>   and do not rely on your own insight.
> In all your ways acknowledge him,
>   and he will make straight your paths.
> Do not be wise in your own eyes;
>   fear the LORD, and turn away from evil.
> It will be a healing for your flesh
>   and a refreshment for your body.

The way in which individuals use their wealth reveals their character. One's attitude toward the poor, and toward poverty itself, reflects personal values. The sages wrestle with the ambiguity of wealth and poverty as a means of

---

32. Ibid., 34–35.

equipping students to assess the values they live by and determine in what or in whom they place their confidence.

CONCLUSION

Because North Americans are immersed in a world of materialism, it becomes difficult to critique financial practices. The instruction of the sages provides an important resource in thinking through one's values about wealth. The sages do not set down hard and fast rules. They give no pat answers. The value of wealth remains equivocal, but not subjective. Concrete patterns of life reveal one's perspective on material goods, whether it is healthy or harmful.

The sage's task was to equip individuals to distinguish between the authentic and inauthentic uses of wealth. How one thought of and used wealth was not a matter consigned to the private realm, as it is in contemporary American culture. The community scrutinized the attitude toward and use of material goods of its individual members. Continued reliance on a faith community as a means of evaluating both attitudes and actions remains crucial for receiving a clearer understanding of who we are. Just "as water reflects the face," so others help us to see more clearly the materialism that embeds itself in the very fiber of our being.

The issues surrounding economics, wealth, and poverty are multifaceted and must be treated accordingly. The responsibility for church leaders to address the subject is demanding and the cost high for listeners willing to take the arduous journey from greed to generosity.[33] As Proverbs demonstrates, the path to generosity does not always or usually follow a straight line. It is filled with twists and turns and contradictions and tension and conflict. The results, however, are a more mature character.

Our culture is jaded with materialism and greed, which directly influences our spiritual diet. Many whose lives are consumed by the acquisition of more possessions destroy themselves and contaminate the environment in which they live. Those in leadership positions are called on to identify and name those powers and principalities that promote greed.[34] The advertising world is one of those powers. Advertising slogans feed the self-indulgence

33. Marjorie Thompson describes spirituality as dynamic. It "is continually challenging, changing, and maturing us." *Soul Feast*, 8.

34. I understand this task in a way similar to what I believe Charles Campbell advocates when he argues that preachers have the responsibility to name the powers and principalities that are at work in our world. Further Campbell states that one of the purposes of preaching is to form a people who can resist the powers. Campbell, *The Word before the Powers*, 92, 94.

of Americans. For example, a GMC slogan from a number of years ago claims of a product, "It's not more than you need, just more than you're used to." Such commercial "wisdom" incites greed. Many others like it generate a craving for more and lead individuals to embody characteristics of the gang described in Proverbs chapter 1. Following the pedagogy of the sages, however, contemporary leaders can rely on the abundant resources that Proverbs provides to guide the faith community into a more responsible use of wealth leading them ultimately to a lifestyle that embodies generosity. Such a lifestyle is a way in which Proverbs puts working clothes on godliness.

Chapter Eight

Yahweh and Character Formation
(Proverbs 15:33—16:9)

The belief that random or arbitrary chance is a driving force in human affairs is quite popular. Over thirty years ago, Harold Kushner in his best seller, *When Bad Things Happen to Good People*, concluded that, when bad things happen, God can do very little about it.[1] God's hands are tied because of God's limited power. When bad things happen, it is primarily because people are victims of lousy luck.

The gambling industry has built a multi-billion dollar business based on people who believe in the idea of luck. Luck becomes the way by which we explain our lives. Life is like a game of roulette. You spin the wheel and when your time has come, that is it. You can do nothing about it. We are at the mercy of fate. Postmodern people do not believe in a purposeful God who directs life.

One unconscious reason underlying why so many people believe in luck may be because it absolves them of taking responsibility. We simply are victims of circumstances. So we describe a person as being "lucky at play, but unlucky at love." The only response is just to kick back and go with the flow, *que será será*.

As much as people believe in luck, there is an equally prevalent and totally contrary belief that humans possess the power to control their own destiny. Thus on the flip side of the secular coin of luck appears the human potential philosophy. Humans take pride in their ability to succeed. Many

---

1. Kushner, *When Bad Things Happen to Good People*.

contemporary proverbs reflect this "possibility thinking" mind set: "the sky's the limit," "where there's a will there's a way," and "if at first you don't succeed, try, try again." These "can do" proverbs convey the power of the human spirit to achieve: "if it's going to be, it's up to me."

On a more aggressive level, beyond the "can do" proverbs, is a genre known as the "No Fear" proverbs. Alyce McKenzie refers to these as "can do" proverbs on steroids.[2] "No Fear" proverbs take the human potential movement to new heights: "Know your own limits, then break 'em," "Living with boundaries is not living," "I don't come here to play, I come here to win."[3] These proverbs express a level of competitiveness that comes at the expense of anyone who gets in the way of an individual's personal goals.

"Can do" proverbs express the popular philosophy that we are the captains of our own ships, the masters of our own fates. Destiny lies within our hands. Those who work hard flourish. Those who practice prudence in financial investments reap economic success. Through wise planning, discipline, and industry one can achieve independent wealth. If parents work hard and sacrifice, their children will most assuredly succeed. If individuals eat right, exercise regularly, and take care of their bodies, long life is the compensation. Hard work and discipline are rewarded. As communicated by celebrities, athletes, and entrepreneurs through the media, "You can do whatever you make up your mind to do!" We are self-made individuals.

In contrast to these two secular views, wisdom brings a different perspective to the table. On the one hand, the idea of luck or chance does not exist in wisdom's vocabulary. Contrary to seeing humans as simply victims of circumstances, wisdom holds to a high view of human potential. Those who live responsibly achieve health, wealth, and wisdom. When individuals adhere to the order of creation, success follows naturally. Most of the proverbs in chapters 10–15 emphasize a character-consequence perspective. That is, the kind of character habits one develops produces direct consequences. So those who work hard prosper. Those who act responsibly succeed. We determine our own future. On the other hand, wisdom does not believe that humans completely control their own destiny. Wisdom maintains a healthy and honest view of its own limitations and lives within those constraints. What Proverbs brings to the situation, which secular philosophies disregard, is a fundamental belief in the active presence of God.

With the beginning of Proverbs chapter 16, the number of proverbs often referred to as the "Yahweh proverbs" increases.[4] In addition, the

---

2. McKenzie, *Preaching Proverbs*, 82, 83–84.
3. Ibid., 86.
4. Yahweh proverbs are those proverbs that explicitly refer to the name of "Yahweh"

concentration on the act or character-consequence scenario, so prevalent in chapters 10–15, shifts. Exceptions to the rule now appear more frequently. Proverbs 15:33—16:9 brings into sharp relief the tension that exists in the relationship between what humans accomplish and what God designs. These theologically daring proverbs present human freedom in tandem with divine sovereignty:

> The fear of the LORD is instruction in wisdom,
>   and humility goes before honor.
> The plans of the mind belong to mortals,
>   but the answer of the tongue is from the LORD.
> All one's ways may be pure in one's own eyes,
>   but the LORD weighs the spirit.
> Commit your work to the LORD,
>   and your plans will be established.
> The Lord has made everything for its purpose,
>   even the wicked for the day of trouble.
> All those who are arrogant are an abomination to the LORD;
>   be assured, they will not go unpunished.
> By loyalty and faithfulness iniquity is atoned for,
>   and by the fear of the Lord one avoids evil.
> When the ways of people please the LORD,
>   he causes even their enemies to be at peace with them.
> Better is a little with righteousness
>   than large income with injustice.
> The human mind plans the way,
>   but the LORD directs the steps.

This series of proverbs holds together nicely as a single unit. Several good reasons exist for understanding this text as a tightly knit cluster.

First, all of the sayings, with the exception of verse 8, are Yahweh proverbs.[5] It is interesting to note that the highest number of direct references to the Lord in the book of Proverbs is in 10:1—22:16.[6] In addition, the thickest concentration of Yahweh proverbs occurs in chapters 15 and 16.[7] Therefore the text serves as the theological center of chapters 10–22.

in one of their two lines.

5. Yet verse 8 is not out of place. It serves as an example of what pleases the Lord in verse 7. An overlapping proverb, in fact, appears in 15:16a: "Better is a little with the fear of the Lord." "Fear of the Lord" is substituted for "righteousness" in 16:8.

6. The lowest number of references is in chapters 25–29. In chapters 25–27 there are only two references to God: 25: 2, 22. Proverbs refers to the Deity almost exclusively by the name Yahweh (eighty-seven times). The more generic term, God, (Elohim, Eloah) is used only six times (2:5, 17; 3:4; 25:2; 30:5, 9).

7. Chapters 15–16 contain twenty Yahweh references out of a total of sixty-six in

Second, whereas one line of each of the proverbs contains the catchword "Lord," the other half of each verse usually refers to human activity of some kind. Listen to some of these references: "the plans of the mind belong to mortals" (16:1) and "the human mind plans the way" (16:9). The sages speak of human arrogance (16:5), loyalty and faithfulness (16:6), and righteousness (16:8). Tension exists in each proverb between divine sovereignty and human freedom, the activities of God and the activities of people.

Third, a group of royal proverbs (16:10–15) succeeds this text. The two units are intentionally placed together. Similar terminology is used to describe God and king in both sections.[8] It appears then that in 16:1–15 an editor has skillfully assembled two collections of proverbs, the first half on the actions of Yahweh and the second half on the nature of kingship, so that the reader must reflect on the relationship between the two clusters. In Old Testament theology, Yahweh and the monarchy stand in close relationship (see 21:1). The monarchy serves as the earthly representative of the divine. The Lord upholds the moral order of the world (16:4–9) through the just rule of an earthly king (16:10–15).

Fourth, 15:31–33 serves as an introduction to this cluster of proverbs. With the exhortation to hear, listen to, and heed instruction, the text is similar to the admonitions to a son to listen to the instructions of his father that mark the major units in chapters 1–9 (e.g., 1:8–9; 3:1–2; 4:1–3). This introduction encourages the youth to accept instruction that gives wisdom.

Finally, 16:1 and 9 form an inclusion, with both verses confirming that humans strategize but God decides the final outcome. The inclusion sets in bold relief the theme of this unit of material.

HUMAN FREEDOM AND DIVINE SOVEREIGNTY

This cluster of proverbs raises the long-standing issue of the relationship between human and divine activity in Proverbs. Some scholars view the human and divine elements in the book as distinct spheres of life. The "mundane" or secular proverbs are the earliest and are concerned with the success and harmonious life of the individual. Later the sages added the Yahweh proverbs to the collection to give it a more theological tone.

---

the whole of 10:1–22:16.

8. For example, there are certain attitudes and activities that are an "abomination" (תּוֹעֵבָה; vv. 5, 12) to the Lord and to the king. In contrast there are certain activities that "delight" (רָצוֹן; vv. 7, 13, 15) Yahweh and the king. Interestingly these two terms are often contrasting pairs in proverbial descriptions of Yahweh's attitude toward human actions: 11:1; 11:20; 12:22; 15:8.

One of the primary proponents of this view is William McKane who classifies the proverbs according to three phases of development.[9] The first and earliest phase he calls Class A proverbs. These "secular" proverbs focus on the individual. In the second phase, the center of concern shifts from the individual to the community. These he refers to as Class B proverbs. The proverbs in the third phase, Class C, are the latest editions to the collection and are the most theological. These include the Yahweh proverbs. The Yahweh proverbs reinterpret the earlier secular proverbs. The historical development in McKane's scheme, then, moves from the secular to the sacred.[10]

While R. N. Whybray also believes that the Yahweh proverbs were introduced later to reinterpret the secular proverbs, he does not believe, like McKane, that the Yahweh proverbs were randomly thrown into the collection.[11] Whybray asserts that it makes little sense for the reinterpretation process to proceed in a haphazard manner. He argues for a reinterpretation that took place in some orderly fashion. In regard to the sentence literature in 10:1–22:16, "the greatest concentration of Yahweh sayings occurs in the exact centre of this section, chapters 15 and 16."[12] Chapter 15:33–16:9 represents the theological kernel of these chapters.[13] Furthermore, while 15:33–16:9 is the center of gravity for the whole of Proverbs 10–22, the individual proverbs of chapters 10–22 cluster around the Yahweh-sayings peppered all through the Proverb collection. These Yahweh-sayings are intentionally placed beside "mundane" proverbs to reinterpret the adjacent sayings.[14]

Both McKane's and Whybray's approaches put human and divine action at opposite poles. In Proverbs, they see sharp polarity existing between

---

9. McKane, *Proverbs*, 11, 415.

10. Gerhard von Rad identifies in Proverbs a "tension between a radical secularization on the one hand and the knowledge of God's unlimited powers on the other." *Wisdom in Israel*, 98.

11. Whybray, "Yahweh-Sayings and Their Contexts in Proverbs, 10:1—22:16."

12. Ibid., 158. Whybray notes that the Massora points to the fact that 16:17 is the middle verse of the book of Proverbs.

13. Ibid., 159, 160.

14. The following Yahweh proverbs are the examples he uses: 10:3, 22, 27, 29; 11:20; 12:2, 22; 14:2; 15:3, 8, 9, 11, 16; 16:20, 33; 17:3; 18:10; 19:21; 20:10, 12, 22, 23, 24, 27; 22:12. Whybray, "Yahweh-Sayings and their Contexts in Proverbs, 10:1–22:16." Elsewhere, Whybray offers other examples. For instance, he sees 16:33 and 17:3 as forming a framework to 17:1–2 which have a certain thematic affinity. "The two Yahweh proverbs, which assert Yahweh's control over human affairs (16:33) and his assessment of the human heart (17:3) make the point that family life, like the other aspects of human existence and decision making, is ruled by an all-seeing and hidden God." *Wealth and Poverty in the Book of Proverbs*, 111. Whybray continues to develop this line of reasoning in his commentary, *Proverbs*.

sacred and profane wisdom. Therefore, the profane proverbs are in desperate need of a theological foundation.[15]

The main problem with their views is that, in Israelite thought, there never was a division between the sacred and the secular. For Israel, all of life was sacred and under the rule of Yahweh. There was no secular realm.[16] Even though many proverbs do not directly use religious language, wisdom always assumes a faith perspective.[17] In fact, separation of secular and theological thinking seems suspiciously modern and postmodern. McKane's approach views Proverbs as "a house divided against itself."[18] The Yahweh proverbs do not turn the secular sayings into something more religious.[19] No evidence exists to indicate a battle raging between the sages regarding a sacred and secular domain of life.

So what is the relationship between the anthropocentric and theocentric dimensions? A perspective more in keeping with the nature of Proverbs is that the human element looms large in the book. The student must take responsibility to choose the right path (chapt. 9). Yet while humans take responsibility for their own destiny, their decisions are always made within the larger context of a Yahwistic view of the world. Human and divine activity are not mutually exclusive. All through Proverbs these two relationships compliment as well as stand in tension with one another.[20] Therefore, while the theocentric view remains foundational,[21] it is not in the foreground in

---

15. Since these proverbs dominate the book, some have viewed Proverbs as the first cousin to secularism. Horst D. Preuss is extreme in seeing the book as completely secular. According to him, the Yahweh of Proverbs is not the Yahweh of Israel. *Theologie des Alten Testaments*. But if Preuss is right, then why was Proverbs retained as Jewish Scripture?

16. Fredrick M. Wilson offers a strong critique of McKane's position. See his "Sacred and Profane?" Wilson asks a provocative question: If Israel's sages intended the kind of radical revision that McKane suggests, then why are so many of the secular (and misguided!) proverbs still preserved (323)? Frydrych also has a strong critique of McKane in *Living under the Sun*, 176-77.

17. This is the position of Perdue in *Wisdom and Creation*, 46. See also Farmer, *Proverbs and Ecclesiastes*, 1-2.

18. Wilson, "Sacred and Profane?," 327.

19. Duane Garrett maintains that "the Book of Proverbs does not simply attach the caboose of Yahwism to the train of secular, international wisdom." *Proverbs, Ecclesiastes, Song of Songs*, 54.

20. Christine Roy Yoder borrows an image from another writer who likens the divine/human relationship to "circus performers balancing on two speeding side-by-side horses." She explains the analogy saying its comparable to having "one foot on the horse of divine power and freedom and the other on the horse of human autonomy—or, variously, straddling divine determination and human freewill." *Proverbs*, 179.

21. There are scholars that argue for a theocentric view of Proverbs. See, for example,

Proverbs. Human action remains front and center.[22] The concern for the success of the individual and the community takes precedence. Proverbs begins and ends with a focus on human responsibility (1:8; 31:10–31).

HUMAN ABILITY: WISDOM'S RESOURCES

Since human activity stands in bold relief in Proverbs, it is necessary to reflect more closely on the nature of such activity. To do so better equips one to understand the human/divine relationship. The sages have a tremendous respect for what humans can accomplish. Wisdom affirms that individuals are capable of making wise choices and displaying responsible behavior. In so doing, such people will live healthy, prosperous, successful lives. Because they value human ability and understanding, the sages use all the resources at their disposal to discover the means of living a successful life. They use the resources around them as well as the resources within themselves.

For one, the sage actively seeks to learn from others, including those outside the Israelite community. Wisdom views individuals as human beings rather than Jews or Gentiles. Thus the sage is able to converse respectfully with any person who demonstrates insight into living life more fully. It is part of the task of wisdom to identify insight and truth wherever it is found. Consequently, it comes as no surprise that biblical wisdom is international in scope. No one culture or group can claim a monopoly on truth. With an international outlook, the sage leaves no stone unturned in aggressively pursuing wisdom. The wise are those who appropriate into their own community the best learning, the best knowledge, and the most ingenious cultural achievements from other peoples.

Clear evidence of this exists in the book of Proverbs itself as one reads the gnomic sayings a foreign king's mother taught him in Proverbs 31:1–9.[23] The major block of material found in Proverbs 22:17–24:22 also exhibits close parallels to the thirty sayings of an Egyptian sage, Amenemope.[24] The

---

Leo Perdue, *Wisdom and Creation*.

22. See Walter Zimmerli, "Zur Struktur der alttestamentlichen Weisheit;" Brueggemann, *In Man We Trust*.

23. Further 30:1–9 contains a Transjordan collection.

24. Pritchard, "The Instruction of Amen-em-opet," 421–424. Scholars have debated the similarities of the Egyptian sayings with the sayings of Proverbs for some time. But that there are some affinities between the Egyptian and Israelite works at least expresses an international dimension to wisdom. See Whybray, *The Book of Proverbs*, 6–14. Richard Clifford identifies the parallels between Proverbs 22:17–23:11 and the Instructions of Amenemope. See Clifford, *Proverbs*, 199–211. It is sometimes difficult even to distinguish between certain proverbs that are from Israelite culture and proverbs from other

prudent ones do not stand trembling in the face of culture. Because of the deep respect for human ability, wisdom opens herself to insight about life wherever it might be found. By observing the whole realm of creation and culture, the wise are able to discover a level of truth and order that equips them to cope with life. Their task was simply this: to discover insights from the world around that better equipped them to function responsibly in the day to day affairs of life and to contribute to the greater good of the community. Once discovered, these principles or insights were filtered through a Yahwistic worldview and incorporated into the value system of Israel. So the sages stayed in constant dialogue with the world around. They fine-tuned their faculties to learn from their environment.

Not only does wisdom actively seek out the insights of other cultures, wisdom also takes advantage of the insights of those in its own community. The sages did not rely exclusively on their own mental resources, but depended on the council of others. A number of proverbs urge the individual to seek out advice from others:

> Where there is no guidance, a nation falls,
>   but in an abundance of counselors there is safety. (11:14)

> Without counsel, plans go wrong,
>   but with many advisers they succeed. (15:22)

> . . . . in abundance of counselors there is victory. (24:6; 20:18)

Wisdom clearly believes that two heads are better than one. Because sages highly regard human ingenuity, they seek out the insights of others, whether in the cultures of foreign peoples or in the counsel of the wise in their own community.

Finally, the sages capitalize on the resources within themselves: their own ability to observe, to think, and to plan. One resource the sage used for ordering life was learning from experience and creation. One observes creation and the world around and extracts the truths that God has placed there (cf. Prov. 3:19-20; 8:22-31). The sapient understands the importance of observing the world from the least significant creature (the ant; 6:6-11) to the most significant (the lion; 30:29-31). The wise become participant observers. But they do not simply observe. They filter and rethink observations, conserving and preserving them.[25]

Based upon all the resources available to them, the judicious ones then use their minds to think, discern, set goals, and make decisions; planning

---

ancient Near Eastern cultures.

25. The book of Ecclesiastes is a good example of this.

is their forte. The proverbs in 16:1–9 contain a number of allusions to this human activity. Humans plan (v. 1), they work (v. 3), they use their minds (v. 9).[26] The gift of wisdom is the competency to devise and carry out plans.

In Proverbs, humans live life with purpose and forethought. Only the most foolish give little consideration to tomorrow.[27] Even the ant knows to store up food during the summer for future use (Prov. 6:6–8).[28] Proverbs advises: "The plans of the diligent lead surely to abundance, but everyone who is hasty comes only to want" (21:5). Humans work and plan and utilize their skills in order to live productive lives. As Brueggemann has observed, in the eyes of God, humanity "is the trusted creature."[29]

The sage's ability to plan brings a sense of order to her life. In fact, one of the goals of Wisdom was to enable the wise person to live by the order of the universe. The sages exerted much energy in discovering this physical and moral order. They believed that the world was created in an orderly fashion.[30] Living in harmony with the order of the universe brings longevity of life, wealth, and fortune. When an individual integrates daily life into the order of creation, success results. Neglecting order brings failure. The sage, however, has sometimes been accused of having too mechanical a view of such order, namely, that the wise believe in a world that is automatically programmed to pay the pious and punish the perverse. Such a view perceives the world as operating on a rigid system of rewards and punishments.

Now it is true that many of the proverbs appear to reflect this worldview. The classic example is Proverbs 26:27: "Whoever digs a pit will fall into it, and a stone will come back on the one who starts it rolling." In addition, as has already been observed, a good number of the proverbs in chapters 10–15 reflect an act-consequence mindset. Still, while it is true that the sages developed plans and strategies by which to live, they did not believe in a created order that operated mechanically. The sages do attempt to establish order to life. They have an interest in discovering certain predictable patterns of experiences. Even given this interest, the order which they discover underlying the experiences of life are not fate producing. They did not see

26. In verse 1 the Hebrew term is "arrangement" (מַעֲרָךְ). In verses 3 and 9 it is "think" (מַחֲשָׁבָה).

27. Proverbs 24:27 counsels a young man to make sure he has the resources available before building a house or establishing a home. He must develop the ability to set priorities.

28. There is similar advice given in 27:23–27. Know the condition of your flocks so that you can prepare for the lean times when they come.

29. Brueggemann, *In Man We Trust*, 24.

30. The Egyptian sages referred to this concept as *ma'at*. *Ma'at* has to do with justice, truth, order, etc.

themselves as the captain in creating their own destiny. The sage does not wrestle with the concept of a rigid order as much as with the person of God.[31] A dialectic exists between the predictable order of creation and the free work of God. Wisdom sought not to master life but to navigate it. The sages guided themselves and others through the experiences of life seeking not to dominate but to assume responsibility.

THE LIMITS OF WISDOM

Individuals who use all the resources at their disposal, who learn from the best that culture has to offer, who are keen observers, who use their minds to think and plan, and who handle these resources responsibly achieve success. Thus humans come to have tremendous confidence in what they can accomplish. What is there that humans cannot achieve? We begin to feel like the people of Babel: together we can accomplish anything to which we set our minds. The sky is the limit.

Within such an attitude lie the seeds of destruction. Humans become so confident in their own abilities that they all but forget the need for God in their lives. Skillful planning and creative use of resources has led individuals to feel self-sufficient. We are in control. We order our own lives. We are the master of our own fate. Arrogance dominates the human realm.

The Yahweh proverbs in 15:33–16:9 speak to this state of affairs. Total confidence in human abilities leads to what this text considers as the most heinous of all sins: pride. Pride is a refusal to admit that humans are not in control of the universe and of their own actions. Chapter 16:2 uses the key phrase: "All one's ways may be pure in one's own eyes . . . ." The phrase "pure in one's own eyes" characterizes hubris.[32] The phrase portrays individuals who perceive no authority or power beyond themselves. They do not need the counsel or advice of others. They trust "in their own wits" (28:26). Pride creates chaos, upsetting the moral order of the community.

In Proverbs and specifically in 15:33–16:9, pride is the fundamental sin of humanity. According to verse 5, the Lord abhors pride: "All those who are arrogant are an abomination to the Lord; be assured, they will not go unpunished."[33] Pride stems from losing sight of the Creator of the universe.

---

31. Crenshaw, "Murphy's Axiom."

32. This phrase, with slight variation, is used repeatedly through Proverbs to describe human pride: 3:7; 12:15; 16:2; 21:2; 26:5,12,16; 28:11; 30:12.

33. The word abomination (תּוֹעֵבָה) is used most frequently in Ezekiel (43 times), Proverbs (22 times) and Deuteronomy (17 times). In Proverbs it is used in regard to God's response to moral and ethical failure. The phrase in the second line of this

Wisdom offers stern warnings about the destructive forces of arrogance.[34] Such a force anesthetizes the need for God, giving humans the erroneous sense of invincibility.

The truly wise, however, know the limits of what humans can accomplish.[35] From the earliest of times, the sages acknowledged the subversive element to human plans.[36] Proverbs 16:1–9 expresses this element in sayings known as "limit proverbs":

> The plans of the mind belong to mortals,
>   but the answer of the tongue is from the Lord.
> All one's ways may be pure in one's own eyes,
>   but the Lord weighs the spirit.
> Commit your work to the Lord,
>   and your plans will be established.
> The human mind plans the way,
>   but the Lord directs the steps. (16:1–3, 9)

Limit proverbs pepper the various collections acknowledging the subversive activity of Yahweh in the midst of human affairs. Limit proverbs concede the limitations of wisdom and the sovereignty of Yahweh: "No wisdom, no understanding, no counsel, can avail against the Lord" (21:30).[37] The sages recognize the limits of what even the wisest person can accomplish. For example, in the numerical saying of 30:18–19, the sage stands amazed at certain phenomena in creation: the way of an eagle, a snake, a ship, and a man with a woman. All of these are a wonder to the sage who

---

proverb, translated "be assured," is a Hebrew idiom literally meaning "hand to hand" (cf. 11:21). This probably refers to some practice of clapping the hands or extending the hand to assure that what is promised will be completed. One Jewish scholar surmises that since the sin of pride is so heinous God does not leave the punishment to the natural course of events but becomes directly involved in transmitting the penalty. See Malbim, *Malbim on Mishley*, 169. Ronald Clements makes the following observation: When the sages could not appeal to specific punishment that would naturally follow irresponsible actions, to speak of something as "an abomination to the LORD" was a powerful reproof for engaging in wrong activity. See Clements, "The Concept of Abomination in the Book of Proverbs."

34. The most familiar proverb in this regard is 16:18: "Pride goes before destruction, and a haughty spirit before a fall."

35. Gerhard von Rad observes that truly wise people do not consider themselves wise (Prov. 26:12; 28:11; 28:26; 3:5, 7). *Wisdom In Israel*, 101–2.

36. This subversive impulse to wisdom was later brought to the fore by Job and Qoheleth. They are sometimes referred to as "wisdom in revolt." See Scott, *The Way of Wisdom in the Old Testament*.

37. Most of the proverbs in 16:1–9 are limit proverbs. Other limit proverbs include: 16:25, 33; 19:21; 20:24; 21:1, 31.

does not understand how they do what they do. The eagle appears to float through the sky with no physical support; the snake moves across a rock without legs; the ship sails across the sea without any visible propulsion. And the most mysterious phenomenon is the actions of a man toward a woman. Their behavior defies comprehension.

The limit proverbs act as constant reminders that the best laid plans humans can devise still remain under the mercy of a generous but inscrutable God. That is why the wise counsel: "Do not boast about tomorrow, for you do not know what a day may bring forth" (27:1). In spite of what we might think or desire, humans are not ultimately in control. No degree of mastery of the order of creation or the use of the principles of wisdom can assure absolute certainty. Wisdom seeks to manage life's messes, not to master them.

YAHWEH AS SOVEREIGN LORD

The proverbs in 16:1–9 present a comprehensive picture of Yahweh in total control of human affairs. Verse 1 sets the tone: regardless of the plans humans make or the timelines that cultures establish, it is God who determines the final outcome. Verses 1–3 offer a series of vignettes on the establishment of God's will in human life. God's will takes precedence over all human initiative. Then a slight shift in focus occurs in verses 5–8. Here the justice of God prevails over human evil. The Lord upholds the moral order. Verse 4 serves as a transition between these two units.[38] The first line (4a) looks back at the previous subsection summarizing God's sovereign control: "The Lord has made everything for its purpose." The second line (4b) looks forward to the subsequent subsection anticipating God's justice regarding the wicked: "even the wicked for the day of trouble." Finally, verse 9 comes full circle to the original statement made in verse 1: God is ultimately in control.

Verses 1–3 introduce the tension that exists between the human and the divine.

> The plans of the mind belong to mortals,
>   but the answer of the tongue is from the Lord.
> All one's ways may be pure in one's own eyes,
>   but the Lord weighs the spirit.
> Commit your work to the Lord,
>   and your plans will be established.

---

38. Waltke, "The Dance between God and Humanity," 91. Waltke says that verse 4 uses the technique known as "janus" in which it serves the double purpose of both looking back and looking forward.

With the first proverb two possible interpretations exist. On the one hand, the meaning might be that humans have the capacity and the freedom to do their own planning. Then God gives the gift of expression. The knack of giving the right answer, of finding the apt word for the occasion is a gift from God.[39] On the other hand, the second line of the proverb may be a figure of speech for the idea that God makes the final decision. That is to say, humans make their plans but God has the final say.

Eugene Peterson's paraphrase in *The Message* captures the essence: "Mortals make elaborate plans, but God has the last word." This interpretation is more in keeping with the proverb in verse 3 and with the inclusion formed by verse 9. It is thus the better of the two possibilities. In other words, "Man proposes but God disposes." This means that God can and sometimes does foil individual plans. It reminds one of the old saw that exclaims, "There's many a slip 'twixt the cup and the lip." In other words, often between the time we decide to do something and the time we attempt to accomplish it, things go awry. Human schemes frequently verify Murphy's Law: "Whatever can go wrong, will." Though God does not operate under Murphy's Law, God does often impede human schemes. The proverb not only means that God frequently foils plans, it also implies that, through human plans, God can accomplish more than anyone thought possible: "Man's extremity is God's opportunity."

Still another angle on the interaction between God and humans comes in the proverb in verse 3. God ordains only those human proposals that serve God's will: "Commit your work to the Lord, and your plans will be established" (v. 3). Here the term "work" is inclusive of all that goes into accomplishing a goal. To "commit"[40] one's work to the Lord means to turn one's work over to God. The term expresses submission to God's will, admonishing one to a posture of humility (cf. 15:33). The psalmist declares the same thought with the proclamation, "unless the Lord builds the house, those who build it labor in vain" (Ps. 127:1). Verse 3 is not a formula for unfailing success, merely a reminder that success does not ultimately lie in human hands. Considering the thrust of 16:1-9, the point of verse 3 is that humans cannot ultimately control their own affairs; no one can guarantee success. Success comes as a gift from God.

---

39. Whybray, *Proverbs*, 240. This is an important theme in the book of Proverbs. See also Waltke, "The Dance Between God and Humanity," 96.

40. This is the Hebrew term גֹּל which means "to roll." Literally the first line reads "roll on Yahweh your deeds." 1 Peter 5:7 may be similar in thought: cast all your cares on him.

Verses 1–3 picture humans, not God, as taking the initiative. The sages concern themselves with the pragmatics of daily life.[41] So they begin with human responsibility. As humans implement their plans, the Lord responds. The Lord evaluates motives. God "weighs the spirit" (v. 2b), and God's evaluations prevail. Human appraisal remains biased (v. 2a). God establishes only those plans that contribute to the Lord's overall purpose (v. 3). God incorporates those activities into redemptive history.

One of the most difficult proverbs to interpret in this text is verse 4: "The Lord has made everything for its purpose, even the wicked for the day of trouble." On first reading, the proverb appears to communicate a deterministic perspective. God predestines certain people for punishment and, by implication, others for blessing. Such a view completely removes human freedom and relegates the outcome of one's life to the luck of the draw in God's hands.

That perspective, however, misconstrues the proverb's message; the saying certainly does not suggest that God creates certain ones for wickedness. That viewpoint goes against the grain of wisdom thought with its emphasis on individuals making decisions for themselves. Once again, wisdom holds to a high view of humans, their abilities and responsibilities. Rather the term in verse 4 appropriately translated "purpose,"[42] carries the idea that God created everything for a definite goal or end. In other words, God ensures that the ways of the evil will not prevail because God continues to take an active role in the world. Yahweh reserves "the day of trouble," a day of retribution and accountability, for those who refuse to make the right choices. All created things answer to the Lord, including the wicked.

Verse 5 offers further commentary on the last line of verse 4, reassuring God's people that the punishment of the arrogant is certain: "All those who are arrogant are an abomination to the Lord; be assured, they will not go unpunished." At the same time verse 6 affirms that the humble can atone for their iniquity through "loyalty and faithfulness." Evil is avoided by "fear of the Lord."[43] Verse 8 though puts a qualifier on the judgment of God in the here and now. As a better-than proverb, verse 8 implies that God's judgment does not always come immediately: "Better is a little with righteousness than large income with injustice." Sometimes the righteous possess little while unjust activities of the wicked go unchecked. Faithfulness and integrity are not always rewarded in visible ways.

41. The mighty acts of God recorded in the Law and the Prophets remain in the background in the wisdom material.

42. Hebrew מַעֲנֶה, literally "answer, response."

43. Seventeen times the phrase "fear of the Lord" appears in Proverbs: 1:7; 1:29; 2:5; 3:7; 8:13; 9:10; 10:27; 14:2; 14:26; 15:16; 15:33; 16:6; 19:23; 22:4; 23:17; 24:21; 31:30.

The text comes full circle with verse 9, which appropriately summarizes the thought of the passage: "The human mind plans the way, but the Lord directs the steps." Humans think; God directs. Even when plans are meant to do harm, God uses them to bring about good.

The Joseph story in Genesis 37–50 acts as a narrative elaboration of Proverbs 16:1–9. God used the deceptive schemes of Joseph's brothers to bring about a productive result. The sons of Jacob sell their younger brother, Joseph, into Egyptian bondage, intending to eliminate Joseph. But "the best laid plans of mice and men go awry." In their evil conspiracy, God had the final word. After Joseph became second in command over all of Egypt and helped save his family and the whole community from famine, he announced to his brothers:

So it was not you who sent me here, but God; he has made me a father to Pharaoh, and lord of all his house and ruler over all the land of Egypt . . . (Gen. 45:8)

> . . . . Then his brothers also wept, fell down before him, and said, "We are here as your slaves." But Joseph said to them, "Do not be afraid! Am I in the place of God? Even though you intended to do harm to me, God intended it for good, in order to preserve a numerous people, as he is doing today. So have no fear; I myself will provide for you and your little ones." In this way he reassured them, speaking kindly to them. (Gen. 50: 18–21)

God shapes even corrupt plans to fit into God's purposes, including those with the greatest political power. That may be one of the reasons for placing the royal proverbs in 16:10–15 subsequent to the Yahweh proverbs. Kings may have authority, but only as they acknowledge their subordinate status to God and rule in righteousness (16:12–13).

The God of the sages is sovereign Lord. Yahweh's sovereignty, however, does not annul the thoughts and plans of humans. The Lord's supremacy does not create despair about using thought and reason to plan for the future but instead produces hope. God's gracious sovereignty enables those who fear the Lord to face the uncertainties of life with confidence knowing that God's purposes will be done.

Even the greatest care with the most comprehensive plans is never enough to master the risks and problems that face each individual. Therefore, a proper attitude of humility becomes necessary. As confident as the sages are in human ability, ultimately they admonish: "Trust in the Lord with all your heart, and do not rely on your own understanding. In all your ways acknowledge him and he will make straight your paths" (3:5–6).

THE REALM OF GOD'S CONTROL

But exactly how is it that this sovereign Lord works in the lives of people? From the post-exilic period forward, the sages apparently wrestled with this question.[44] All through the Old Testament, Israel frequently witnessed God at work through the mighty acts. The Lord hears Israel's cry and delivers Israel from Egyptian bondage with a mighty hand and an outstretched arm. The Lord dries up the waters of the Red Sea and the Jordan. The Lord leads Israel to conquest over the land of Canaan. The Lord God is the God of history who orchestrated these monumental saving acts, who engaged in miraculous intervention.

Now, however, during the post-exilic period, no king or temple or animal sacrifices exist. Israel no longer possesses land; she is dispersed abroad. So where is God? When it comes to the day-to-day affairs of life during the post-exilic period, the Israelites were left to their own devices; they must get along as best they can. Israel sometimes limited God's work to the mighty acts, the spectacular, or the miraculous.

Such a view persists today. God's people perpetuate the belief that, in the course of the day's events, they basically control the outcome. Only when things get tough does anyone call on God. We foster a God-of-the-gaps mentality: God takes over when we can no longer carry the load. Proverbs offers a corrective to that mind set. The book makes few if any references to the mighty acts of God, to the miraculous, to the major religious institutions of Israel, whether it is the temple, the priest, or the sacrificial system. So then, where is God? God seems almost totally absent, hidden from the human eye.

Yet what seems to be is not the reality. For the sage, God is present even in the littlest details of life. The Lord is involved in the interactions that take place between people. God works through both the good and the bad experiences. Yahweh employs human language to carry out God's purposes. Yahweh uses material wealth and even poverty in the service of maturing people. The Lord is there in the day-to-day routine of life. The collected sayings in chapters 10–22 teach that every moment matters, every activity, regardless of how monotonous, is an opportunity to express wise living. Every decision made concerns God.

God works in the thoughts and plans of humans. In the very realm where individuals believe they exercise the most control, the mind, God establishes a presence. While remaining a mystery, without impeding human freedom God works through the thought processes to bring about God's

---

44. See Bland, "God's Activity as Reflected in the Books of Ruth and Esther."

will. Such an arena of the Lord's activity appears insignificant in the grand scheme of things. But if the search for wisdom is partially an activity of the mind, then it is in the minds of human beings that God is most directly active. Through human thought, which fears the Lord, the individual is brought into an encounter with the divine.

The proverb itself witnesses to God's involvement in the mundane decisions of life. As mentioned earlier, von Rad suggested that proverbs were more important for Israel in making daily decisions than were the Ten Commandments.[45] Israel's fundamental law code highlighted the major ethical obligations that the people must fulfill: do not kill, do not steal, do not commit adultery, etc. Proverbs, in contrast, feature the little, apparently insignificant, decisions that people make day in and day out. So for the book of Proverbs, God is involved in the smallest affairs of life, even in the conversations we enter into with others. Exactly how God does this the sage does not say. The text in 15:33–16:9 does not say.[46] Rather, it assumes that divine sovereignty and human activity exist together in inexplicable ways.

Because God's work includes the whole arena of life, the wise person attends to the little things. The wise woman or man learns from experience, from conversations, from other cultures, and from observing life. The wise actively pursue and develop relationships, they lend a hand to the poor and the oppressed, and they teach others how to live responsibly. In engaging in these activities, they participate in the work of God.

Humans naturally gravitate to the big things in life, to the spectacular, the movers and shakers, and to the sensational as places where God's presence is displayed. Yes, God works in these major events, but the Lord is also actively present in the minor experiences. God is a part of the "coincidences" of life, or what many would label as "luck." God actively engages in the usual, routine, ordinary, modest, and mundane affairs of daily existence. The sage is someone who pays attention to the little things and discovers that the little things are not so little. In the ordinary, God works out God's will for the world. It is as I somewhere read Helen Keller to say, "I long to accomplish a great and noble task, but it is my chief duty to accomplish humble tasks as though they were great and noble."

THE GOAL OF YAHWEH'S WILL

Proverbs 15:33—16:9 begins with an introduction in 15:31–33 to listen to wholesome admonition:

45. von Rad, *Wisdom in Israel*, 26.
46. Neither, for that matter, does any other passage of Scripture!

> The ear that heeds wholesome admonition[47]
>   will lodge among the wise.
> Those who ignore instruction[48] despise themselves,
>   but those who heed admonition gain understanding.
> The fear of the Lord is instruction in wisdom,
>   and humility goes before honor.

This introduction is quite similar to the formulaic sayings that appear in the first nine chapters of Proverbs: "My children listen to your parents' instruction." This text envisions the instruction the sage gives to the youth. It uses the familiar sapiential language of "admonition" or "reproof" (vv. 31, 32). This is not just any kind of reproof; this is wholesome, life-giving instruction (v. 31). Yet the question lingers, How teachable are the youth? Youth are exhorted to heed admonition and discipline. In Proverbs, the instruction a parent offers to a youth parallels Yahweh's admonition to the Lord's children: "My child, do not despise the Lord's discipline or be weary of his reproof, for the Lord reproves the one he loves, as a father the son in whom he delights" (3:11–12).

What is the goal of the Lord's instruction? God purposes are primarily directed toward developing character in people. Character development takes place primarily in the dynamic interaction between human freedom and divine will. God's sovereignty does not cancel out human freedom. Rather it highlights the moral qualities humans choose to nurture within themselves. This is the implication behind verse 4: "The Lord has made everything for its purpose. . . ." God does not predetermine the destiny of anyone, but through divine sovereignty, God brings out the qualities a human chooses to develop, fitting them into the divine scheme. We become what God continues to make us.

God desires to bring out the best in human beings. While the saying is true that God accepts us as we are, God is not willing to leave us as we are. When God encounters individuals through the day-to-day decisions they make, the Lord wills that out of those daily struggles come responsible character that contributes to the wellness of the community and to the purposes of God.

Proverbs 15:33–16:9 places human plans and divine will in dynamic tension. What ties the human (those who fear the Lord) and divine perspectives together in the book of Proverbs is that they serve a common goal.

---

47. The phrase for "wholesome admonition" is תּוֹכַחַת חַיִּים; literally "admonition of life." The word admonition or reproof (תּוֹכַחַת) appears here and in verse 32.

48. מוּסָר (discipline/instruction) appears here and in verse 33.

That goal is the formation of character. Both God and the sages collaborate together in the task of training youth for responsible life in the community.

The result is that the divine and human vistas are no longer perceived as conflicting poles. The goal of shaping character becomes the synthesizing force that engages the two wills. This also explains why the anthropological perspective captures center stage in the book. The sages expressed deep concern over the moral formation of individuals for the sake of maintaining order in the larger community. The question of the sage, however, is not exclusively, "How do I live in God's world?" Rather the question is, "How do I, as a member of the faith community, live in the world?" The anthropological perspective is plainly theocentric.[49]

CONCLUSION

The sages could never fathom a worldview governed by luck. Indeed the most "secular" of their proverbs was under girded with a firm belief in the divine presence. In addition, the wise do not wrestle as we do with the tension between human freedom and divine sovereignty.[50] They regard the anthropocentric and the theocentric as complementary and not mutually exclusive. The anthropocentric proverbs always stand in complementary relationship with the theocentric view. Ultimately, the sages never explain their simultaneous existence. They live with the paradox. Israelite wisdom was an open system, flexible, and adaptable. The worldview of the sages was not built on a concept of an impersonal order, or on actions with automatic built-in consequences but on the active participation of the Lord in the affairs of people in conjunction with their own responsible behavior. The sovereign God operates in close relationship with the order of creation.

How does God work in the world? Ultimately the Lord's actions defy human understanding (16:1, 9). The sages live with openness to the mystery of God. The Lord, in incomprehensible ways, works through the minds of the people. God's sovereignty remains indisputable. God enters into relationship with individuals to work out the divine purposes. Yahweh relates to people like parents to their children. Responsible parents, as they lead and nurture, ultimately allow their children freedom to choose.

Cynthia Rigby uses the image of a woman carrying a baby in her womb to describe the interaction between sovereign God and human will.[51] The child is as distinct from the woman as the world is from God. Yet because

---

49. Dianne Bergant, *What Are They Saying about Wisdom Literature?*, 39.
50. von Rad, *Wisdom in Israel*, 98.
51. Rigby, "Free to Be Human."

God encompasses the world, God and the world exist in mutual relationship. The baby is dependent on the mother for its source of life and nutrients, and the kicks and movements of the baby affect the mother. Just as both woman and child affect one another, so it is in the relationship between God and the world. There is a dynamic in the human/divine relationship. God is one who listens, changes plans, and grieves when people rebel, all the while remaining sovereign. In the divine world, even though human minds choose their own path, the final word rests with the Lord. Those individuals who humbly interact with the divine will produce communities of strong moral character accomplishing the purposes of God.

The God who works in the daily routine of life does so in the context of community. This community is made up not only of the family, as central as family is in the education process, but also of the whole faith community. Proverbs concludes with a portrait of what wisdom looks like within the context of community (31:10–31). The sage uses the "wife of noble character" (NIV) to personify the best of wisdom's virtues. She represents the mature person who is intimately involved in the life of family, neighbors, the larger community, and in relationship with Yahweh.

In light of this, it is fitting to conclude by turning once again to the context in which the development of character is nurtured—in community. The faith community shoulders responsibility for investing in the moral education of its members. The task is formidable, yet through the collaborative effort of parents, church and synagogue, and Yahweh, those open to instruction, like the woman of noble character, will personify the best of wisdom's virtues.

Chapter Nine

Community and Character Formation

(Proverbs 22:6; 31:10–31)

The most climbed mountain in the Western Hemisphere is Oregon's Mount Hood, located about forty miles east of Portland. When my family and I lived in Portland from 1980 to 1993, we enjoyed the beauty of seeing that grand mountain from our home.[1] On May 12, 1986, thirteen high school students from a small private school in Portland set out to climb the beautiful 11,200-foot mountain. It was an annual rite-of-passage for those who had completed their sophomore year. The traditional way to climb Mount Hood is to begin at 2:00 am, reach the summit to see the sunrise, and then descend back to the base camp by noon. The teenagers approached the climb with little thought, little sleep the night before, and no preparation. They wore casual dress and shoes and light coats. They took along no special climbing gear. As they trekked along, a sudden change of weather rolled in, not at all uncommon for that time of year. They found themselves trapped in a snowstorm, a whiteout. The climbers dug a snow cave four feet by six feet for protection. Eleven of the thirteen crammed into the cave. Four days later help finally arrived. But it was too late for most of the hikers whose bodies were so cold that intravenous lines could not even

---

1. I was preaching for the Eastside Church of Christ during this time. Ironically, the first Sunday I preached at Eastside was May 18, 1980, the very day that Mount St. Helens first erupted!

pierce their frozen skin. Rescuers saw bodies stacked in the snow cave like cords of wood. Nine died only four survived.[2]

The group was young, inexperienced, and ill prepared for the climb. Yet it is not just the inexperienced who are vulnerable to this mountain's treachery. Even the most experienced climbers have lost their lives to its unpredictable weather patterns, its hidden crevasses, avalanches, and unexpected drop offs. During a December weekend in 2009, three well-trained and well-equipped climbers were killed as they attempted to scale its summit. What makes experienced climbers vulnerable is that they tend to be overly confident in their skills, equipment, and physical abilities. While the downfall of inexperienced hikers is their naïveté, the downfall of experienced climbers is their pride. Both are vulnerable.

The way climbers approach Mount Hood serves as analogy for the way people often face life's challenges. Life is an exciting journey, an adventure with unknown dangers lurking ahead. For those venturing into adulthood, it is exciting and can appear deceptively easy to manage. But life often throws unexpected twists and turns along the way. While it presents wonderful opportunities and joys, hidden perils and difficult decisions abound. In different ways both the novice and the experienced must remain constantly vigilant.[3] Our world does not adequately prepare individuals for this journey, regardless of the level of experience. James Davison Hunter observes that the "*sanctions* through which morality is validated" no longer resides in the community but is left "to the sovereign choices of the autonomous individual."[4] Managing life's journey successfully demands the support, accountability, and wisdom of a faith community.

It is at this point that Proverbs speaks a profound word. Wisdom capably negotiates the complexities of life. Though the education process in Proverbs showcases youth, the process invites all with open minds, young and old alike, to enter the journey: "Give instruction to the wise and they will become wiser still; teach the righteous and they will gain in learning" (9:9). The teachers use the young adult male as an example for how they engage in the process of character formation, but the instructions of Proverbs apply to all ages and both genders. The sages hold to the conviction that the process must begin in youth, even though those older in years can still learn. Begin at the time when youth prepare for the transition into adulthood, when they are naïve and vulnerable and when their minds are most pliable.

2. See Hallman "Mount Hood's Deadly Deceit: A Remembrance," written on the tenth anniversary of the tragedy.

3. I've referred to this story in an earlier work. See Bland and Fleer, *Preaching Character*, 15–16.

4. Hunter, *The Death of Character*, 146.

During this formative stage, youth face formidable decisions, decisions that affect the direction they take for the rest of their lives.

All through this volume I have highlighted the essential roll the community of faith plays in the process of character formation. In this chapter I want to zero in more closely on this dimension. Wisdom's goal was to assimilate a community into the worldview of Yahweh, to develop a way of life that demonstrated the fear of the Lord. Dialoguing constructively with others in community provided a vital dimension of the formation of character. Such dialogue created a healthy context for reproof, exhortation, and instruction to occur. The interaction process enabled individuals to live responsibly in relationship to their spouse, family, friends, and neighbors. The book of Proverbs witnesses to the effort a whole community takes to instruct a younger generation. The development of relationships, the use of material possessions, engaging in constructive conflict, and the proper use of language are among the resources wisdom relies on for achieving the goal of honing the rough edges of character that lead individuals to fear the Lord.

PROVERBS 22:6 AND COMMUNITY INVOLVEMENT

One proverb worthy of exploring its perspective on the role of collaboration in the educational process is one of the better known. Proverbs 22:6 encapsulates the heavy responsibility placed upon parents, teachers, and community to shape youthful minds:

> Train children in the right way,
>   and when old, they will not stray.

The proverb does not speak per se to the role the community plays in the education process. But in the context of the book of Proverbs, the training of children becomes the responsibility not only of the parents but also the friend or neighbor (25:11–12; 27:6,14, 17) and the wise (1:20–33; 9:9; 15:31–33; 21:11). I will interpret and explore Proverbs 22:6 in the context of the responsibility of the community. Books about raising children frequently quote this proverb. But almost as often as it is quoted, it is misunderstood.[5] Nevertheless, when properly apprehended, the proverb succinctly summarizes the path the community must travel to guide students.

---

5. Rottman, "Introduction."

Training Children

Two words in the first line have been the source of debate: "train" and "children." The first word "train" or "train up" is from the Hebrew term *hanak* (חָנַךְ). Other parts of the Old Testament use the term to refer to the act of dedicating some building or place (e.g., Deut. 20:5; 1 Kgs. 8:63). The Jewish feast of Hanukkah means Feast of Dedication. Ted Hildebrandt argues that the word in Proverbs 22:6 does not mean "to instruct" or "to train" as translators traditionally assume. Rather it means to "dedicate" or inaugurate a young person into the office of life for which he is suited. This is an act of affirmation, a celebration, a dedication ceremony.[6]

Major problems accompany this interpretation. For one, such a dedication ceremony for youth does not seem to be well documented in Israelite culture.[7] That the Jewish practice of Bar Mitzvah could be the ceremony to which Proverbs 22:6 refers seems unlikely. The youth Hildebrandt correctly envisions in Proverbs are in their late teens. Additionally, this interpretation omits the context of Proverbs itself. Nothing in the book indicates that the term *hanak* should be interpreted "to dedicate." For a reader to accept Hildebrandt's view, one must go to other Old Testament texts that use this term (Deut. 20:5; 1 Kings 8:63; 2 Chron. 7:5). In these places, the verb does mean to dedicate or initiate. But is that the determinative meaning of *hanak* for Proverbs?

In the context of the book, *hanak* means the continual training of youth in the proper way of life.[8] When one interprets *hanak* as "to train" or "to instruct," the principle of 22:6 conforms precisely to the instructions of chapters 1–9: namely 2:1–5; 4:10; and 4:20–22. These chapters offer the

---

6. Hildebrandt, "Proverbs 22:6a: Train Up a Child?" Randy Jaeggli takes a similar position. He argues from the use of the word in Genesis 14:14 where Abraham relies on "already initiated" or trained servants to rescue Lot. Thus in Proverbs 22:6 the word refers to initiating or inaugurating an already trained youth into a particular moral lifestyle. So the verse is not about training a youth but initiating him or her into the lifestyle for which they have been trained. Thus he translates the verse as follows, "Initiate the young adult into the lifestyle for which he has been prepared; Even when he grows old he will not turn aside from it" (46). The application of this verse is that parents should take seriously the transition points in a young adult's life, such as high school and college graduations, weddings, and ordinations of young adults into ministry. Parents should see these occasions as opportunities to impress upon their minds the joy of the event as well as the serious responsibility upon which they are about to embark. See Randy Jaeggli, "Interpreting Proverbs 22:6." See also Yoder, *Proverbs*, 224.

7. One parallel that I can think of in the New Testament is Paul laying hands on Timothy and exhorting him not to let anyone look down on his youth. The laying on of hands could represent a rite of passage, or an act of dedication.

8. Dommershausen, "חנך," 20.

proper interpretive framework. Such an interpretation also squares with Proverbs 29:17: "Discipline your children, and they will give you rest; they will give delight to your heart."[9]

The second term in verse 6a that gives interpreters problems is *na'ar* (נַעַר) the word the NRSV translates "children." The Old Testament uses the term to refer to a variety of ages.[10] The context of Proverbs, however, requires that *naar* refer to an older youth and not an infant or child.[11] All through Proverbs the sages offer advice to youth making the transition into adulthood.

The Meaning of "In The Right Way"

Besides the two words, "train" and "children," much misunderstanding surrounds the phrase in 22:6a "in the right way" (NRSV) or "according to his ways." Interpreters offer a variety of explanations. For some the phrase pertains to the vocation a youth chooses. "According to his ways" refers to the kind of career to which a youth aspires. In reality, this interpretation imposes more of the anxiety that contemporary youth face than it deals with what a young Israelite faced. Typically, Israelite youth did not wrestle with such a decision because their fathers trained them to carry on the family trade. Young adults had little choice when it came to matters of occupation. Besides the book of Proverbs is primarily concerned with character not vocation.

Another popular interpretation of the phrase refers to the personal aptitude of the youth. This interpretation maintains that the concern of the proverb lies in discovering a youth's individual interests and talents.[12] In what skill does a child or youth excel? Is the child good in sports, in music, in art, in academics? What hobbies does the child like? The adult seeks to

---

9. Cf. also 19:18: "Discipline your children while there is hope; do not set your heart on their destruction."

10 An infant in 1 Samuel 4:21; Joseph at 17 years old in Genesis 37:2; and Joseph at 30 years old in Genesis 41:12, 46. In Genesis 14:24 the *naar* were trained and experienced young men Abraham sent out to rescue Lot.

11. Whereas Hildebrandt is not willing to use the context of Proverbs to establish the meaning of *hanak*, he does use the context of Proverbs to determine the age of the *naar* (13).

12. Chapter 5 in Johnson and Yorkey, *Faithful Parents, Faithful Kids*; Sell, *The House on the Rock*, 156. Ellen Davis argues that the emphasis should be "according to <u>his</u> way." She writes, "Educating each child according to her own way means that we must relax our theories and pay attention to this particular child, adjust our methods to the way in which she may best learn, nurture her particular gifts, respect her interests." *Proverbs, Ecclesiastes, and the Song of Songs*, 120.

identify and channel a child's early bent or natural talent in much the same way as a river flows naturally through mountains and valleys. Why dam up the river and force it to go a different direction? Again this interpretation reflects more on the individualistic quality of contemporary American culture than it does on the ancient culture of corporate Israel. Nothing in the context of Proverbs substantiates this interpretation.

Still a third interpretation, quite similar to the previous one, argues that it deals with accepting the unique personality of each individual child. As Josh McDowell and Dick Day explain, the proverb urges parents to accept their children as they are, constantly reinforce the child's distinctiveness, and "start recognizing the child's individual personality and work with it to teach and nurture."[13] The phrase admonishes parents to assure children that their parents accept them, trust them, and love them no matter what happens.[14] This view is based on a solid theological principle that God remains faithful to his people, regardless of their behavior. In the same way, godly parents must accept and affirm their children as they are. Actually Proverbs spends a lot of time, work, and energy training children not to cater to their natural tendencies of selfishness and desires.[15]

A little different bent on the interpretation that the proverb refers to the distinctiveness of a child is that it has to do with child development. Parents must take responsibility for understanding and responding appropriately to the different moral developmental phases a child goes through before entering the adult world.[16] However appealing that may look, the question remains is this the focus of Proverbs 22:6a? In the context of Proverbs, simply advising parents to accept the personality of their children as they are is rather anemic in the demanding moral context of wisdom's school.

One final view puts a negative slant on the proverb. "According to his way" means according to the selfish inclinations of the child.[17] The proverb states an irony. If we train up children, allowing them to go their own way, leaving them to their own whims, acquiescing to their own desires, they will turn into selfish adults. But is Proverbs 22:6 irony? Michael V. Fox responds to this interpretation by saying that this is not the meaning of "his way"

---

13. McDowell and Day, *How to Be a Hero to Your Kids*, 58.

14. Ibid., 63.

15. Michael V. Fox also rejects this interpretation. *Proverbs 10–31*, 698.

16. For example, see the developmental phases of Lawrence Kohlberg, discussed in chapter 2.

17. This is the interpretation Richard Clifford gives to the phrase. He paraphrases the meaning, "Let a boy do what he wants and he will become a self-willed adult incapable of change!" *Proverbs*, 197.

in other passages.[18] To follow this interpretation through would mean this youth would enter old age as a fool. In Proverbs old age or gray hair is generally reserved for the wise not the fool (20:29). A more fitting interpretation exists for understanding the phrase.

One must interpret the phrase "in the right way," and this proverb, in light of the educational purpose of the book: the moral training of youth. Therefore the whole covenant community, not only parents, takes responsibility for training youth in the way of righteousness, justice, and equity. As youth attain maturity, they will develop the moral instruction given to them in their early years and will persevere "in the right way." Parents and community take responsibility for instructing youth in the elementary principles of right and wrong. Therefore, "when old, they will not stray" (22:6b). Having been given fundamental principles by which to live, as youth mature they build on those principles and persist in being true to what is righteous and fair.

What the Proverb Promises

In quoting this proverb, many quickly point out the exceptions to it. Sometimes they see youth from godly homes rebel against the moral training given to them. Thus many apologetically quote the proverb, hastening to add the qualifier, "But we know there are exceptions." Such a practice destines the proverb for impotence. Through observation and experience, we all know of children, raised in the homes of loving godly parents, who jettison their faith as they enter into adulthood. So how do we explain this proverb in light of our experiences?

Like all proverbs, this one does not make an unconditional promise. If a reader reads only this proverb and assumes it is exhaustive, then the logical conclusion is that youth have no moral responsibility and that guilt for how children ultimately behave is completely on the shoulders of the parents. If that were in fact the case, then the whole of Proverbs ought to address parents. In reality, the responsibility of the individual is taken very seriously in Proverbs, something evidenced by the fact that the majority of the book is addressed to the youth.

Other proverbs in the book qualify the thought of 22:6. All through the hallways of Proverbs, pictures of rebellious youth line the walls. The sages speak of youth who do not listen to parents' instructions. So Proverbs 13:1 observes: "A wise child loves discipline, but a scoffer does not listen to rebuke." The very first proverb of the sentence literature contrasts the wise

---

18. Fox, *Proverbs 10–31*, 698.

and the foolish son: "A wise child makes a glad father, but a foolish child is a mother's grief" (10:1). In addition, God, the perfect parent, had rebellious children (Hos. 11:1–11)—and still does. Individuals often tend to make this proverb say more than it was intended to say. The proverb does not make parents totally responsible for the lifestyle their children choose so that the faith of the child completely depends upon the faith and training of the parent. Children who rebel against godly parental instruction will be held accountable for their own actions.[19] Once again even though Proverbs 22:6 does not speak directly to the responsibility of the community for training children to morally follow the right path, the proverb is embedded in a book that assumes the wise in the community, not just the parents, naturally take responsibility for engaging youth in the education process (1:20–33; 9:1–12).

Proverbs 22:6 in Dialogue with Proverbs 2:1–9

In many ways Proverbs 22:6 should be interpreted in light of what is said about the educational process in Proverbs 2:1–9. The wisdom poem in 2:1–9 describes a collaborative effort at work in the process of instructing youth:

> My child, if you accept my words
>   and treasure up my commandments within you,
> making your ear attentive to wisdom
>   and inclining your heart to understanding;
> if you indeed cry out for insight,
>   and raise your voice for understanding;
> if you seek it like silver,
>   and search for it as for hidden treasures—
> then you will understand the fear of the LORD
>   and find the knowledge of God.
> For the LORD gives wisdom;
>   from his mouth come knowledge and understanding;
> he stores up sound wisdom for the upright;
>   he is a shield to those who walk blamelessly,
> guarding the paths of justice
>   and preserving the way of his faithful ones.
> Then you will understand righteousness and justice
>   and equity, every good path;

---

19. "The person who sins shall die. A child shall not suffer for the iniquity of a parent, nor a parent suffer for the iniquity of a child; the righteousness of the righteous shall be his own, and the wickedness of the wicked shall be his own" (Ezek. 18:20).

The voice heard in this poem is that of the parent or wisdom teacher. The phrase "if you accept my words" implies that the adult teacher initiated the education process (v. 1). The teacher does not leave this process to chance believing that proper training takes place simply through the natural cycles of life (e.g., Kohlberg). Rather the teacher takes deliberate steps to initiate and fulfill the responsibility.

The wisdom teacher, however, is not the only player involved in the task. Verses 3–5 describe the role youth play in the effort. Youth must take responsibility to open their minds and actively seek out instruction. The text describes the intensity of the search. Notice the phrases used: "cry out for insight," "seek it like silver," "search for it as for hidden treasures." This is no casual endeavor; the search is passionate. The youth exerts rigorous effort to acquiring insight.

The educational process involves yet another key player. Verses 6–8 portray God as the one who "gives wisdom" and the one who protects youth from evil men and the evil woman (vv. 12–19). God acts as a "shield."[20] The cumulative image that unfolds in this passage is of a community working toward a common goal. Character is not generated in a vacuum. It flows out of a vision of the nature of God. Character can only develop in the context of a community and in the presence of a goal that is greater than the self. The following is how James Davison Hunter describes the context in which character manifests itself:

> It will be found . . . within families and communities that still, somehow, embody a moral vision. . . . In such settings people will not merely acquire techniques of moral improvement but rather find themselves encompassed within a story that defines their own purposes within a shared destiny, one that points toward aims that are higher and greater than themselves.[21]

Proverbs 2:1–9 draws a picture of such a community. It is a community sustained by the strength and power of the Lord, deliberately at work in training those with open minds to understand wisdom and to acquire "the knowledge of God."

It takes a particular kind of village to raise a youth in this neighborhood; it takes a community of believers. The community engages in a collaborative

---

20. Fox says that the lecture in 2:1–22 describes "a well-thought-out idea of the learning process: (1) Elementary moral conscience (fear of God) motivates one to seek wisdom (1:7). (2) One seeks wisdom diligently (2:1–4 and other exordia). (3) God grants wisdom (2:6). (4) Wisdom brings with it a higher level of moral conscience (2:5a) and knowledge of God (2:5b), so that (5) one can better discern what God wants in all circumstances (2:9; 3:6). " Fox, *Proverbs 1–9*, 133.

21. Hunter, *The Death of Character*, 227.

effort to train up youth in the right way. This educational process, however, is not primarily intellectual. Its goal is not to raise up intellectual giants who possess a wealth of information in their field of expertise. Rather, the educational process is primarily relational. Through entering into relationship with Yahweh, with parents or spouse (5:15–19; 12:4; 31:10–31) and with one's neighbor the open-minded gain wisdom and learn to live responsibly. The process culminates in a people whose lives manifest "righteousness and justice and equity" (2:9) in the presence of the living God. Because Proverbs 2:1–9 speaks of the education process, it serves as a helpful context in which to understand 22:6.

As an admonition, 22:6 does not place blame on a particular adult who conscientiously fulfills his or her responsibility to instruct when youth do not display the desired results. The proverb does not serve as a weapon to accuse or to create unnecessary guilt. At the same time, one must not run to the other extreme when quoting the proverb by hastening to add a disclaimer: "Yes, we know the proverb is true, but we all know there are exceptions." Those who quote the proverb emphasize the disclaimer so frequently that it strips the proverb of its power.

Of course, the proverb does not carry an unconditional promise, but neither does it intend to induce guilt or place blame. Rather, it serves as a word of exhortation to parents, teachers, and the whole faith community. It also serves as a fitting summary of wisdom's goal: train those with open hearts and minds in the right way, and the right way will develop into habits and the habits will develop into character and that character will create one's destiny.

THE COMMUNITY AND THE WISE WOMAN OF PROVERBS 31:10–31

The goal the sages set for both the inexperienced and the experienced is the same: to strive for mature character. After all of the proverbs, all of the advice, and all of the exhortation given in chapters 10–29, in the final chapter the sages hold up the paradigm of what mature character looks like. One would expect after reading through the collection of proverbs from King Solomon's collection (chapts. 10–22) and then Hezekiah's collection (25–29) and the words of King Lemuel (31:1–9) that the ultimate paradigm of wisdom would be a king or a well-known sage. Surprisingly whom they present is an ordinary person (31:10–31)! They put forward an unknown woman of wisdom.

This picture of the wise woman at the end of chapter 31 is often misunderstood. For one, some conclude that this is an idealized description. No person could ever expect to come close to doing all the things she does.[22] The description, therefore, is unrealistic. That view, however, is myopic because it does not consider the agrarian environment in which she lives.[23] Keep in mind this is a picture of a woman who lives and works on a farm! Therefore it is not at all an unreasonable portrayal of the tasks she does. Even women who work on farms today take on similar kinds of rigorous duties. In addition what she does is not all in a day's work. What is portrayed is a lifetime of discipline, instruction, hard work, and fearing God that is condensed into a single poem.

For another, some do not like this poem because it depicts the woman in a subservient role to her husband. She does all the hard work while her husband sits in the gate with the other city elders making the decisions. However, this woman by choice lives to serve and empower others. She lives to serve her husband, her household, her neighbors, and her community. Because this wise woman is identified as the model for others to emulate, the husband remains in the background. Other passages of Scripture describe the man's responsibility to serve others (Prov. 24:27). A fundamental quality of all Christians is that God calls males and females alike to serve others. Proverbs 31 contains a description of a wise woman who disadvantages herself for the sake of advantaging others. That is the definition of a righteous person.

A God-centered community of which she is a part shapes this wise woman. She is intimately involved in the life of the community, is accountable to the community, upholds community standards, and serves the community. As a result she has spent her lifetime pursuing wisdom and developing the qualities of trust (v. 11), service (v. 15), prudence (v. 16), discipline (v. 17), generosity (v. 20), courage (vv. 21, 25), hard work (v. 27), and most importantly the fear of the Lord (v. 30). The community has been instrumental in forming her character. At the beginning of the book the sages described how a different kind of community shaped the character of the members of a gang (1:8–19). That all-too-common type of community is cliquish and sectarian. No individual member possesses a unique identity. All must conform to rigid standards. As a result, the individual is completely absorbed into the persona of the gang no longer able to think or choose for herself.

22. Yoder says this woman "embodies not *one* woman but the desired aspects of many...." She is a "superwoman." *Proverbs*, 299.

23. For an excellent treatment of this poem, see Davis, *Scripture, Culture, and Agriculture*, 147–54.

In contrast, the God-centered community supports its members but at the same time it enables each member, like the woman of wisdom, to maintain her own identity. The community supports the individual and the individual serves the greater good of the community. Wisdom engenders character that is both shaped by and shapes community.

CONCLUSION

The sage wants students to know that as they begin to seek wisdom, they will find the pursuit wearisome and at times discouraging (2:1–5). The desire for wisdom is not a natural desire; one must acquire a taste for it. The way one acquires such a taste is to work through the initial struggles and tedium while maintaining openness and patience in the process. The process of acquiring wisdom is compared to miners digging for precious metal (2:4). True, the task is arduous. It involves diligence and commitment but what one pursues is of extraordinary value.

The instruction poem of 2:1–9 (as well as others, e.g. 4:1–9 and 4:10–19) focuses not on the content of wisdom but on the attitude toward seeking it. To gain wisdom is not only to gain insight into life. Wisdom is also an attitude, a posture; it is the desire to pursue what is right which one must cultivate. What the sages concern themselves with early on in the book of Proverbs is not the transfer of information from the wise to the naïve, nor the acquisition of a body of skills. Rather they are about developing a kind of attitude that passionately drives a person to want to continue to learn and grow. This is the task for the contemporary sage as well. It is to instill within the hearts and minds of Christians an unquenchable thirst for wisdom, righteousness, justice, and equity (2:9).

Again wisdom is not primarily focused on particular decisions made or isolated acts of speech and behavior but on the embodiment of character. Proverbs is not so much a "How To" manual as it is a "How To Be" resource. So the most important question that faith communities must ask themselves is not what are we doing but who are we becoming. My grandmother quoted the following nursery rhyme to me when I was a youth:

> Rich man, poor man, beggar man, thief
> Doctor, lawyer, Indian chief

One of the traditions in saying the rhyme was to pull the pedals off a flower while quoting it. Wherever one landed when the last pedal was removed was the kind of character you were going to be. The rhyme poses the most important question one can ask. *Who are we going to be*? Not what are we going to do?

"Who are we going to be" is the question the wise pose to their communities. Our concern is not primarily with activities or programs or image or status but with character. Our concern is developing a hunger and thirst for a clear vision of the character of God. It does not matter whether a person is sixteen or ninety-six, that question always remains appropriate. It gives perspective as we face the daily issues and frustrations in life. The sage stimulates within people and within the church and synagogue a desire, a longing to *become*. We are becoming what God continues to make us.

Bob Keeshan, known to millions as Captain Kangaroo, was for decades the beloved host of a morning television show for children. When he began his role as the grandfatherly Captain in 1955, Keeshan was only twenty-eight years old; and so to look the part, he had to wear a great deal of make-up, fake whiskers, and a wig. But as he played the role through the years, his hair turned white and wrinkles appeared. Keeshan found that he needed less and less make-up. Near the end of his career he could say: "I have grown into the part."[24] The goal of the people of God is to grow into the character of God.

---

24. See Tippens, *Pilgrim Heart*, 203.

Bibliography

GENERAL BIBLIOGRAPHY ON PROVERBS AND WISDOM

Aitken, Kenneth T. *Proverbs*. Daily Study Bible Series. Philadelphia: Westminster, 1986.
Allen, Diogenes. "Wisdom of the World and God's." *Princeton Seminary Bulletin* 23 (2002) 195–99.
Alter, Robert. *The Art of Biblical Poetry*. Boulder, CO: Basic Books, 1985.
———. *The Wisdom Books: Job, Proverbs, and Ecclesiastes, A Translation with Commentary*. New York: Norton, 2010.
Barton, Stephen C., ed. *Where Shall Wisdom Be Found? Wisdom in the Bible, the Church and the Contemporary World*. Edinburgh: T. & T. Clark, 1999.
Beardslee, William. "Uses of the Proverb in the Synoptic Gospel." *Interpretation* 24 (1970) 61–73.
Bergant, Dianne. *What Are They Saying About Wisdom Literature?* New York: Paulist, 1984.
Bland, Dave. "The Biblical Quest for Wisdom." Major Review of Roland Murphy's *The Tree of Life*. *Interpretation* 46, no. 2 (1992) 183–84.
———. "Formation of Character in the Book of Proverbs." *Restoration Quarterly* 40 (1998) 221–37.
———. "Iron Sharpens Iron: From Exposition to Sermon (Proverbs 27:14–19)." *Leaven* 8.1 (April 2000) 70–74.
———. "A New Proposal for Preaching from Proverbs." *Preaching* 13.6 (1997) 28–30.
———. *Proverbs, Ecclesiastes, Song of Solomon*. College Press NIV Commentary. Joplin, MO: College Press, 2002.
———. Review of *Preaching Proverbs: Wisdom for the Pulpit* by Alyce McKenzie. *Princeton Seminary Bulletin* 19 (1998) 84–85.
———. "Right Timing: Proverbs 26:1–9." *Preaching* 13.6 (1997) 31–33.
———. "The Use of Proverbs in Two Medieval Genres of Discourse: 'The Art of Poetry' and 'The Art of Preaching.'" *Proverbium: Yearbook of International Proverb Scholarship* 14 (1997) 1–21.
———. "Wisdom." In *Baker Illustrated Bible Dictionary*, edited by Tremper Longman et al., 1718–20. Grand Rapids: Baker, 2013.
Bland, Dave, and David Fleer, eds. *Preaching Character: Reclaiming Wisdom's Paradigmatic Imagination for Transformation*. Abilene, TX: ACU Press, 2010.

Blenkinsopp, Joseph. *Sage, Priest, and Prophet*. Library of Ancient Israel. Louisville: Westminster John Knox, 1995.

———. *Wisdom and Law in the Old Testament: The Ordering of Life in Israel and Early Judaism*. Oxford Bible Series. Oxford: Oxford University Press, 1983.

Brown, William P. *Character in Crisis: A Fresh Approach to the Wisdom Literature of the Old Testament*. Grand Rapids: Eerdmans, 1996.

———. "The Pedagogy of Proverbs 10:1–31:9." In *Character & Scripture: Moral Formation, Community, and Biblical Interpretation*, edited by William P. Brown, 150–82. Grand Rapids: Eerdmans, 2002.

———. "To Discipline without Destruction: The Multifaceted Profile of the Child in Proverbs." In *The Child in the Bible*, edited by Marcia J. Bunge, 63–81. Grand Rapids: Eerdmans, 2008.

———. *Wisdom's Wonder: Character, Creation, and Crisis in the Bible's Wisdom Literature*. Grand Rapids: Eerdmans, 2014.

Brueggemann, Walter. *In Man We Trust: The Neglected Side of Biblical Faith*. 1972. Reprinted, Eugene, OR: Wipf & Stock, 2006.

———. "What You Eat is What You Get: Proverbs 15:17." In *The Threat of Life: Sermons on Pain, Power, and Weakness*, edited by Charles L. Campbell, 116–21. Minneapolis: Fortress, 1996.

Bryce, Glendon E. "'Better'—Proverbs: An Historical and Structural Study." *The Society of Biblical Literature Book of Seminar Papers*, edited by L.C. McGaughy, 343–54. Missoula: SBL, 1972.

Camp, Claudia. *Wisdom and the Feminine in the Book of Proverbs*. Bible and Literature Series 11. Decatur, GA: Almond, 1985.

Clements, Ronald E. "The Concept of Abomination in the Book of Proverbs." In *Texts, Temples and Traditions: A Tribute to Menahem Haran*, edited by Michael V. Fox et al., 211–25. Winona Lake, IN: Eisenbrauns, 1996.

———. "The Good Neighbour in the Book of Proverbs. In *Of Prophets' Visions and the Wisdom of Sages*, edited by Heather A. McKay and David J. A. Clines. Journal for the Study of the Old Testament Supplements 162. Sheffield: JSOT, 1993.

Clark, Ronald R., Jr. "Schools, Scholars, and Students: The Wisdom School *Sitz im Leben* and Proverbs." *Restoration Quarterly* 47 (2005) 161–77.

Clifford, Richard J. *Proverbs*. Old Testament Library. Louisville: Westminster John Knox, 1999.

———. *The Wisdom Literature*. Interpreting Biblical Texts. Nashville: Abingdon, 1998.

Collins, John J. "Proverbial Wisdom and the Yahwist Vision." *Semeia* 17 (1980) 1–17.

Crenshaw, James L. "The Acquisition of Knowledge in Israelite Wisdom Literature." *Word & World* 7 (1987) 245–52.

———. "Education in Ancient Israel." *Journal of Biblical Literature* 104 (1985) 601–15.

———. *Education in Ancient Israel: Across the Deadening Silence*. New York: Doubleday, 1998.

———. *Old Testament Wisdom: An Introduction*. 3rd ed. Louisville: Westminster John Knox, 2010.

———. "Murphy's Axiom: Every Gnomic Saying Needs a Balancing Corrective." In *The Listening Heart: Essays in Wisdom and the Psalms in Honor of Roland E. Murphy, O. Carm*, edited by Kenneth G. Hoglund et al., 1–17. Journal for the Study of the Old Testament Supplements 58. Sheffield: JSOT Press, 1987.

———. *Urgent Advice and Probing Questions: Collected Writings on Old Testament Wisdom.* Macon, GA: Mercer University Press, 1995.

———. "Wisdom and Authority: Sapiential Rhetoric and its Warrants." *Vetus Testamentum Supplement* 32 (1980) 10–29.

Collins, John J. *Proverbs, Ecclesiastes.* Knox Preaching Guides. Atlanta: Knox Press, 1980.

Day, John, Robert P. Gordon, and H. G. M. Williamson, eds. *Wisdom in Ancient Israel: Essays in Honour of J. A. Emerton.* Cambridge: Cambridge University Press, 1995.

Davidson, Robert. *Wisdom and Worship.* London: SCM Press, 1990.

Davies, G.I. "Were there Schools in Ancient Israel?" In *Wisdom in Ancient Israel: Essays in Honour of J. A. Emerton*, edited by John Day et al., 199–211. Cambridge: Cambridge University Press, 1995.

Davis, Ellen F. *Proverbs, Ecclesiastes, and the Song of Songs.* Louisville: Westminster John Knox, 2000.

———. *Scripture, Culture, and Agriculture: An Agrarian Reading of the Bible.* Cambridge: Cambridge University Press, 2009.

Dundes, Alan. "On the Structure of the Proverb." In *The Wisdom of Many: Essays on the Proverb*, edited by Wolfgang Mieder and Alan Dundes, 43–64. Garland Folklore Casebooks 1. New York: Garland, 1981.

Eaton, John. "Memory and Encounter: An Educational Ideal." In *Of Prophets' Visions and the Wisdom of Sages: Essays in Honour of R. Norman Whybray on His Seventieth Birthday*, edited by Heather A. McKay and David J. A. Clines, 179–91. Journal for the Study of the Old Testament Supplements 162. Sheffield: JSOT Press, 1993.

Estes, Daniel J. *Hear, My Son: Teaching and Learning in Proverbs 1–9.* Grand Rapids: Eerdmans, 1997.

Farmer, Kathleen A. *Proverbs and Ecclesiastes: Who Knows What is Good?* International Theological Commentary. Grand Rapids: Eerdmans, 1991.

Fontaine, Carole R. "The Sage in Family and Tribe." In *The Sage in Israel and the Ancient Near East*, edited by John G. Gammie and Leo G. Perdue, 155–64. Winona Lake, IN: Eisenbrauns, 1990.

———. *Traditional Sayings in the Old Testament: A Contextual Study.* Sheffield: Almond Press, 1982.

Fox, Michael V. "Ideas of Wisdom in Proverbs 1–9." *Journal of Biblical Literature* 116 (1997) 613–33.

———. "The Pedagogy of Proverbs 2." *Journal of Biblical Literature* 113 (1994) 233–43.

———. "The Social Location of the Book of Proverbs." In *Texts, Temples and Traditions: A Tribute to Menahem Haran*, edited by Michael V. Fox et al., 227–39. Winona Lake, IN: Eisenbrauns, 1996.

———. "Unity and Diversity in Proverbs." Paper presented at the Society of Biblical Literature, San Francisco, CA, November 1992.

———. *Proverbs 1–9.* Anchor Bible 18A. New York: Doubleday, 2000.

———. *Proverbs 10–31.* Anchor Bible 18B. New Haven: Yale University Press, 2009.

———. "Wisdom and the Self-Presentation of Wisdom Literature." In *Reading from Right to Left: Essays on the Hebrew Bible in Honour of David J. A. Clines*, edited by J. Cheryl Exum and H.G.M. Williamson, 153–72. New York: Sheffield Academic Press, 2003.

———. "Words for Folly." *Zeitschrift für Althebraistik* 10 (1997) 1–12.

Frydrych, Tomás. *Living Under the Sun: Examination of Proverbs and Qoheleth.* Boston: Brill, 2002.

Gammie, John G., and Leo G. Perdue, eds. *The Sage in Israel and the Ancient Near East.* Winona Lake, IN: Eisenbrauns, 1990.

Goldingay, John. *Proverbs, Ecclesiastes and Song of Songs for Everyone.* Old Testament for Everyone. Louisville: Westminster John Knox, 2014.

Gordis, Robert. "The Social Background of Wisdom Literature." *Hebrew Union College Annual* 18 (1943-1944) 77-118.

Harrelson, Walter. "Wisdom and Pastoral Theology." *Andover Newton Quarterly* 7 (1966) 6-14.

Heskett, Randall J. "Proverbs 23:13-14." *Interpretation* 55 (2001) 181-84.

Hildebrandt, Ted. "Motivation and Antithetic Parallelism in Proverbs 10-15." *Journal of Evangelical Theological Society* 35 (1992) 433-44.

———. "Proverbial Strings: Cohesion in Proverbs 10." *Grace Theological Journal* 11 (1990) 171-85.

———. "Proverbs 22:6a: Train Up a Child?" *Grace Theological Journal* 9 (1988) 3-19.

———. "Proverbial Pairs: Compositional Units in Proverbs 10-29." *Journal of Biblical Literature* 107 (1988) 207-24.

Hoglund, Kenneth G., Elizabeth F. Huwiler, Jonathan T. Glass, Roger W. Lee, eds. *The Listening Heart: Essays in Wisdom and the Psalms in Honor of Roland E. Murphy.* Journal for the Study of the Old Testament Supplements 58. Sheffield: JSOT, 1987.

Jacobson, Arland D. "Proverbs and Social Control: A New Paradigm for Wisdom Studies." In *Gnosticism and the Early Christian World: In Honor of James M. Robinson,* edited by James E. Goehring et al., 75-88. Forum Fascicles 2. Sonoma, CA: Polebridge, 1991.

Jaeggli, Randy. "Interpreting Proverbs 22:6." *Biblical Viewpoint,* 33 (1999) 41-48.

Kidner, Derek. *The Wisdom of Proverbs, Job and Ecclesiastes: An Introduction to Wisdom Literature.* Downers Grove, IL: InterVarsity, 1985.

———. *The Proverbs.* Tyndale Old Testament Commentaries. London: Tyndale, 1964.

Kugel, James. *The Idea of Biblical Poetry: Parallelism and Its History.* New Haven: Yale University Press, 1981.

Lang, Bernhard. *Wisdom and the Book of Proverbs: A Hebrew Goddess Redefined.* New York: Pilgrim, 1986.

Longman, Tremper III. *How to Read Proverbs.* Downers Grove, IL: InterVarsity, 2002.

———. *Proverbs.* Baker Commentary on the Old Testament Wisdom and Psalms. Grand Rapids: Baker Academic, 2006.

Malbim on Mishley: The Commentary of Rabbi Meir Leibush Malbim on the Book of Proverbs. Edited by Rabbi Charles Wengrov. Jerusalem: Feldheim, 1982.

Martin, James D. *Proverbs.* Old Testament Guides. Sheffield: Sheffield Academic, 1995.

McKane, William. *Proverbs: A New Approach.* Old Testament Library. Philadelphia: Westminster, 1970.

McKay, Heather A., and David J. A. Clines, eds. *Of Prophets' Visions and the Wisdom of Sages: Essays in Honour of R. Norman Whybray on His Seventieth Birthday.* Journal for the Study of the Old Testament Supplements 162. Sheffield: JSOT Press, 1993.

McKenzie, Alyce M. *Hear and Be Wise: Becoming a Preacher and Teacher of Wisdom.* Nashville: Abingdon, 2004.

———. *Preaching Proverbs: Wisdom for the Pulpit.* Louisville: Westminster John Knox, 1996.

———. *Preaching Biblical Wisdom in a Self-Help Society*. Nashville: Abingdon, 2002.

———. "The Incredible Shrinking God: Biblical Wisdom as Antidote." The Academy of Homiletics Annual Papers, 1998.

———. "'Different Strokes for Different Folks': America's Quintessential Postmodern Proverb." *Theology Today* 53 (1996) 201–12.

Melchert, Charles F. *Wise Teaching: Biblical Wisdom and Educational Ministry*. Harrisburg, PA: Trinity, 1998.

Murphy, Roland E. *Proverbs*. Word Biblical Commentary 22. Nashville: Nelson, 1998.

———. *The Tree of Life: An Exploration of Biblical Wisdom Literature*. 2nd ed. Grand Rapids: Eerdmans, 1996.

———. *Wisdom Literature and Psalms*. Interpreting Biblical Texts. Nashville: Abingdon, 1983.

Murphy, Roland E., and Elizabeth Huwiler. *Proverbs, Ecclesiastes, Song of Songs*. New International Biblical Commentary. Peabody, MA: Hendrickson, 1999.

Niditch, Susan. "Folklore and Wisdom: Mashal as an Ethnic Genre." In *Folklore and the Hebrew Bible*, 67–87. Minneapolis: Fortress, 1993.

O'Connor, Kathleen M. *The Wisdom Literature*. Message of Biblical Spirituality 5. Wilmington, DE: Glazier, 1988.

Orlinsky, Harry, M., ed. *Studies in Ancient Israelite Wisdom*. Library of Biblical Studies. New York: Ktav, 1976.

Packer, J. I., and Sven K. Soderlund, eds. *The Way of Wisdom: Essays in Honor of Bruce K. Waltke*. Grand Rapids: Zondervan, 2000.

Pemberton, Glenn D. "It's A Fool's Life: The Deformation of Character in Proverbs." *Restoration Quarterly* 50 (2008) 213–24.

———. "The Rhetoric of the Fathers: A Rhetorical Analysis of the Father/Son Lectures in Proverbs 1–9." PhD diss. Iliff School of Theology and University of Denver, 1999.

Perdue, Leo G. *Proverbs*. Interpretation: A Bible Commentary for Teaching and Preaching. Louisville: John Knox, 2000.

Perdue, Leo G., Bernard Brandon Scott, and William Johnston Wiseman, eds. *In Search of Wisdom: Essays in Memory of John G. Gammie*. Louisville: Westminster John Knox Press, 1993.

Scherer, Andreas. "Is the Selfish Man Wise?: Considerations of Context in Proverbs 10.1–22.16 with Special Regard to Surety, Bribery and Friendship." *Journal for the Study of the Old Testament* 76 (1997) 59–70.

Scott, R. B. Y. *Proverbs, Ecclesiastes: Introduction, Translation, and Notes*. Anchor Bible 18. Garden City, NY: Doubleday, 1965.

———. *The Way of Wisdom in the Old Testament*. New York: Macmillan, 1971.

Sell, Charles. *The House on the Rock: Wisdom from Proverbs for Today's Families*. Wheaton, IL: Victor, 1987.

Setzer, Timothy Nathan. "God's Governance in the Book of Proverbs." *Henceforth* 19.1 (1991) 17–28.

Shupak, Nili. "The Sitz im Leben of the Book of Proverbs in the Light of a Comparison of Biblical and Egyptian Wisdom Literature." *Revue Biblique* 94 (1987) 98–119.

Sneed, Mark. "The Class Culture of Proverbs: Eliminating Stereotypes." *Scandinavian Journal of the Old Testament* 10 (1996) 296–308.

———. "Is the 'Wisdom Tradition' a Tradition." *Catholic Biblical Quarterly* (2011) 50–71.

Thompson, John Mark. *The Form and Function of Proverbs in Ancient Israel*. The Hague: Mouton, 1974.
Van Leeuwen, Raymond C. "Liminality and Worldview in Proverbs 1–9." *Semeia* 50 (1990) 111–44.
———. "Proverbs." In *The New Interpreter's Bible*. Edited by Leander E. Keck. Vol. 5. Nashville: Abingdon, 1997.
———. "Wealth and Poverty: System and Contradiction in Proverbs." *Hebrew Studies* 33 (1992) 25–36.
Waltke, Bruce K. *The Book of Proverbs: Chapters 1–15*. New International Commentary on the Old Testament. Grand Rapids: Eerdmans, 2004.
———. *The Book of Proverbs: Chapters 15–31*. New International Commentary on the Old Testament. Grand Rapids: Eerdmans, 2005.
Washington, Harold C. *Wealth and Poverty in the Instruction of Amenemope and the Hebrew Proverbs*. SBL Dissertation Series 142. Atlanta: Scholars, 1994.
Weeks, Stuart. *Early Israelite Wisdom*. Oxford Theological Monographs. Oxford: Clarendon, 1994.
Wells, David. *Losing Our Virtue: Why the Church Must Recover Its Moral Vision*. Grand Rapids: Eerdmans, 1998.
———. "The Weightlessness of God." Christian Life Conference. Second Presbyterian Church, Memphis, TN. January 21–23, 2000.
Westermann, Claus. *Roots of Wisdom: The Oldest Proverbs of Israel and Other Peoples*. Translated by J. Daryl Charles. Louisville: Westminster John Knox, 1995.
Whiting, Bartlett Jere. "The Nature of the Proverb." *Harvard Studies and Notes in Philology and Literature* 14 (1932) 273–307.
———. "The Origin of the Proverb." *Harvard Studies and Notes in Philology and Literature* 13 (1931) 47–80.
Whybray, R. N. *The Book of Proverbs: A Survey of Modern Study*. History of Biblical Interpretation Series 1. Leiden: Brill, 1995.
———. *The Intellectual Tradition in the Old Testament*. Beihefte zur Zeitschrift für die alttestamentliche Wissenschaft 135. Berlin: de Gruyter, 1974.
———. *Proverbs*. New Century Bible Commentary. Grand Rapids: Eerdmans, 1994.
———. *Wealth and Poverty in the Book of Proverbs*. Journal for the Study of the Old Testament Supplements 99. Sheffield: JSOT, 1990.
Williams, James G. "The Power of Form: A Study of Biblical Proverbs." *Semeia* 17 (1980) 35–58.
Willis, John T. *The Old Testament Wisdom Literature: Job, Proverbs, Ecclesiastes, Song of Solomon*. Abilene, TX: Biblical Research Press, 1982.
Wilson, Fredrick M. "Sacred and Profane? The Yahwistic Redaction of Proverbs Reconsidered." In *The Listening Heart: Essays in Wisdom and the Psalms in Honor of Roland E. Murphy*, edited by Kenneth G. Hoglund et al., 313–34. Journal for the Study of the Old Testament Supplements 58. Sheffield: JSOT, 1987.
Witherington, Ben III. *Jesus the Sage: The Pilgrimage of Wisdom*. Minneapolis: Fortress, 1994.
Yoder, Christine Roy. *Proverbs*. Abingdon Old Testament Commentaries. Nashville: Abingdon, 2009.
Youngblood, Kevin J. "Cosmic Boundaries and Self-Control in Proverbs." *Restoration Quarterly* 51 (2009) 139–50.

Zuck, Roy B., ed. *Learning from the Sages: Selected Studies on the Book of Proverbs*. Grand Rapids: Baker, 1995.

THEOLOGY OF WISDOM

Boström, Lennart. *The God of the Sages: The Portrayal of God in the Book of Proverbs*. Stockholm: Almqvist & Wiksell, 1990.
Brown, William P. "Character and Crisis in Proverbs, Job, and Ecclesiastes." Paper presented at SBL in San Francisco, 1992.
———. *Character in Crisis: A Fresh Approach to the Wisdom Literature of the Old Testament*. Grand Rapids: Eerdmans, 1996.
Clements, Ronald, E. "Wisdom and Old Testament Theology." In *Wisdom in Ancient Israel: Essays in Honour of J. A. Emerton*, edited by John Day et al., 269–86. Cambridge: Cambridge University Press, 1995.
———. *Wisdom for a Changing World: Wisdom in Old Testament Theology*. Berkeley: BIBAL, 1990.
———. *Wisdom in Theology*. Grand Rapids: Eerdmans, 1992.
Crenshaw, James. "The Concept of God in Old Testament Wisdom." In *In Search of Wisdom: Essays in Memory of John G. Gammie*, edited by Leo G. Perdue et al., 1–18. Louisville: Westminster John Knox, 1993.
Perdue, Leo G. *Wisdom and Creation: The Theology of Wisdom Literature*. Nashville: Abingdon, 1994.
Rad, Gerhard von. *Wisdom in Israel*. Translated by James Martin. Nashville: Abingdon, 1972.
Waltke, Bruce K. "The Book of Proverbs and Old Testament Theology." *Bibliotheca Sacra* 136 (1979) 302–17.
———. "Proverbs: Theology of." In *New International Dictionary of Old Testament Theology and Exegesis*, edited by Willem A. VanGemeren, 4:1079–94. Grand Rapids: Zondervan, 1997.

THE LITERARY AND RHETORICAL COMPOSITION OF THE SENTENCE LITERATURE

Bland, Dave. "A Rhetorical Perspective on the Sentence Sayings of the Book of Proverbs." PhD diss., University of Washington, 1994.
Bryce, Glendon E. "Another Wisdom-'Book' in Proverbs." *Journal of Biblical Literature* (1972) 145–57.
Finkbeiner, Douglas. "An Analysis of the Structure of Proverbs 28–29." *Calvery Baptist Theological Journal* 11 (1995) 1–14.
Garrett, Duane. *Proverbs, Ecclesiastes, Song of Songs*. New American Commentary. Nashville: Broadman, 1993.
Goldingay, John. "The Arrangement of Sayings in Proverbs 10–15." *Journal for the Study of the Old Testament* 61 (1994) 75–83.
Hildebrandt, Ted. "Proverbial Pairs: Compositional Units in Proverbs 10–29." *Journal of Biblical Literature* 107 (1988) 207–24.

———. "Proverbial Strings: Cohesion in Proverbs 10." *Grace Theological Journal* 11 (1990) 171–85.
Huwiler, Elizabeth Faith. "Control of Reality in Israelite Wisdom." PhD diss., Duke University, 1988.
Malchow, Bruce V. "A Manual for Future Monarchs." *Catholic Biblical Quarterly* 47 (1985) 238–45.
Meinhold, Arndt. *Die Sprüche. Teil I. Sprüche Kapitel 1–15*. Zürcher Bibelkommentare. Zurich: TVZ, 1991.
Murphy, Roland E. "Proverbs 22:1–9." *Interpretation* 41 (1987) 398–402.
Perry, S. C. "Structural Patterns in Proverbs 10:1–22:16: A Study in Biblical Hebrew Stylistics." PhD diss., University of Texas at Austin, 1987.
Perry, T. A. *Wisdom Literature and the Structure of Proverbs*. University Park: Pennsylvania State University Press, 1993.
Scherer, Andreas. "Is the Selfish Man Wise?: Considerations of Context in Proverbs 10:1–22:16 with Special Regard to Surety, Bribery and Friendship." *Journal for the Study of the Old Testament* 76 (1997) 59–70.
Snell, Daniel C. *Twice-Told Proverbs and the Composition of the Book of Proverbs*. Winona Lake, IN: Eisenbrauns, 1993.
Van Leeuwen, Raymond C. *Context and Meaning in Proverbs 25–27*. Atlanta: Scholars, 1988.
Waltke, Bruce, K. "The Dance between God and Humanity." In *Doing Theology for the People of God: Studies in Honor of J. I. Packer*, edited by Donald Lewis and Alister McGrath, 87–104. Downers Grove, IL: InterVarsity, 1996.
Weeks, Stuart. "Context in the Sayings Collections." In *Early Israelite Wisdom*, 20–40. Oxford Theological Monographs. Oxford: Clarendon, 1994.
Whybray, R. N. *The Composition of the Book of Proverbs*. Journal for the Study of the Old Testament Supplements 168. Sheffield: JSOT, 1994.
———. "Yahweh-sayings and Their Contexts in Proverbs, 10:1–22:16." In *La Sagesse de L'Ancien Testament*, edited by Maurice Gilbert, 153–65. Bibliotheca Ephemeridum theologicarum Lovaniensium 51. Leuven: Peeters, 1990.

ADDITIONAL WORKS CITED IN THIS VOLUME

Abrahams, Roger. "Proverbs and Proverbial Expressions." In *Folklore and Folklife: An Introduction*. Chicago: University of Chicago Press, 1972.
Arewa, Ojo E., and Alan Dundes. "Proverbs and the Ethnography of Speaking Folklore." *American Anthropologist* 66 (1964) 70–85.
Arthurs, Jeffrey D. "Proverbs in Inspirational Literature: Sanctioning the American Dream." *Journal of Communication and Religion* 17 (1994) 1–15.
———. "Words Fitly Spoken: Rhetorical Characteristics of Proverbs." Paper presented at the Speech Communication Association Annual Meeting, Miami, FL, 1993.
Atkinson, David. *The Message of Proverbs*. Downers Grove, IL: InterVarsity, 1996.
Barns, Daniel R. "Telling it Slant: Emily Dickinson and the Proverb." In *Wise Words: Essays on the Proverb*, edited by Wolfgang Mieder, 439–65. Garland Reference Library of the Humanities 1638. New York: Garland, 1994.

Bascom, W. R. "Four Functions of Folklore." *Journal of American Folklore* (1954) 333–49. Reprinted in *The Study of Folklore*, edited by Alan Dundes, 279–97. Englewood Cliffs, NJ: Prentice-Hall, 1965.

Bennett, William. *The Book of Virtues*. New York: Simon & Schuster, 1993.

———. "Moral Literacy and the Formation of Character." In *Moral, Character, and Civic Education in the Elementary School*, edited by Jacques S. Benninga, 131–38. New York: Teachers College Press, 1991.

Blackaby, Henry, and Richard Blackaby. *Spiritual Leadership*. Nashville: Broadman & Holman, 2006.

Bland, Dave. "God's Activity as Reflected in the Books of Ruth and Esther." *Restoration Quarterly* 24 (1981) 129–47.

Brenner, Athalya. "Proverbs 1–9: An F Voice?" In *On Gendering Texts: Female and Male Voices in the Hebrew Bible*, edited by Athalya Brenner and Fokkelien Dijk-Hemmes, 113–30. Biblical Interpretation Series 1. Leiden: Brill, 1993.

Brown, Francis, S. R. Driver, and Charles Briggs. *A Hebrew and English Lexicon of the Old Testament*. 2nd printing. Oxford: Clarendon, 1975.

Brown, H. Jackson. *Life's Little Instruction Book: 511 Suggestions, Observations, and Reminders on How to Live a Happy and Rewarding Life*. Nashville: Rutledge Hill, 1991.

Brueggemann, Walter. *Texts Under Negotiation: The Bible and Postmodern Imagination*. Minneapolis: Fortress, 1993.

Burke, Kenneth. *The Philosophy of Literary Form: Studies in Symbolic Action*, 3rd ed. Los Angeles: University of California Press, 1973.

Campbell, Charles L. *The Word before the Powers: An Ethic of Preaching*. Louisville: Westminster John Knox, 2002.

Campbell, John Angus. "Review of *Truth and Method* by Hans-Georg Gadamer." *Quarterly Journal of Speech* 64 (1978) 101–22.

Cloninger, C. Robert. "Book Forum: *Character Strengths and Virtues: A Handbook and Classification*." *American Journal of Psychiatry* 162 (2005) 821.

Clouse, Bonnidell. *Teaching for Moral Growth: A Guide for the Christian Community*. Wheaton, IL: Bridgpoint, 1993.

"Conflict in the Church: Division or Diversity?" Produced by the Mennonite Central Committee, Akron, PA. 1999. Videocassette.

Covey, Stephen R. "Seven Habits of Highly Effective People." New York: Simon & Schuster, 1989. Audiotape.

Crossan, John Dominic. *Cliffs of Fall: Paradox and Polyvalence in the Parables of Jesus*. 1980. Reprinted, Eugene, OR: Wipf & Stock, 2008.

Cueni, R. Robert. *Dinosaur Heart Transplants: Renewing Mainline Congregations*. Nashville: Abingdon, 2000.

Culpepper, R. Alan. "Education." In *The International Standard Bible Encyclopedia*, edited by Geoffrey W. Bromiley 2:21–27. Rev. ed. Grand Rapids: Eerdmans, 1982.

Dommershausen, W. "יכח." In *Theological Dictionary of the Old Testament*, edited by G. Johannes Botterweck and Helmer Ringgren, 5:19–21. Translated by David Green. Grand Rapids: Eerdmans, 1986.

Eaton, John. *The Contemplative Face of Old Testament Wisdom in the Context of World Religions*. Philadelphia: Trinity, 1989.

Elliott, Mark Barger. *Creative Styles of Preaching*. Louisville: Westminster John Knox, 2000.

Fackre, Gabriel. *The Christian Story: A Narrative Interpretation of Basic Christian Doctrine*. 3rd ed. Grand Rapids: Eerdmans, 1996.

Fowler, James W. *Stages of Faith: The Psychology of Human Development and the Quest for Meaning*. San Francisco: Harper & Row, 1981.

Fussell, George. *The Power of Vision: How You Can Capture and Apply God's Vision for Your Ministry*. Ventura, CA: Barna Research Group, 1992.

Fussell, R. Curtis. *Deadly Sins and Living Virtues: Living beyond the Seven Deadly Sins*. Lima, OH: CSS Publishing, 1997.

Gadamer, Hans-Georg. *Truth and Method*. Translated by Joel Weinscheimer and Donald G. Marshall. 2nd rev. ed. New York: Crossroad, 1991.

Gese, Hartmut. "Wisdom Literature in the Persian Period." In *The Cambridge History of Judaism: Introduction; The Persian Period*, edited by W. D. Davies and Louis Finkelstein, 1:189–218. Cambridge: Cambridge University Press, 1984.

Greenhaw, David. "As One with Authority: Rehabilitating Concepts for Preaching." In *Intersections: Post-Critical Studies in Preaching*, edited by Richard Eslinger, 105–22. Grand Rapids: Eerdmans, 1994.

Grossman, David. "Trained to Kill." *Christianity Today* 42.9 (August 10, 1998) 30–39.

Hallman, Tom, Jr. "Mount Hood's Deadly Deceit: A Remembrance." *The Sunday Oregonian*, May 12, 1996.

Hallo, William W., ed. *The Context of Scripture*. Vol 1, *Canonical Compositions from the Biblical World*. New York: Brill, 1997.

Hauerwas, Stanley. *A Community of Character: Toward a Constructive Christian Social Ethic*. Notre Dame: University of Notre Dame Press, 1981.

Hirsch, E. D., Jr. *Cultural Literacy: What Every American Needs to Know*. New York: Vintage, 1988.

Hirsch, E. D., Jr., Joseph F. Kett, and James Trefil. *The Dictionary of Cultural Literacy*. Boston: Houghton Mifflin, 1988.

Howard, Robert W. "Lawrence Kohlberg's Influence on Moral Education in Elementary Schools." In *Moral, Character, and Civic Education in the Elementary School*, edited by Jacques S. Benninga, 43–66. New York: Teachers College Press, 1991.

Hunter, James Davison. *The Death of Character: Moral Education in an Age without Good or Evil*. New York: Basic Books, 2000.

Jackson, Vera R. "Proverbs: A Tool for Work with Older Persons." In *Aging Families and Use of Proverbs for Values Enrichment*, edited by Vera R. Jackson, 5–13. New York: Haworth, 1994.

Janis, Irving. *Victims of Groupthink*. Boston: Houghton Mifflin, 1972.

Johnson, Greg, and Mike Yorkey. *Faithful Parents, Faithful Kids: A Strategy for Passing the Baton of Faith—From Those Who've Done It*. Wheaton, IL: Tyndale, 1993.

Johnson, Thomas H., ed. *The Complete Poems of Emily Dickinson*. Boston: Little, Brown, 1960.

Kierkegaard, Søren. *Concluding Unscientific Postscript*. Princeton: Princeton University Press, 1941.

Kirshenblatt-Gimblett, Barbara. "Toward a Theory of Proverb Meaning." In *The Wisdom of Many: Essays on the Proverb*, edited by Wolfgang Mieder and Alan Dundes, 111–21. Garland Folklore Casebooks 1. New York: Garland, 1981.

Kohlberg, Lawrence. "Education for Justice: A Modern Statement of the Platonic View." In *Moral Education: Five Lectures*, edited by Nancy F. Sizer and Theodore R. Sizer, 57–83. Cambridge: Harvard University Press, 1970.

———. *Essays on Moral Development, The Psychology of Moral Development: The Nature and Validity of Moral Stages.* Vol. 2. San Francisco: Harper & Row, 1984.
Kushner, Harold. *When Bad Things Happen to Good People.* New York: Schocken, 1981.
Lemaire, André. "Education: Ancient Israel." In *The Anchor Bible Dictionary*, edited by David Noel Freedman, 2:305–12. New York: Doubleday, 1992.
Lewis, C. S. *Mere Christianity.* New York: MacMillan, 1977.
Long, Thomas G. "Preaching the Pronouncement Stories in Luke." In *Preaching from Luke/Acts*, edited by David Fleer and Dave Bland, 34–49. Abilene, TX: ACU Press, 2000.
———. "Beavis and Butt-Head Get Saved." *Theology Today* 51 (1994) 199–203.
———. *Preaching and the Literary Forms of the Bible.* Philadelphia: Fortress, 1989.
———. *The Senses of Preaching.* Atlanta: John Knox, 1988.
McAdoo, Harriette P., and Linda A. McWright. "The Roles of Grandparents: The Use of Proverbs in Value Transmission." In *Aging Families and Use of Proverbs for Values Enrichment*, edited by Vera R. Jackson, 27–38. New York: Haworth, 1994.
Marketos, B. J. *A Proverb for It: 1510 Greek Sayings.* Translated by Ann Arpajoglou. New York: New World, 1945.
Massey, Morris E., and Michael J. O'Connor. "Values Profile System." Minneapolis: Carlson Learning, 1989.
McClure, Cynthia Rowland. *The Courage to Go On: Life after Addiction.* Grand Rapids: Baker, 1990.
McDowell, Josh, and Dick Day. *How to be a Hero to Your Kids.* Dallas: Word, 1991.
McKinlay, Judith E. *Gendering Wisdom the Host: Biblical Invitations to Eat and Drink.* Sheffield: Sheffield Academic, 1996.
Mieder, Wolfgang. "Paremiological Minimum and Cultural Literacy." In *Wise Words: Essays on the Proverb*, edited by Wolfgang Meider, 297–316. Garland Reference Library of the Humanities 1638. New York: Garland, 1994.
———. *Proverbs Are Never out of Season: Popular Wisdom in the Modern Age.* New York: Oxford University Press, 1993.
———. "The Essence of Literary Proverb Study." *Proverbium*, edited by Wolfgang Mieder, 23 (1974) 892.
Mieder, Wolfgang, and Deborah Holmes. *Children and Proverbs Speak the Truth: Teaching Proverbial Wisdom to Fourth Graders.* Burlington: University of Vermont Press, 2000.
Mieder, Wolfgang, and Anna Tóthné Litovkina. *Twisted Wisdom: Modern Anti-Proverbs.* Burlington: University of Vermont Press, 1999.
Mieder, Wolfgang, Stewart A. Kingsbury, and Kelsie B. Harder. *A Dictionary of American Proverbs.* New York: Oxford University Press, 1992.
Northcutt, Wendy. *The Darwin Awards: Evolution in Action.* New York: Plume, 2002.
Paterson, Katherine. *Bridge to Terabithia.* New York: HarperCollins, 1977.
———. "From Story to Stories." Keynote speech delivered at the meeting of the Academy of Homiletics, Atlanta, December 1, 1995.
———. *Jacob Have I Loved.* New York: HarperCollins, 1980.
Peck, M. Scott. *Further along the Road Less Traveled.* New York: Simon & Schuster, 1993.
Pei, Mario. "Parallel Proverbs." *Saturday Review* (May 2, 1964) 16–17, 53.
Peterson, Christopher, and Martin E. P. Seligman. *Character Strengths and Virtues: A Handbook and Classification.* New York: Oxford University Press, 2004.

Peterson, Eugene. *The Message: The Wisdom Books*. Colorado Springs: NavPress, 1996.

Plantinga, Cornelius, Jr. *Reading for Preaching: The Preacher in Conversation with Storytellers, Biographers, Poets, and Journalists*. Grand Rapids: Eerdmans, 2013.

Postman, Neil. *Amusing Ourselves to Death: Public Discourse in the Age of Show Business*. New York: Penguin, 1985.

Preuss, Horst Dietrich. *Theologie des Alten Testaments*. 2 vols. Stuttgart: Kohlhammer, 1991–92.

———. *Old Testament Theology*. Old Testament Library. Westminster John Knox, 1995–96.

Pritchard, James B., ed. *Ancient Near Eastern Texts Relating to the Old Testament*. 3rd ed. Princeton: Princeton University Press, 1969.

Raths, Louis Edward, Merrill Harmin, and Sidney B. Simon. *Values and Teaching: Working with Values in the Classroom*. Columbus, OH: Merrill, 1966.

Rigby, Cynthia. "Free to be Human: Limits, Possibilities, and the Sovereignty of God." *Theology Today* 51 (1996) 47–62.

Rogers, Tim B. "The Use of Slogans, Colloquialisms, and Proverbs in the Treatment of Substance Addiction: A Psychological Application of Proverbs." *Proverbium: Yearbook of International Proverb Scholarship*, edited by Wolfgang Mieder, 6 (1989) 103–12.

Rokeach, Milton, and Sandra J. Ball-Rokeach, "Stability and Change in American Value Priorities, 1968–1981." *American Psychologist* 44 (1989) 775–84.

Rottman, John M. "Introduction: Literary Forms." In *The New Interpreter's Handbook of Preaching*, edited by Paul Scott Wilson, 65. Nashville: Abingdon, 2008.

Sample, Tex. *Ministry in an Oral Culture: Living with Will Rogers, Uncle Remus, & Minnie Pearl*. Louisville: Westminster John Knox, 1994.

Scott, Bernard Brandon. *Hear Then the Parable: A Commentary on the Parables of Jesus*. Minneapolis: Fortress, 1989.

Seitz, Christopher R. "Old Testament or Hebrew Bible?" In *Word without End: The Old Testament as Abiding Theological Witness*, 61–74. Grand Rapids: Eerdmans, 1998.

Shawchuck, Norman, and Roger Heuser. *Leading the Congregation: Caring for Yourself While Serving the People*. Revised ed. Nashville: Abingdon, 2010.

Skehan, Patrick A. "A Single Editor for the Whole Book of Proverbs." In *Studies in Ancient Israelite Wisdom*, edited by James L. Crenshaw, 329–40. Library of Biblical Studies. New York: Ktav, 1976.

Steele, Edward D., and W. Charles Redding. "The American Value System: Premises for Persuasion." *Western Journal of Speech Communication* 26 (1962) 83–91.

Stewart, John. *Language as Articulate Contact: Toward a Post-Semiotic Philosophy of Communication*. New York: State University of New York Press, 1995.

Taylor, Archer. "The Study of Proverbs." *Proverbium* 1 (1965) 1–10.

Thompson, Margorie J. *Soul Feast: An Invitation to the Christian Spiritual Life*. Louisville: Westminster John Knox, 2005.

Tippens, Darryl. *Pilgrim Heart: The Way of Jesus in Everyday Life*. Abilene, TX: Leafwood, 2006.

Wells, David. "The Weightlessness of God." Speech delivered at the Second Presbyterian Church's Christian Life Conference, Memphis, TN, January 21–23, 2000.

———. *Losing Our Virtue: Why the Church Must Recover Its Moral Vision*. Grand Rapids: Eerdmans, 1998.

Willimon, William. "Hunger in This Abandoned Generation." In *Sharing Heaven's Music: The Heart of Christian Preaching*, edited by Barry L. Callen, 21–32. Nashville: Abingdon, 1995.

———. *Pastor*. Nashville: Abingdon, 2002.

———. *Proclamation and Theology*. Nashville: Abingdon, 2005.

Willis, Timothy. "'Obey Your Leaders': Hebrews 13 and Leadership in the Church." *Restoration Quarterly* 36 (1994) 316–26.

Wuthnow, Robert. *God and Mammon in America*. New York: Free Press, 1994.

Zimmerli, Walter. "Zur Struktur der alttestamentlichen Weisheit." *Zeitschrift für die alttestamentliche Wissenchaft* 51 (1933) 177–204.

www.ingramcontent.com/pod-product-compliance
Lightning Source LLC
Chambersburg PA
CBHW031429150426
43191CB00006B/462